REBEL
without
A CLUE

REBEL
without
A CLUE

a memoir

JANET GREEN

Matador
9 Priory Business Park,
Wistow Road, Kibworth Beauchamp,
Leicestershire. LE8 0RX
Tel: 0116 279 2299
Email: books@troubador.co.uk
Web: www.troubador.co.uk/matador
Twitter: @matadorbooks

ISBN 978 1785891 083

British Library Cataloguing in Publication Data.
A catalogue record for this book is available from the British Library.

Printed and bound by CPI Group (UK) Ltd, Croydon, CR0 4YY
Typeset in 11pt Bembo by Troubador Publishing Ltd, Leicester, UK

Matador is an imprint of Troubador Publishing Ltd

Dedicated to Debbie and Dany
With love and thanks

Introduction

Oy! What a life I've had! A mad mother, sexually abused at fourteen years old, promiscuity, sexual experimentation, considerable nudity in many guises, recreational drugs, male and female lovers (sometimes both at the same time). Then there were the jobs: secretary, shop assistant, nurse, topless waitress, stripper, glamour model and, finally, social worker.

And secrets – some kept for many years.

When I've told people I'm writing my memoirs, their reaction has often been one of surprise. I see myself through their eyes for a moment. I am now a short, plump, elderly spinster, complete with cats and a dog. I am a picture of respectability, having retired from my job as a social services manager. They've even said occasionally, "You? Memoirs? What on earth have you got to write about?"

And, of course, some younger people think that it is only their generation who use drugs, who are sexually promiscuous, who are out and proud.

So I thought I had an interesting, sometimes shocking, sometimes funny story to tell, particularly as it is set largely in the sixties and seventies, when life in Britain was changing so rapidly.

Some, although not all, names have been changed to protect people from information about their wild youth becoming public. Some characters don't deserve this protection, but others were innocents who just happened to feature in my life at this point.

And if some people recognise themselves, in spite of the name changes, they might like to reflect on what I've missed out of the story. (You know who you are!)

I believe that what I've written is a truthful account of the first half of my life. It may not always be in exactly the right order, but I have referred to my old diaries, letters and journals to try to keep it accurate. And I have been surprised at how many actual conversations I can recall. The memory is an amazing muscle.

L. P. Hartley wrote in *The Go-Between*, 'The past is a foreign country. They do things differently there.'

Well, yes and no. My past, in the fifties, sixties and seventies, may be atypical of the time, yet there are many similarities with modern life. Or maybe the story is less unusual than I believe. Maybe many now elderly people had similar experiences.

I hope that my readers (assuming there will be more than one) will be entertained and interested in this tale of a rebel without a clue.

1

A New Career Move

Listen. I don't know how it happened, OK? By rights, at twenty-seven years old I should have been married to a Jewish accountant, having had two children and with another on the way. Probably living in Croydon.

As it turned out, at that age I was a dope smoking, stripping lesbian. What can I tell you?

As Philip Larkin wrote (and Sigmund Freud might have said), 'They fuck you up, your Mum and Dad', so perhaps that's the answer. On the other hand, one person's fuck-up is another person's lucky break.

★

So there I was at my first stripping job. It was at a pub in Hackney, a lunchtime gig. Phil drove me and would be in charge of the music cassette. I did my make-up and hair at home, then got dressed, preparing to get undressed, in the 'dressing room' (AKA the ladies' toilet), helpfully sited next to the stage. I was very nervous, although found that smoking a little joint helped a bit. I heard the potty-mouthed MC announce my name and climbed the couple of steps onto the makeshift stage, where there was a wooden chair, but nothing else.

A sea of men's faces gazed up at me, expectantly. They were loud and cheering, but thankfully didn't seem too drunk. This was during the days of restricted pub opening hours, so at twelve midday they hadn't had too long to get pissed. I made no eye contact, fixing my gaze off in the distance to the back of the bar.

The strains of 'Just an Old Fashioned Girl' came through the loudspeakers and I started the routine. All went fairly well until I got to the point of taking my heeled shoes off. They had a T-bar, secured with a small buckle. I knew that my hands were shaking too much to attempt this delicate task, so gestured to a young man in the front row to undo them for me. As he fiddled, I heard him mutter, "I can't do this. My hands are shaking too much."

After a lifetime, he got both shoes undone and I was able to kick them off to one side. I unhooked my black satin basque without too much trouble, but then realised I hadn't yet undone the stockings from the suspenders. Oh no! I had to think quickly. Sitting on the upright chair, I managed to take the stockings off while draping the loosened corset over my torso until I'd finished. Not ideal, but it was an emergency.

I got through it, leaving my G-string on until the very last second, and then grabbed my clothes, dumped throughout my performance in a heap by the side of the stage, and ran into the dressing room/ladies' toilet. I knew that items of clothing or props were liable to go missing if left on the stage, taken as souvenirs. It wasn't a graceful exit. What the hell. A girl's gotta do…

The sound of applause reached me through the doors of the lavatory. Blimey. I didn't think they'd noticed my slip-ups.

I had a brief respite while the comedian did his stuff and then there was a break in the proceedings. I guess this was to extend the show and keep the punters drinking while they waited for the next part.

The second spot, in my nurse's uniform and with a huge silver-coloured syringe, used for dramatic effect to squirt baby lotion over my breasts, went down even better. Thankfully, I had a different pair of shoes for this spot. No buckles, but not exactly regulation lace-ups either.

It was cash in hand and, even after buying Phil a drink for driving me, I found that I had enough spare dosh to buy an ounce of hash that week.

★

Where It all Started

The house was so quiet. It was never usually this silent. My mum and dad might be having their weekly row, or my brothers would be hammering something, and my sisters would be tearing up and down the stairs, getting ready to go dancing or on a date.

Everyone was out, except me and Mum. I could hear the clock ticking, and Mum humming to herself as she peeled potatoes in the scullery.

"Dum, de de de dum, always. Dum de de de dum, always, always."

She was having a good day. No shouting at me, no slamming down of the china mugs, no muttering about "… that no good *schlemiel*. What a *meshugener*." I was wary of disturbing the peaceful place I found myself in, but was getting bored with my colouring book.

I'd listened to *Children's Favourites* on the radio with Uncle Mac, sung along with the good ones – 'Oh, the runaway train went over the hill and she blewwww'. I wanted to get my comics from round the corner, but didn't have any money. I'd have to sweet talk Mum.

"Mum?"

"Mmm… always, always…"

"How did you meet Dad?"

She put down the potato peeler and came to sit at the kitchen table with me.

Uh, oh. Long story coming up. I hoped that they wouldn't have sold out of *The Dandy* and *The Beano*.

"Well, I was born in Russia, but we had to leave when I was a baby because of the pogroms."

"What's pogroms?" I asked.

"It was horrible people who didn't like us because we were Jewish."

"What, like Mrs Barrows?"

"Very similar. So, anyway, my mother and father and me came over to England in a boat. We had nothing except what we stood up in, but we had relatives in the East End, so we headed there. They couldn't speak a word of English, but found the streets full of Jewish people and even a synagogue.

"It was just like the village we'd left behind, where everyone knew everyone else, and knew their business, too."

"But how did you meet Dad?" I interrupted.

"I'm getting to that. My parents were very strict and religious. Not like us. My father saved up and eventually bought a sewing machine. He started making hats and then had a factory. He was very successful, and being so religious, gave donations to the synagogue. They even put his picture up in the entrance hall.

"I'd started off with the name Mila, but by the time I grew up I didn't want to have such a foreign-sounding name, so I changed it to Milly. I had six brothers and sisters and I was the oldest."

"Like me," I said. "I've got four brothers and two sisters. And I'm the youngest."

"That's right. You're the baby of the family. Anyway, as the oldest I had to look after the others, but I went to work in the family business when I was only thirteen years old. I was a good girl. Very obedient and religious.

"When I was twenty, though, the First World War was over and the East End was full of young people, like me, who wanted to dance and have a good time.

"I would tell my parents that I was going to see my friend and would stay there for dinner, then me and the other naughty girls would go to a dance hall and wait for a young man to ask us to take to the floor.

4

"It was at a dance hall that I met a young man with blond hair and blue eyes. He was short, stocky and cocky, and looked rather like James Cagney, smartly dressed in shoes with spats, and seemed very debonair. He had the gift of the gab, too. He told me 'You're the best-looking girl here.' He had the sweet talk, alright."

"Was that Dad?" I asked.

"Yes. That was him. Morry was also from a family of seven children. The boys were boxers at The Boys' Club in Bethnal Green, runners for the petty criminals of the area, known to be handy with their fists and, being handsome chaps, popular with the girls. And they ate bacon sandwiches.

"He was so different from anyone I'd met before, and I fell for him. My parents didn't approve. He was of a lower class, but at least he was Jewish. They had no idea just how un-Jewish Morry's family really were.

"Somehow we found places to canoodle and, inevitably, canoodling led me to getting pregnant."

"Is canoodle how babies are made, Mum?"

"Yes. I'll tell you more about that another time. Now go and tidy your room."

"Aw, Mum! Tell me some more."

But that was the end of the story for that day. She'd got carried away with the telling of it, and realised at that point that the rest of it might not be suitable for young ears. I missed out on my comics that week and it was a few years before I was told what happened next.

He did the decent thing and they got married in Bethnal Green Register Office, very quietly, with only her best friend and his brother as witnesses. There was only one small problem: neither of them felt brave enough to tell her parents, so Milly went on living at home, her relationship with my dad a clandestine one.

The weeks went on. Her pregnancy was not showing quite yet, when she decided to join the fashion of the day, by having her long hair cut into an up-to-the-minute short bob. When she got home from the hairdressers, her mother was appalled.

"You look like a slut. How could you do such a thing to me? What will the neighbours think when they see you looking like some *shikse* from the streets?"

When her father saw the new hairstyle his reaction was even worse. Being a strict father, he removed his belt and proceeded to thrash her, even as she crouched in the corner, crying.

At this very moment, Morry turned up to take her out for the evening. Her younger sister, Rae, opening the door, said with a smirk, "She's really in trouble tonight."

Morry, hearing the wails of distress, rushed into the sitting room, where he caught hold of my grandfather's arm, stopping him from beating Milly, and shouted, "That's my wife you're hitting, and she's having my baby!"

When the dust had settled, arrangements were quickly made for another wedding, this one to be in a synagogue, with all the trimmings. Morry hired a suit, complete with a top hat, held up by his rather large ears. Milly wore a knee-length dress of white lace, with a veil and headdress of stiffened white satin. She carried an enormous bunch of flowers, which she was careful to hold over her belly for the entire service.

Later, people looked knowing, but marvelled that such a premature baby could look so healthy and bonny.

So that's how Mum and Dad met.

Laying the Foundations

Before I was born, the family lived in the East End of London, in the charmingly named 'Spittle Street'. Mum, Dad and six children living in a two up, two down hovel with no running water and a shared lavatory.

Money was always short, not helped by the fact that my dad had an ongoing love affair with the bow-wows. He was an upholsterer and often spent his weekly wages on the way home, via the racing stadium, not even keeping enough by for the housekeeping.

So Mum always had to work to keep food on the table, unless she was in the last stages of pregnancy. She never wanted such a big family. On finding herself pregnant yet again, she would try the age-old remedy of hot baths and gin, sometimes with a successful outcome. Or she would seek help (heart in mouth, because everyone knew that things could go wrong) from a woman she knew, who was experienced in such skills. She tried to save for a Dutch cap, but every time she'd raised enough money, one of the boys would need new shoes or their often-patched trousers would be beyond further repair.

It probably helped the household expenses that all the kids were evacuated during the war. Although she had this vast brood of children, Mum was never particularly maternal, except perhaps when she was breastfeeding, which she did for as long as possible. Maybe it gave her a closeness she could not otherwise express… or perhaps she used it as a means of avoiding further pregnancies.

The East End had long been a magnet for various immigrant groups, and at this time it was the Jews who made up the majority of the local community. Following the bomb damage to the East End, my family had been moved to a house in Tottenham, North London. It wasn't a luxurious place, but it was much better than the slum of Spittle Street. When we moved to Brunswick Road, we were the only Jewish family in the street, a fact we did not advertise. Anti-Semitism was rife in London and there were still those well-documented signs in the windows of lodging houses stating 'No Irish, No Jews and No Dogs'.

We were completely assimilated and never kept a kosher house, or went to the synagogue, except for weddings and bar mitzvahs. I think that Mum rebelled against her religious parents, because she really went the whole nine yards in rejecting Judaism. We had a big fried breakfast every Sunday, complete with bacon and sausages, although she did nod in the direction of her heritage by serving proper Jewish chicken soup for dinner.

Mum was forty-seven when she had me. She'd started the menopause and never dreamt that she'd get pregnant again with a seventh child. Debbie, my next sibling up, was nine years old, and Mum thought that she'd finished with nappies and sleepless nights. Never a patient woman, she more or less turned over my care to my oldest sister, Sheila, who was nineteen when I was born. So Mum looked after my nutritional and disciplinary needs; Sheila, who was sweet natured, took care of childrearing; but it was Debbie, a feisty tomboy, who was my playmate and tutor.

She would take me in my pram to the park, which had a very steep incline, let go of the pram handle and race it down the hill, both of us screaming with delight. We had another game that involved her lying on the big bed she shared with Sheila, and I would put my feet in her hands, and my hands on her feet. Then she would raise her arms and legs and, hey presto! We were acrobats! Even more importantly, she taught me to read, using cards with letters and words, such as 'nose' or 'apples', on them.

I was lucky that our financial fortunes were looking up by the time I was born in 1947. My eldest brothers, Ron and Charlie, were both in the Merchant Navy, sending money home, and Sheila was working in a shop, so we had more household income. By the time I was five years old, my two other brothers, Joe and Ivor, were employed, and Debbie would soon be leaving school. They all put something into the domestic purse, so things became easier, although Dad was still gambling his wages away, and arguments between my parents were a regular feature of the week.

Brunswick Road was made up of small terraced houses, each with a back yard that had its very own outside toilet. We had a bucket on the landing for night time pees, which was not emptied frequently enough.

Sometimes I would squat over the bucket to do a wee, and my bottom would get cold and wet from its contents. It never bothered me though, except in winter, when it took ages for my bum to get warm again.

My two sisters and I shared one bedroom, with them in a double bed and me in a single. Ron, Charlie and Ivor shared another bedroom, with just enough room for a wardrobe and a chest of drawers. Joe had a small bedroom all to himself, because he had passed the scholarship and needed somewhere to do his homework. Mum and Dad had a room downstairs in the middle of the ground floor.

Overlooking the road was The Front Room. This was rarely used and kept for visits from relatives and the welfare lady, who would run her finger along the mantelpiece and berate Mum about the amount of dust she found there. Whenever the welfare lady visited, she would be served tea in the best china. Unfortunately, it all bore the legend 'J. Lyons', and was a souvenir of when Mum worked there, as she only ever took jobs where there was some perk or another. At J. Lyons she had gradually acquired a whole tea service.

When she worked at the clothing factory, she would secrete a sleeve here and a collar there about her person, until she had an entire coat for someone in the family. Then it would all be sewn together at home. During the smoked salmon factory period, even the cat eventually refused to eat smoked salmon. And in the biscuit factory, the workers were allowed to bring home the broken biscuits… Mum made sure that some were always smashed on her shift. We never went short of biscuits. The welfare lady would also be presented with some of these fragmented biscuits on a J. Lyons plate.

It was the kitchen, though, that was the hub of the family. It was there that we ate, bathed in front of the fire and argued. It was also where I put on my all-singing, all-dancing shows for the family. 'How Much Is That Doggie in the Window?' was a favourite, with Debbie providing the 'Woof, woof' bit. It was where I put Dad's thinning hair into lots of little curls, held in place with ribbons. Actually, they were not ribbons at all, but strips of cut-up lining from the coat factory. Still, they looked pretty in Dad's hair, I thought.

At the very back of the house, there was a scullery, where a copper for heating water was installed. It had to be lit from underneath, with the cold water from the tap at the sink transferred to it, bucket by bucket. Once the water was hot it could be taken, again bucket by bucket, to the tin bath set up in the kitchen. The cooker was in there, too. The scullery was Mum's domain, and you ventured in there when she was cooking at your peril. "This kitchen's not big enough for two people!" she'd yell.

The tin bath hung on the wall in the back yard, ready for the Friday night ablutions. There was a hierarchy to the order in which we bathed and had the privilege of clean water. Modesty would be ensured by the knowledge that it was bath night; nobody went in the kitchen unless it was their turn to bathe, the tub placed in front of the fireplace. First in was Dad, followed by Mum, and then one of the boys, each person getting a top-up of hot water. The next lot of clean water was for the baby – me – followed by Debbie, who tells me she would complain, "I don't want to get into that. The baby's been in there covered in wee and number twos."

When it was Ivor's turn, he would also grumble, "I don't want to get in there. Two girls have been in that water." The next batch of fresh water would be for Sheila first (being a girl and therefore cleaner), then the remaining two boys. It was like a military operation and took several hours.

★

When I was four years old, Mum told me to get into my pushchair because we were going to the park. I was thrilled. Mum never took me to the park. We went on a bus first, and then into a place with green, well-clipped lawns and clumps of bushes.

I couldn't see any swings, but thought there must be a playground further on. It was odd, though, because we went into a big building where ladies in blue and white dresses, their fronts covered with white aprons, rushed about. They put me into a cot in a room with other children, and then my mum left. I watched her through the bars of the cot, and although my eyes welled up, I didn't cry.

I had a tonsillectomy the next day, waking from the operation dozy, feeling sick and with a very sore throat. Mum didn't come to see me that day, but she did come the day after that, bringing Ozzie, my stuffed koala bear, brought back from Australia by my brother Ron. The nurses said Ozzie had to be made clean, and took him away to be sterilised. He was never the same after that; his long, silky fur became all dull and stiff. Still, I was glad to have him there to cuddle, familiar and comforting in the lonely nighttimes.

When it was finally time to go home, Mum came to collect me with the pushchair. She brought me a big bottle of Lucozade, which I'd never tasted before. It was absolutely delicious, so I suppose that was one good thing to come out of the whole experience.

I had started school at three and a half. Debbie had been badly bullied at her school by other children, who would surround her in the playground, shouting "Kill the Yid!" The teachers were equally anti-Semitic, if rather more subtle. How they found out that she was Jewish was a bit of a mystery. She didn't look particularly Jewish, being fair skinned with green eyes and light coloured hair. But if she could be found out, then I would certainly be a more obvious target, being olive skinned with dark hair and eyes.

The family pooled their resources to send me to a little private school. The fees were five shillings a week, and that included lunch. Norton School was just round the corner from home, but in a rather posher street. It was in a terraced house with a proper garden. The classroom was in the front, and held four rows of desks and benches, with a couple of single desks in the alcoves on either side of a blackboard, which was fixed to the boarded-up chimney breast. All the children, who were aged between three and twelve, were taught in the same classroom.

The owner of the school, Mrs Norton, was an elderly lady. We didn't see much of her, as all the lessons were taught by her daughter, Miss Queenie. Miss Queenie was tall and slim, with frizzy red hair, always caught up in an unruly bun. She was actually married, with two daughters: one attended our lessons and the other went to the grammar school. They had a cat and an Old English Sheepdog called Bisto, but us kids called him 'Gravy Face'. Both animals wandered in and out of the classroom; Gravy Face was a bit smelly, but we didn't mind because he would lie down under a desk and we could put our feet on him.

Thanks to Debbie I could already read, and I'm sure that my family would have explained this to Miss Queenie and Mrs Norton, but maybe they didn't understand the extent of my ability. On my first day at school, Miss Queenie was very kind, talking to me in a low, gentle voice. She told me to sit at one of the desks in an alcove, and gave me a page from a newspaper and a pencil.

"I'm busy at the moment," she said "but I will come and help you shortly." Pointing at the paper, she went on, "Now, this is the word 'the'. I want you to go through the paper and mark it each time you see that word."

I nodded and set to, finishing the task in a few minutes. When she saw me gazing around the room, Miss Queenie asked me why I wasn't doing what she'd asked me. I was a bit scared, but told her that I'd finished.

She was suitably impressed, and from that day onwards, whenever a school inspector came to visit, I was always called upon to read aloud. I was very proud to be a star pupil, getting lots of praise and attention.

Unfortunately, my arithmetic was not on a par with my reading. This was not picked up, however, until I was asked to solve a sum written on the blackboard. I then had to admit I couldn't see that far, and my extreme short sight was exposed.

Spectacles were the order of the day, each pair more hideous than the last. I never did catch up with sums, though, and to this day cannot recite the seven, eight or nine times tables.

As all the adults in the family were working, and did not get home until early evening, arrangements were made for me to stay after school and have my tea there for a small charge, so I was able to spend extra, special time with Miss Queenie and could cuddle Gravy Face, a very patient animal, in their kitchen. I loved Miss Queenie, so this arrangement was all good.

The lessons were sometimes a bit haphazard. We did the three Rs, of course, but never had games or PT. There just wasn't anywhere to do them. We did use the garden for 'Nature Study', though, cutting up flowers to examine the sap, petals and stems. Catching caterpillars was also a popular pursuit. We'd put them into jam jars with a hole in the lid, shove in a few leaves, then wait and watch until they became a chrysalis. They would sometimes survive to become a butterfly, but many a caterpillar had a sad and lonely end to its life, forgotten in its jam jar at the back of the greenhouse.

Miss Queenie sang with a choir, led by Sir Malcolm Sargent. When she'd had an evening of rehearsals, she would regale us the next day with accounts of what had happened, what the great conductor had said or done, and might even sing the songs she had been practising.

She was learning Esperanto, the new universal language, so as she found a new phrase or word, would teach it to us. She was convinced that '*Kiom kostas la kuko?*' ('How much does the cake cost?') would stand us in good stead, should we ever travel outside of the United Kingdom.

Mornings were always a bit fraught in our house. There were a lot of people to get washed, dressed and off to work or school.

"Have you got everything?" my mum asked. "Have you had a wee?"

"I'm going to be late," I said, worrying the front door latch – a stretch for a seven year old.

"Where's your milk?" I had to take milk for the morning break. I liked the milk, but hated the cod liver oil I had to have once a week. It was slimy in my mouth and smelt stinky.

I ran back down the passage to get the milk from the larder, and came back with a bottle. My hair was already escaping from its beribboned plaits and I was getting hot.

"Right. Off you go then. Ask someone to take you across the road." My mum had to get her sandwich and flask ready before she went to work. Being late ran in the family. There was a big road to cross and I'd been told to always wait for a grown-up ('only ask a lady') to take me over it.

I slung my bag around my body, holding the milk tightly to my chest. "Bye!" I shouted, running now along the narrow terraced street, then onto the pavement of the main road.

Seven Sisters station was nearby, along with a row of shops. There was the Swap Shop, an Aladdin's cave of floor-to-ceiling junk, where old copies of *The Beano* could be bought for a penny, and the bakers', tempting with doughnuts, squishy with red jam, and iced fingers that could be licked until the white icing was all gone, then eaten as a bun.

There was a paper shop, too. My big sister Debbie would tell me to ask for "Ten unmarried men, please." Wally would grin and give me a pack of ten Bachelor cigarettes.

Waiting for someone to take me across the road, I jumped when a fire engine passed within inches of me, making a terrible noise. I could see that it stopped outside the station. There was a lot of shouting, people running about and loads of smoke coming out of the dark bricked entrance. I thought it was the most exciting thing I'd ever seen – apart from when Lassie rescued that little boy from down the well.

I wanted to wait and see what happened next, but a woman with curlers under her headscarf, coming out of the butchers on the corner, exclaimed, "What are you up to? You should be in school."

"Can you take me across the road, please," I asked, as rehearsed at home.

Safely over the way, I was even later now, so ran, puffing hard. The milk bottle was wet and slippery and, as I reached the front door of the school, it slipped out of my hands. Bits of glass and milk splattered all over the place. It all seemed to happen in slow motion. Then, suddenly, I was wetting myself, a stream of wee running down my bare legs, straight into my white ankle socks.

I opened my mouth and howled with shame, anger and shock as Miss Queenie opened the door, taking in the sorry scene in a moment. She took me into the kitchen where I was given a hug and a cup of warm milk to drink, while my knickers and socks dried on the fender in front of the fire.

Outings and Treats

In 1953, the Coronation gave rise to huge excitement everywhere. A street party was to be held, with a fancy dress competition for the kids, followed by a special tea. I was five years old and Debbie was fourteen. Debbie was dressed as a pirate; she looking suitably threatening as she sulked, saying, "I don't want to go. I'll be the oldest one there." Mum made me an Elizabethan dress out of Union Jacks. It even had a hooped skirt. I looked the business.

A boy wearing a shop-bought cowboy outfit won first prize, and we were all outraged, although he did have a squint and wore glasses with one side patched up with pink sticking plasters, so perhaps he needed a treat.

Tea was set out on long tables down the road, each family having provided a table and chairs for their kids. The sun shone weakly and we had meat paste sandwiches, followed by jelly and custard, then fairy cakes topped with icing. There was orange squash to drink, and we were all given a toy Coronation coach, painted in gold and red.

Only one family in the street had a television: the Barrows, who lived two doors down from us. They were a bit on the rough side, and I wasn't encouraged to play with the two girls, Sally and Georgina, who were around my age. On Coronation Day, though, we would have given our eye teeth to be best friends with them, as it was those neighbours who were invited into their house to watch the procession on the ten-inch screen. As for the rest of us, we had to crowd around their window to try to catch a glimpse of the pretty young woman, who looked like she had stepped out of a fairy tale.

It wasn't too long after this that we acquired our own telly. It was installed in The Front Room, which immediately stopped being used only on high days and holidays, and became the place where we all crowded in to watch *Opportunity Knocks* and *I Love Lucy*. I really did love Lucy, too. I would fall off the sofa with laughter at her antics.

Mum was a Liberace fan, entranced by his perfect smile and charming ways, not to mention his extraordinary talent at the keyboard. She had no idea that he was 'one of them', growing quite cross when one of my brothers suggested that he was a bit of a pansy. "Just because he's got clean nails and dresses nicely, doesn't mean that he's like that, you know," she'd comment. "You could learn something from him," she'd added. The boys would guffaw knowingly, but they didn't dare argue with her.

We all knew that Mum was not one to be crossed lightly. Sometimes we'd all be sitting around the kitchen table and something would get her goat. Her voice would go ominously quiet and she would declare, "I'm a very placid woman, BUT..." and at this point she would raise her fist then bang it on the table with such force that the whole table (a very sturdy utility model) would shake – as would all the family.

Although she was the least maternal of women, one way she did demonstrate caring was through food. She would cook huge meals for all nine of us. Sometimes, looking at the mound of food overflowing on my plate, I would say, "I can't eat all this." She was surprisingly flexible and would reply, "Just eat what you can and leave the rest."

So I would do just that. But when she saw that I hadn't eaten all of the meal, she would say, "What's the matter? You don't like my cooking?" in the most defensive tone. Not wanting to upset her (because who knew what that could lead to?) I would force myself to clear my plate.

And so began my complicated relationship with food, which lasts until this day, and which has seen me on and off diets for most of my adult life.

On a Saturday, I would go with Mum to get the week's shopping. A favourite place was Durley Road market in Stoke Newington. My favourite auntie, Eva, Mum's sister, lived there with her husband and their only child, Marsha, so we would sometimes visit them before going shopping. Auntie Eva was everything Mum was not: affectionate, warm and loving. She would often slip me half a crown, saying, "Don't tell Uncle Jack", who was known to be mean.

Marsha was a year older than me, so I got all her cast-offs. The only problem was that by the time they came to me, Auntie Eva had already added a panel here, let down a hem there, so that these frocks often had a patchwork effect. I didn't really mind. Marsha had nice clothes, usually carefully made by her mother, or bought for her by Auntie Rita, another of Mum's sisters. Rita doted on Marsha, but referred to our bit of the family as 'Milly's brats'. Ah well, can't win 'em all. Marsha went to dancing classes and elocution lessons. There was a huge photo of her over the mantelpiece in their best room. She was posing in a dancing costume, wearing a smug smile, holding out the skirt, her feet just so in fourth position (learnt at ballet class), and her long red hair all glossy and tidy, held in place by a wide ribbon. Although Marsha and I were friends, I was so jealous of her. I wanted Auntie Eva for my mum, and I wanted a new dress that no one had ever worn before.

After a cup of tea and a slice of Auntie Eva's homemade cake, Mum and I would make our way to the town centre and do the shopping. We might go into Woolworths, on the corner of the market, where the counters were raised on foot-high legs. The space underneath the counter was used for storage. If not many people were around, Mum would say to me, "See that box over there? Go and get it." And off I'd go, somehow picking up on the need for caution, bringing the package back to her, whereupon she'd stuff it into her shopping bag on wheels, to be examined later.

As an occasional treat, we'd go for a late lunch at the pie and mash shop. The seating was on long benches, set into semi-private alcoves with marble-topped tables. There was sawdust on the floor and steam rising from the high counter, where ladies in hairnets served the pies, thick with meat and gravy, mashed potato on the side, and the whole lot covered with a parsley sauce, known as 'liquor'. Outside the shop they kept live eels, all gleaming and black, in trays of shallow water on a table. The eels usually kept very still, but if you poked one, they would all start to slither around, slightly threatening, although not really, because they could not escape from their box.

We'd go to the pictures, too. There were two cinemas in Tottenham: the ordinary one and another one, only known as 'The Bug 'Ole'. It had seen better days, and the once-red velvet seats were now faded and sticky with unknown substances, but the tickets were cheap. We'd go and see the blockbuster of the day or a Disney film. As soon as the lights went down, Mum would produce a Spam sandwich, and a flask of tea or a bottle of orange squash. These would sustain us through the rigours of *Bambi* or *The King and I*.

Now and then, Mum and I would go on holiday to the seaside – Clacton or Southend. Just the two of us. I guess it was an opportunity for her to have a break, justified by taking me with her. She was often easier and less likely to lose her temper when we had time away.

Self-catering apartments were unheard of in those days, so we would stay at a bed and breakfast. The rules of the establishment often required guests to leave at nine thirty in the morning and not return to their accommodation until five o'clock.

By the time I was ten years old I was already having periods and had little buds of breasts. I hated it all, being the only girl in the whole school who had hair under her arms, not to mention other places, and whose chest now protruded with two lumps. I had a way of buttoning my cardigan at the top, so that it fell straight down over my bosom. I wore a cardigan all year round.

That year Mum and I went to Hastings for a week. She was determined that I should go on the beach.

"It'll be good for you, get some sun to your body."

"No, Mum, I don't want to. Why can't I just read my book?"

"You can read it on the beach. Now get your swimming costume on."

"No. I'm not going to. I'll be cold."

What it was really about, of course, was my self-consciousness at revealing my body to the world. We didn't talk about this, but Mum must have picked up on some of my anxiety.

That evening, without any warning, she announced she would shave my legs, and without so much as a 'by your leave', proceeded to do so. I certainly liked the finished result, turning my legs this way and that and admiring the new smoothness, like a baby's bottom. So that was one less problem, although I still had those damned tits to contend with. Still, at least I could now wear shorts and get onto the beach, which kept her quiet for a bit.

The next afternoon the sky blackened and it started to rain. It rained for days, unremitting, heavy, great dollops of water constantly soaking us. Our B&B was cold, and being wet made it colder. After several days of this and a constant diet of pork pies, Mum said, "Shall we go home?" I packed in five minutes flat.

Sometimes my dad took me places, too. It might be just a ride around the block as a pillion passenger on his little motorbike, with me holding onto his waist very, very tightly. One night we went to the dog track in Haringey, and he let me choose a dog to put a bet on. I liked it, seeing all those daft dogs chasing a pretend rabbit.

Another time we went to watch a Spurs football game, but that was a bit scary when the crowd of men surged forwards following a goal, and the rules of the game were a mystery to me – they still are.

We would go and see his mum and brothers at their house in Stepney. I was frightened of Grandma Green. I often couldn't understand what she was saying, as she mostly spoke Yiddish. Not that she said much from her deep armchair. Mostly "Have a *kichl, kinder. Esn, esn.*"

The *kichl* were hard little biscuits, which needed to be dunked in tea for ages before they became edible. Still, my uncles would always give me half a crown each, or sometimes five shillings. As we left, with the money tucked away in my pocket, Dad would ask, "How much did you cop then?" and we'd add it up before getting on his motorbike to go home.

Once he took me to Uncle Reg and Uncle Sam's shop on Whitechapel Road. It appeared to be a café. There was a long counter, with a glass display case containing several dry-looking buns. An old woman, behind the counter with a cigarette in her mouth, was washing up a few tea cups. She nodded to Dad as we went past her. There was only one customer, a man wearing a cloth cap and a tweed jacket. He nodded at Dad, too.

At the back of the shop there was a door leading to stairs. We went up the stairs and came to another door. Dad knocked on the door – 'tat, tat, tattity, tat' – and the door opened to reveal a right commotion. There were a lot of men in there, all smoking up a storm, all shouting. There was a radio tuned into a racing commentary, and a tick-tack machine in the corner, pumping out a stream of paper. It was an illegal betting shop.

As we moved through the room, one man after another asked Dad, "Is this your kid then, Morry?" I felt very shy, and peeped at them from behind my dad's stout frame. They kept giving me a shilling here, ten bob there, and even a pound note from one of them. I really copped a lot on that outing.

Mum used to send me off every week to Sunday school at the Salvation Army, not really for any religious education, but to be shot of me for a couple of hours. Naturally, no one was told that we were really Jewish, and I enjoyed the singing and bible stories. Sometimes there would be a discussion, too, like why the Good Samaritan was so named. We got milk and biscuits, not to mention a present at Christmas, so that was alright.

When Auntie Eva told Mum that Marsha went to Hebrew classes on Saturdays, Mum saw a new window of opportunity. She could get rid of me for a while on Saturdays, too.

It was duly arranged that I would accompany Marsha next week. We went to her local synagogue and I found myself in a classroom with about a dozen other children. The teacher was an ordinary-looking man, apart from wearing a black skullcap.

The lesson began. It was all gobbledegook to me and I found it very dull. I drifted off into my usual daydreams, wondering what we would have for dinner, whether I would get time to go to the library today and so on.

Suddenly, immediately over my head, there was a loud crack and I found myself showered with glass. For one terrifying moment I was convinced that God himself had noticed that I was not paying attention, and had sought to punish me in this way. It was with some relief that I realised a light bulb had exploded. I wasn't about to risk it again though, and refused to return to the Hebrew classes, just in case.

There was one time when I found myself going 'on holiday' without any family. I can't remember the journey to the big house, only that it was enormous with dark corridors, locked rooms and lots of children. I'm not even sure why I went there. I think I was about eight years old. Debbie had often been sent away to children's homes when she was little, so perhaps Mum had found it a useful way to have a break from the minimal childcare she provided.

I remember Mum taking me to the Jewish Board of Guardians to ask for money. Was that to finance this place she'd taken me to?

The 'holiday camp' was run by religious Jews, that I do remember, because it was all quite strange to me. We had religious instruction and Hebrew classes. I didn't understand any of it, although most of the other children seemed to. There was one class where I had a tummy ache and needed to blow off. It was only after I broke wind that I realised I had done a number two. The shame prevented me from telling anyone and I inexpertly washed my dirtied knickers myself, secretly, in the bathroom.

We slept in dormitories, separate ones for boys and girls. The dormitories held about eighteen beds. We each had a small bedside locker for our belongings. At night there were often snuffles of tears shed, giggles of the more bold, and a hum of little girls talking about the things little girls talk about.

A nurse would come in at certain times to tell us to be quiet and go to sleep. She never comforted the weeping ones, or checked to see if everyone was present and correct. There was a night when she had made one entrance, then came back again to find that I was still chatting. She grabbed my arm and took me off down the dormitory to a broom cupboard at the end of the room. She told me that there were rats in there and that I would have to stay until I learnt to be quiet at bedtime. With that she pushed me into the cupboard and I heard the lock turn.

There was no window. It was very, very dark. It smelt of mustiness and disinfectant. I couldn't tell if there was anything to sit on, so I sank to the floor, terrified that the rats would run all over me. I didn't cry, but felt a constriction in my throat and chest that made breathing difficult. How long was I there? Ten minutes? Half an hour? Four hours? I have no idea, but eventually I was released and told to go back to bed.

I suppose it was effective as a punishment because I hardly spoke to anyone after that, either during the day or night. I kept my head down and did my time until I could go home again.

Changes and Challenges

I was eight in 1955 when we moved to a new house, still in Tottenham, but much grander than the one in Brunswick Road.

Semi-detached, at the end of a row, not only was there a back yard with an outside lavatory, but also a proper front garden. We had two enormous reception rooms, one of which became Mum and Dad's bedroom, a dining room with a hatch through to the kitchen, four bedrooms upstairs and an indoor toilet and bathroom, with running hot water. A palace.

Even better, I got my own room for the first time. It was the box room, about eight feet square, so there wasn't a lot of space, but it didn't matter. It was mine. Somewhere I could escape the hurly-burly and noise of the family, and read until my eyes felt like sandpaper. I arranged all my toys – poor Ozzie and Harvey, my rabbit, together with the bear with no name and a particularly ugly doll that Ron had brought me back from Singapore – onto the top of the chest of drawers, where they glared at me with their beady eyes.

There was a family living next door with a daughter, Sylvia, who was about my age. She was tall and thin, in contrast to my short plumpness, but we became instant friends, along with Linda, who was just over the road. We'd play dressing up, acting out all our favourite films and books. *The Famous Five* was a popular one, with Sylvia being Julian, Linda as George and, being the youngest, I usually got stuck with being Anne. Timmy the dog was imaginary, while we just dispensed with Dick, who was a bit of a drip anyway.

It was around this time that I saw a black person for the first time. I was playing in the street with Sylvia, Linda and the twins when a black woman crossed the road just in front of us. We all stopped our game and just stared at her in fascination. I knew about black people from the books that my brother Ron brought me back from his travels, so I understood different skin colours, but I had never seen one in real life.

Apart from her skin colour, this lady looked very ordinary and rather smart, dressed in a grey coat and matching hat. She wore lipstick and carried a shiny, brown handbag. As I watched her, my skipping rope drooping onto the ground, I saw that she was headed towards my house. As she went up the path, I dropped the rope and tore over the road, yelling, "I've got to go home now!"

As I got to the front door, my mum was letting the black lady in and ushering her into our new front room.

"This is Winifred, who works with me," Mum said.

"Hello. And what's your name?" Winifred asked me.

Her voice was like nothing I'd heard before. She was almost singing the question. When she smiled at me, her teeth were astoundingly white against the red of her lipstick and the darkness of her skin.

"This is Janet, my youngest," Mum replied for me.

All I could do was to sit on the pouffe, in front of her, and stare. I wanted to hear her talk some more, but felt too shy to ask or answer questions. I was saved when Ron and Sheila came in to help entertain our guest.

Later, after she left, it emerged that Winifred had recently come to England from Trinidad, leaving behind all her family. She hoped they would be able to join her eventually, but for the moment did not know anyone in England. Having started work at the same factory as my mum, they had got talking. Mum, being partial to rescuing waifs and strays, had invited Winifred round for tea. And perhaps she remembered how it felt to be from an immigrant background, often reviled and misunderstood.

I liked our new house and my new friends. It was all going so well. Too well. Towards the end of that long summer holiday, before I turned nine, I asked when school would be starting. There was a long silence, and then Mum said, "You're not going back to Miss Norton's. You'll be starting a new school."

What? I couldn't quite believe what I'd heard. What did it mean?

Mum continued, "They don't do the Eleven Plus at Miss Norton's, so you need to go to a different school. We're going to meet the headmaster next week."

My head reeled. I would have to leave my beloved Miss

Queenie. Leave the safe place where I knew everyone, and was a star pupil. I would have to learn how to do sums and do PE. I was devastated, grief-stricken and my heart was broken for the first time. I crouched behind the kitchen door and keened like a stricken animal, sobbing, unable to stop, even when Mum said, "Right. That's enough now. Stop crying or I'll give you something to cry about."

In the end it was Sheila who coaxed me out of the dark corner, promising me some hot chocolate in bed. I hiccupped my way to the asylum of my room feeling so very sad. I never said goodbye to Gravy Face or Miss Queenie. I never saw them again.

Going to my interview at the new school I was still in a very low mood, and going into the huge building, with seemingly endless corridors, was scary. Making our way to the head's office, we passed through the assembly hall, an imposing room with a stage at one end, together with a piano by its side. There were what looked like ladders along all the walls, for what use I couldn't begin to imagine.

The headmaster sat behind a solid desk. He seemed to be a large person, taking up a lot of space in the small room. He had very little hair on his head, but sported a large ginger moustache. He asked me two questions.

"What is nine times nine? And how do you spell the word 'sugar'?"

I panicked. I tried to think of the table, but just couldn't make sense of the numbers. It was all a jumble in my head. My heart was pounding. My mouth was dry. I took a guess.

"Er… Is it eighty-seven?"

I paused, trying to catch my breath.

"Now spell 'sugar'," he boomed across the table.

Sugar? Sugar? I knew this, but my brain had closed down with anxiety and fright.

"S-H-U-G-E-R," I haltingly replied.

And that was it. When I started my new school that autumn,

I was put into the lowest stream, and there I stayed until the end-of-year tests. I came top of the class in many subjects, so went into the highest stream the next year, my last at junior school. It would prove, though, to be too late to catch up for the Eleven Plus syllabus, even if I had known how to change fractions into percentages – which I didn't.

It didn't really matter because everything changed during the following summer holiday.

A Summer to Remember

Mum wasn't exactly an advert for *Homes and Gardens*. In fact, she was a dreadful housekeeper. If someone knocked unexpectedly on the door of our house, we would all rush around throwing stuff into cupboards, behind the sofa and under cushions so as to create some semblance of order and tidiness in the front room, where visitors were always invited to sit.

It was my job when I got back from school, as the first person home in the afternoon, to clear away the breakfast things and wash up, but I hadn't done it. Then I would pay the price, as Mum would chase me around the table in the kitchen, trying to catch up to give me a good hiding – a slap on the legs or a clip round the ear. The problem was that when I had a good book on the go, I would forget to do my chores. Then Mum would get home and she'd go bananas when she saw the mess left from the morning. Good job I was quicker on my feet than she was. I'd keep saying, "Sorry, sorry. I'll do it now", but it would take a few laps of the table before she would stop shouting, "When I get my hands on you, I'll kill you", and she'd calm down a bit.

That year, in the summer holidays, I was playing with my gang in the street. It started to rain, so we all went into my house, climbing the stairs to the bedroom shared by my older sisters. None of the grown-ups were at home. I was nearly nine years old, and didn't need to be babysat.

One thing led to another. Peter said that he'd show us his thing if one of the girls showed theirs. The twins giggled, but didn't make a move. Sylvia said to me, "Go on. You do it." So I did. Peter and I flashed at the same time. It was just a glimpse and I think the girls got the better deal – well, there was more to see. And that was it, really. We pulled our pants back up and went to the sweetshop to get Sherbet Fountains and lemonade powder.

That evening, after I'd been really good and done the washing up, I was in my room, head in a book as usual, when I heard Mum shout, "When I get my hands on you…"

Quick as a flash, I dashed into the toilet – a previously proven safe haven – and bolted the door. I put down the toilet lid, preparing to sit there for a long time until I felt safe. She banged on the door, huffing and puffing, but there was no way that I was going to unlock it. I didn't know how she'd found out about me and Peter, but there was no doubt in my mind that this was the problem.

After a while she went away. I allowed myself a sigh of relief. She must be calming down. It would be safe to come out soon for my dinner. A short time later I recognised her footstep on the stairs again. It was very quiet. I could hear my own breathing.

Suddenly, and completely without warning, the blade of an axe broke through the wooden door. The sound of wood cracking was almost as loud as the noise my heart made. The splintered white gloss paint from the door flaked off and fell to the ground. I stared at the silver blade just inches from my face, becoming quite fixated by the sharp, shiny oblong, unable to tear my gaze away.

Taking a sudden breath, something between a gasp and a sob, I backed up against the wall as she bellowed her usual refrain, "When I get my hands on you, I'm going to kill you." I didn't scream, but I thought, *She means it this time.* The blade was pulled out of the door and I heard Joe, one of my big brothers, exclaiming, "What the hell are you doing?"

It went very quiet out there for a long time. Eventually, I

opened the door, planning to creep out to see if it was safe. She must have been waiting for me, because the next thing I knew I was trapped on the three steps that led to my other sanctuary: my bedroom.

She hit me over and over again, anywhere she could land a swipe: on my legs, arms, head, back. All the time she was shouting, yelling, shrieking like a mad thing. Once again, I was rescued by Joe, who pulled her off me, saying, "That's enough." I crept into my bedroom and stayed there until the next morning. When I came down the stairs for breakfast, nothing was said about yesterday. Not ever.

And then my dad died.

He always had a Capstan fag on the go. Sticking to his lower lip, it was as much a part of his face as his nose. He was a short, tubby bloke, with grey thinning hair and an easy smile.

Once I heard two girls talking in the playground. One of them said, "Who do you love more, your mum or your dad?" I was astounded. I never knew it was possible to love your mum. For me there was no contest.

The only tactile affection I got at home was from Dad. I always kissed him goodnight, and always shared his Sunday breakfast, snuggled up next to him in his bed. Other than that, we didn't do hugs, kisses or cuddles in our house.

Dad was fifty-five years old when he became ill. He would go into hospital for short periods and then come home again. He'd had to stop work and was in bed a lot. There came a time when he went into hospital for a long time. Everyone in the house was very quiet, very tippy-toed. They took me to the hospital, and we went into a side room where there was a very thin, tiny, old man lying in bed. He was all eyes and teeth. I didn't know who he was, but then someone gave me a gentle push and said, "Go and give Dad a kiss."

I couldn't see any resemblance between this person and my daddy, but I went up to the bed and looked into the face of the stranger. He smiled at me and, suddenly, I recognised him.

Climbing on the bed to lie next to him as I always did, I chattered about this and that until Sheila said that it was time to leave.

Our house became even quieter over the next few days, until there was such an atmosphere that I became convinced that he had died and that no one was telling me.

Alone in the house, I went into the lounge and threw myself face down onto the sofa. I sobbed into the cushions. I felt sick, choking on my tears, wanting and yet not wanting to know the truth. I was so muddled. Why wasn't I being told that Dad had died? Was it to be a secret? Would it be a secret forever?

It was actually the next day that Mum came back from the hospital, sat on the stairs, and told me, "You haven't got a daddy anymore." She was crying. I'd never seen her cry before and it was so shocking that it immediately triggered my own grief.

I was shipped off to some relatives until after the funeral, and when I came back it was as if I'd dreamt the whole thing, because he was never mentioned again, at least not in front of me. I took refuge in numbness, an invisible barrier, where I could protect myself from the pain of losing him. It was a long time before I would let myself cry again.

Mum had some sort of mental breakdown after my dad died. I think she became very depressed and missed his presence, in spite of their regular arguments. She went into hospital. Electro-convulsive treatment was the dish of the day in the fifties, so she had that. This was followed by a lobotomy.

It sounds so extreme to us now, but using these brutal treatments to cure mental health problems was new and modern at that time. It seemed to work, too, because her depression lifted. But she was never the same. Her personality changed, making her far less volatile, but also a bit wishy-washy, without her usual anger and passion.

I failed the Eleven Plus exam and went to the local secondary modern, Risley Avenue. I couldn't have cared less. It was an all girls' school, where we had to wear a horrible uniform in green and yellow. Mum had bought the skirt and blazer two sizes too big for me, in the belief that I would grow into them. I didn't, and spent the next few years in a skirt turned over several times at the waist, and a blazer that almost reached to my knees.

The Prime Minister, Mr Macmillan, declared we'd never had it so good, and rationing had finally ended. We were on the cusp of a new decade, and I was on the cusp of adolescence, about to become a rebel after a short pause.

I discovered sex and rock 'n' roll. The drugs came later.

2

The Dangers of Rock 'n' Roll

Going to Big School was a revelation. For a start, it was all girls – something I'd never come across before. For another thing, it was even more enormous than my junior school. And it was far enough away to have to get a bus.

I was put in the top stream. Although I struggled with the maths, I did well in other subjects. I soon belonged to a gang of first year pupils with whom I'd play skipping or hand clapping games in the breaks. We also had a habit of sitting on the playground floor with our coats over us, and having a fiddle with each other. Jolly interesting it was, too.

In the summer holidays, at the end of the first year in secondary school, I became friends with Jenny. She was in my class and she turned up one day at my house, just when I was in the middle of a game of dressing up with Sylvia and Linda. It was 'The King and I', and we had made authentic-looking pantaloons by tucking a full skirt between our legs and securing the hem into the waistband at the back.

When Jenny arrived I felt a bit silly. She seemed far more grown up than me, wearing make-up and having pierced ears. Obviously, the game stopped there and then, with Sylvia and Linda drifting off elsewhere. Jenny said that we should go to the Royal dance hall on Saturday afternoon where they had a disco for under-sixteens.

"I can't dance," I said, a bit shamefaced.

"I can. I'll teach you."

And she did. We'd play records at her home and mine. Cliff

Richard featured widely, along with Billy Fury, Marty Wilde and the cheerful shouting of Joe Brown and The Bruvvers. She'd swing me round and show me complicated moves, involving arms and twisting our bodies in unison, all the while mouthing instructions at me.

"Now you go under."

"Do that three times."

"Give me your other hand."

I must say we got it down to a fine art, and I learnt to love both rock 'n' roll music and dancing. We never missed a Saturday afternoon at the Royal.

I was mad for Cliff Richard. I loved every aspect of him. His voice, of course, which was like honey, smooth and sweet, but also his big brown eyes, the way his hair hung in a quiff over his forehead, his almost swollen lips, which held such promise. The trouble was that I didn't quite understand exactly what the promise involved.

I'd been fascinated by sex and sexuality since I was about ten. Sylvia and Linda and I had had some fumblings when we were playing, particularly in the game we called 'Master and Servants'. We nearly got caught once by Linda's uncle when we were in the toy teepee erected in her garden, so we stopped that particular game and went onto one of the others. 'The Famous Five' was usually a pretty safe bet. No fumbling in that one.

Somewhere I'd heard about a book called *The Origin of Species* by Charles Darwin. Maybe Miss Queenie had talked about it. I suspected it held the answers I wanted. I took myself off to the library, where I'd been a regular for years, and asked the librarian where I'd find this book. If she was surprised by this request from a twelve year old, she hid it well, and just told me that it was for reference only, and that I would not be allowed to take it home. Settling myself at a table with this weighty tome, I scanned it for some time. The pictures were interesting, but I just couldn't find a chapter on 'Doing It'.

It was a couple of years before I found out more. Sylvia was a year older than me and went to the Girls' High School. They had sex education lessons there. And as she learnt about semen, ovaries, vaginas and penises, she told me about it. She even did some drawings of sperm for me, but suggested that I destroy these in case my mum found them – although it only looked like a picture of tadpoles to me.

So now I had the knowledge, but was still lacking the practice. I met a boy on holiday and we went to the pictures. Naturally, we sat in the back row. When he kissed me, with his tongue in my mouth and my nose all squashed, I felt that I might suffocate. By the end of the film, we'd got a bit better at it and he'd touched my breasts – outside of my clothes, but not for want of trying to get under my jumper. It was all rather exhausting, and I wasn't at all sure that I wanted to repeat the experience.

I would turn fourteen in October 1961, and decided that I wanted to celebrate by booking tickets for Jenny and me to go to a Cliff Richard concert. After school, we found a phone box with the plan of phoning the theatre to find out how much the tickets were. Two boys passed by, did a double take, and came back. They squeezed into the phone box with us. One of them, who was very tall and thin with a lot of spots, put one arm around me, pulling me towards him and trying to kiss me. His other hand found its way up my school skirt and was sliding into my knickers. I was terrified, and promptly bit the hand that was over my shoulder.

"Ouch!" he exclaimed. "Doesn't your mother feed you enough?"

With this he pulled me out of the phone box and down an alleyway. He pinned me against the wall and then started shaking. I thought that he was having a fit of some kind. It was all very scary and I was still trying to get away, but he was much stronger than me, in spite of his apparent affliction. He finally stopped shaking, which was a great relief, and just walked away. I was quite shaken myself, but ran back to the High Road, looking for Jenny. There was no sign of her, so I went home.

It was a couple of days later that Mum suddenly looked at my clothes and asked, "What's that down the front of your skirt?"

I looked and saw a widely spread stain of white stuff. "I don't know," I replied, surprised. "I must have spilt some milk down me."

"Hmm. Well, you'd better wash it."

It wasn't dry enough to wear the next morning, so I had to go to school in a non-uniform skirt, getting told off by the headmistress in the process. Jenny asked me why I wasn't wearing uniform, so I explained about the mysterious stain.

"That wasn't milk, you wally," she said. "That was spunk."

A thought entered my head. How did she know?

"Have you Done It yet?" I asked her.

"Yeah. A few times."

I was shocked. Jenny was six months younger than me, so was only thirteen years old. At the same time, I was fascinated and, it has to be said, quite envious that she'd completed that particular hurdle of The First Time.

Now I knew a bit more, my crush on Cliff Richard took on a few more details. I would daydream about those lips kissing me, his hands gently, yet firmly, running themselves over my body… Then there came a bit of a blank. I wasn't absolutely sure how it went after that.

My fourteenth birthday came and went. We'd gone to the Cliff Richard show and, although I hadn't been able to bring myself to scream with the other girls, seeing him in the flesh with those tight trousers and crisp shirt gave yet more fuel to that particular fantasy.

Sometimes, when I looked in the mirror, all I saw was someone who was short, fat and ugly. I looked different from most of the girls I knew. I had olive skin and thick, almost black hair, full lips and wide, brown eyes. I had a big nose. A Jewish nose. Not hooked, thankfully, but definitely not *retroussé*, either. I looked different. Foreign.

My figure had developed earlier than other girls', too, giving me a generous bust, with a small waist, flaring out to womanly hips. And I was tiny, just less than five feet. I wished I looked like everyone else. I felt sure that no boy would ever want me for a girlfriend, and Cliff certainly wouldn't look twice.

Jenny and I had started going to the Lynch House Youth Club a few evenings each week. They had records and dancing for the girls, with pool and table tennis for the boys. The youth workers didn't seem to get very involved, but mostly sat in their office smoking and drinking coffee. Occasionally they would take a walk around the club to make sure no one was fighting or getting drunk. Alcohol wasn't allowed, but lots of the kids smoked.

There was this boy, Barry, who went to the club. He was older than me, about eighteen. He had brown eyes, dark hair greased into a plumage, plump lips. If I half closed my eyes, he was a dead ringer for Cliff, apart from being about six inches shorter.

But, Oh My God, I wanted him. I would follow him around the club, hopefully unobtrusively, just to look at him. I found out that he lived in one of the prefabs behind the High Road, and that he had a motorbike.

When he finally noticed me and said he'd walk me home, I thought I'd died and gone to heaven. As I gave my hair a final brush and put on more lipstick, I dreamt that now we would be a couple. He would be my boyfriend, bring me chocolates and flowers, let me sit on his lap and tell me he loved me. I'd read all about it in *Honey* magazine.

The fact that he could barely string two words together didn't bother me. After all, he only needed to know three little words. The rest of it would follow naturally, as I found out his favourite meal, what music he liked and his best subject at school.

He put his arm around me as we walked and, when we passed his place, a low-lying prefab erected just after the war, he asked me if I wanted to have a coffee before he took me home. As we went into the darkened hall, he pulled me to him and started kissing me. Oh, yes! I kissed him back with much enthusiasm. Whilst kissing me he edged me along the hallway and into one of the rooms, lowering me onto a bed, still kissing.

"Barry," I said shyly, "I, um, haven't done this before."

He didn't respond, just kept taking off more and more of my clothes, until I was naked. This was it. I was about to Do It with the boy I loved.

There was no foreplay. No stroking or affection or sweet nothings. He just tore into me. It hurt like hell and I gasped with pain, but thankfully it didn't last long. He left the room without a word.

"Is that it?" I thought. I couldn't understand what all the fuss was about. I sat on the bed, trying to sort out my thoughts, my clothes and my wobbly legs.

Before I could gather myself together, another boy came in. All the lights were off, but I was sure I didn't know him. He pushed me back on the bed, and then fucked me as quickly and as brutally as Barry had done, in spite of my struggling and trying to push him off. He left just as abruptly.

Crying now, I got dressed while trying to make sense of what had happened.

There was one thing for sure: there was no point now in saving myself for Mr Right.

The only person I told was Jenny. I somehow felt I'd done wrong, which led to the awful situation I'd found myself in. After all, these things were a mystery to me. I had no idea of whether I'd behaved properly or what. So I played it down, not wanting to look a fool.

The next time we went to the youth club, there were knowing looks from both the boys and other girls. My card, apparently, was marked. I was a slag. The local bike. A tart. Betrayed by Barry, I was now fair game for any bloke who fancied a shag. And when do young men not fancy a shag?

Sometimes they would sweet talk me into fucking them; other times there were threats of violence – they'd threaten to kick me in the teeth or break my arm. Once a boy waved a knife at me and said he would slash my face.

Leaving the youth club became a game of who would catch me first to take me off to a dark place and screw me. There was one evening I remember when I was too frightened to leave, as a gang of about fifteen young men stood in the club's car park chanting, "We want Janet!"

It got later and later, and the youth workers clearly wanted to go home, but none of them offered me any help or suggested escorting me to the bus stop, although they did look worried. In the end, I had to just run like hell for leather into the relative safety of the brightly lit high street. I got away that time.

I wrote a poem. It's not a great masterpiece, but tells of how I was feeling then.

> I am fourteen.
> Young and nubile, skin clear, eyes bright,
> Breasts proud and high.
> I look good.
> Men look at me as I walk,
> Hips swinging, down the road.
> Eyes brushed with illicit mascara
> (Oh shit! Mum would have a fit.)
> I know about men and what they want.
> I have read Lolita.
> I have read
> Lady Chatterley's Lover
> (Well, I read the dirty bits.)
> I look clean, innocent.
> Virginal, untouched.
> You would never know from looking
> The cesspools of my mind.
> The ravages of my body.
> The sadness of my life.

I stopped going to the club. Jenny and I would go instead to Wood Green, where we would spend a whole evening walking from one end of the main street to the other and back again. Or up to the West End, strolling between Trafalgar Square and Leicester Square, usually with a transistor radio held to our ear, trying to listen to the awful reception of pop music from Radio Luxembourg, although we switched off when Horace Batchelor started his usual rant on his method to win the football pools.

We were often chatted up by boys, of course. I still had that dream of being someone's real girlfriend, of being special to him, holding hands and doing ordinary teenage things together, like going to the cinema, having picnics, talking about our futures together.

It never happened, and I found myself being screwed by yet another bloke, who probably couldn't believe his luck. I never experienced any pleasure from these encounters. In fact, I didn't know that women could have orgasms.

It all seemed to be happening to someone else. A recurring nightmare, but I couldn't work out how to wake up and make it end.

In the summer there was a fair at Alexandra Palace, so we would go there if we had some money.

One evening, we prepared to head to the fairground. We backcombed and lacquered our hair, and covered our spots with Max Factor Pan Stik before we went out. We wore matching white stilettos and handbags. We were fourteen years old and thought we were the bee's knees.

As we moved around the fair, the music changed every few moments, each ride having its own sound system. The mechanical noises of the rides themselves, the shouting of the stallholders, screams from the girls on the scarier rides... all combined, resulting in a mad cacophony.

Then it started to rain.

"I'm going home," I said. "I'm getting soaked."

"No, don't go," Jenny responded. "It's only a shower. Anyway I've got a brolly. We can share it."

"Nah. I'm fed up. We've done the best rides, and those swing boats made me feel sick. I'm off."

Jenny pouted. "Look, let's have a sit down and a cup of tea. Then see how you feel and it might stop raining."

"But it's noisy. And I've got a headache."

"Aah. You poor little cow." Jenny grinned.

I couldn't help but smile back at her. I knew I was being boring, but this was the third time we'd come to the fairground this week. It was something to do on those long summer evenings. And, since it was August, there was no school to worry about the next day.

I was edging towards the bus stop when the aroma of onions and hotdogs hit our senses.

"Shall we get…?" she started to say.

"No! We might get off with someone and then we'll have onion breath!" I exclaimed.

"So you're staying then?"

"Alright, but only for another half hour."

We were just about to get into a bumper car when two boys came alongside us. One of them got into the car with me and the other dragged Jenny by the hand to another one.

"Oi!" I said indignantly. "I was with my friend. What do you think you're doing?"

"Oh, come on," he replied. "We can have a laugh. We'll give those two a right bashing. You can drive."

I sneaked a look at him. He had dark hair, slicked back, and was wearing jeans and a striped shirt. Nice looking, a bit like Marty Wilde. He was definitely older than me, about nineteen, I guessed.

"Oh, OK, but then I'm going home. I've got to be back by half past ten, or my mum will kill me."

"You've got loads of time. Tell you what, I'll walk you to the bus stop. OK?"

My imagination immediately went into overdrive. He liked me, fancied me, and wanted to be with me. This could be the

Proper Boyfriend. When he put his arm around me, I didn't protest.

We hurtled around the bumper car rink, laughing each time we banged into Jenny and the other bloke, or I screamed when someone crashed into us, knocking the breath out of me. As the ride ended, I conferred with Jenny.

"I've got to go or I'll be late. He's going to walk me to the bus stop. Are you coming?"

"Yeah. I've got to be back by eleven, so I might as well go now."

We could see that the boys were talking together, although they fell silent as we approached them. They were obviously talking about us – probably saying they wanted us to be their girlfriends.

We all started to walk to the main road, then paired off so that Jim and I were in front, followed by Jenny and Bill. Jim pulled me into a darkened shop doorway and we kissed. It was not a great kiss. Too wet and too much tongue, but I didn't stop him. After all, this is what you do to get A Boyfriend. Isn't it?

After a while, we carried on walking. Jim said, "Tell you what. I'll take you all the way home. Then we can make a date to meet up again. What d'you reckon?"

"Mmm. If you want to," I replied, playing it cool.

"I just need to pop into my house to get some money for our fares. I only live round the corner. Come on, it'll only take a minute."

"Alright. Where's Jenny and your mate? I'll tell her what I'm doing."

He told me that they were still snogging way back along the road and they'd catch us up. Jenny was allowed out later than me so I wasn't too bothered.

As we went into the house he started kissing me again. The house was very quiet and when he started to edge me up the stairs, I let him take me into a bedroom. We lay down on the bed, gradually taking my clothes off. There was not a lot of petting and, just as he was about to enter me, I became aware of someone else coming into the room.

"Who's that?" I asked. "What do they want?"

"Well, I think we know what he wants, don't we?"

I could hear the smirk in his voice, and I realised that this was not going to be the romantic interlude I'd imagined. I started to struggle with him and tried to push him off, but he was strong. The person who had entered the room came over to the bed and held my arms above my head, while Jim used his knees to separate my legs. He finished quickly and changed places with the stranger. I was sobbing, begging, "Please don't. Please stop. Please let me go." I was pathetic in my futile demands. I did not notice that a third person was watching from the foot of the bed, until the second man rolled off me.

I don't know exactly how many of them raped me. I think it was six or seven, but it might have been more. One boy even said to me, "Don't cry. You'll spoil it if you cry."

And, even more strangely, a young woman came in at one point and told them to shut me up, to stop me from making so much noise. I think she was Jim's sister. I was bewildered that she, another girl, could see what was happening but not help me. Her comment resulted in one of them putting his hand over my mouth, and I struggled to breathe. I felt that I was suffocating and that I might die here in this unknown house.

They finally let me get dressed and I stumbled back into real life where I felt as if I were in a trance, not really in this world at all. The street lights seemed too bright, the pavements were all slanted and the world looked strange. I wondered if the bus conductor could tell what had happened just from looking at me. I felt so ashamed, dirty and humiliated. I noticed that my stockings were shredded. When did that happen?

It was way beyond my curfew by the time I got home, but I managed to avoid seeing my mum or siblings by going straight upstairs, calling out "Sorry I'm late." I headed for the bathroom, where I scrubbed myself with the nailbrush until my skin was red and sore.

And that was that. I told no one. I felt sure I must have been responsible in some way. Perhaps it was because of how I was dressed, or because I had kissed him, or because I wasn't a virgin.

Somehow I managed to push it to the back of my mind, except for the nightmares and flashbacks I had for years and years. It was my burden, my secret, my shame.

In fact, it was thirty years before I talked about it. The frequent flashbacks and nightmares finally resulted in me asking my doctor for a counselling referral. She told me that I was clearly suffering from post-traumatic stress disorder and gave me some antidepressants and an appointment to see the practice's counsellor.

On that first appointment I found myself sobbing for the whole fifty minutes of the session. The counsellor, a lovely Indian woman wearing a sari in sunset shades, was so kind and patient as the story came out between the tears and snot.

From that day onwards I never had another flashback or nightmare about being gang raped when I was fourteen, although I still find my stomach clenching whenever I come across a rape scene in a film or on television. I have to close my eyes until it's over.

Mods Rule

Sometimes I would stay the night with Jenny. We would wear our chaste cotton pyjamas and talk into the night. When we finally went to sleep, she would throw an arm over me as we lay like spoons in her single bed, cocooned in warmth, affection and nylon sheets.

It was when I came back home from one of these sleepovers that Sheila met me with my diary, which had been hidden under my mattress, in her hand. Although some of it had been written in code, I guess it wasn't that difficult to decipher. It was all in there. I felt so ashamed, but also incredibly angry that she had read my most secret thoughts and actions. At fifteen, surely I was entitled to some privacy? Not according to Sheila. I wouldn't talk to her about it, but a few days later my brother Joe, who was married by then, came over and took me out for a drive.

"Sheila says you've been getting up to all sorts," he ventured calmly, in a low voice.

I immediately burst into noisy tears, but still couldn't talk about it, or what had really been happening, or how powerless I had felt to stop it. I just didn't have the words.

"It's alright," he went on. "It's not the end of the world. We think it would be a good idea for you to get away for a while, to come and stay with me and Helen. Would you like that?"

I hiccupped an agreement, and the deal was done. I would go to their new home in Hertfordshire, and attend a local school for the summer term. When I came back to Tottenham, I wouldn't go back to my senior school, but would be going to Pitmans College to learn how to be a secretary.

No one asked me if I wanted this as a career, but it seemed a good option. For a working-class girl, to become a secretary was quite an accomplishment. My secondary modern school gave little attention to academic achievements, as most of us were expected to end up working in a shop or a factory.

To be accepted into the new school I had to meet with the headmaster. He was kindly, but when he said, "I hear you fell in with the wrong crowd", I became defensive and just shrugged my shoulders. It was probably as a result of this that I ended up in the lowest stream – again.

Actually, it was alright. It meant that I could just sail through that term at school, coming top in almost every subject (except maths). I soon made new friends, and even acquired a boyfriend from the year above… that was a bit of a coup. To my amazement, he didn't try anything on with me. He was just content to hold hands and kiss, and occasionally cuddle on a sofa. I had a revelation: this is what other girls did. This was a normal teenage relationship. I wish I could remember his name. I'd like to thank him for helping me bring an end to that lost year.

Two of the girls I became friendly with asked me what music I liked. Naturally, I mentioned Cliff and my other passions. They looked at me with affectionate amusement, and one of them said, "You're a rocker, aren't you?"

"What's that, then?" I asked.

"Well, you can either be a mod or a rocker. It all depends on what music you like and what you wear."

It took me a moment, but then I realised that they looked quite different from me. I wore full skirts, with stiffened petticoats, a fitted blouse and a nipped-in waist. On my feet were my beloved white stilettos. I had tightly curled, permed hair. They wore pencil skirts, with crew-neck jumpers, finished off with Hush Puppies brogues. Their hair was straight and cut symmetrically. And they just looked very cool.

So it came to pass that Cliff, Marty and what's-his-name fell off my radar, being replaced by the Beatles, the Rolling Stones, The Who and The Animals. Their music was different, too. They sang with ragged voices, dragged over razor blades, to a persistent beat.

The only exception really was Paul McCartney. He had that softness to him that rather reminded me of Cliff. A smoother voice, too, than John Lennon or Eric Burden. So Paul became my new passion. He was the good boy among all those bad boys with knowing eyes, looking at me from my bedroom wall.

By the time I came back to London, I was a mod through and through. I'd kept in touch with Jenny, although my family was disapproving of this, and we found that we'd changed. We were both mods now, but we also found that our short separation had ended that wild time for us. We had altered our behaviour and, if we hadn't quite become models of good conduct, we were certainly more selective than we had been. And we were still best friends.

I settled into the private Pitmans College, taking up shorthand (which I struggled with), typing, English, book-keeping and commerce. It felt very grown up, as we did not have to wear a uniform, and were addressed as Miss This or Miss That. I took my first ever exams, and did well in English, surprisingly OK in book-keeping, and just about alright in everything else except shorthand, which continued to puzzle me.

I had a couple of boyfriends. Real ones. There was Terry who wore an anorak with a red, white and blue target on the back. Very mod. Going out with Terry gave me a lot of points in our circle, especially as he had a scooter. We'd sit kissing and petting for hours on his mum's sofa while she was out, but never went the whole way. At some point in the evening he'd excuse himself and go off to the bathroom for five minutes. Then he'd take me home. On his scooter. A perfect evening, from my point of view. Eventually, though, it just tailed off, which was a bit irritating, as I'd covered that year's diary with hearts and inscriptions stating 'I love Terry'.

My sister Debbie and brother Charles had bought a small hairdressing shop in Hackney. This gave me my first Saturday job, sweeping the floor and doing shampoos, for which I received tips from the customers. So what with my wages, tips and pocket money, I could afford to buy mod clothes, or to make them myself. Not that I was very good at these efforts of making my own clothes. They were often not quite right, but I would state, "Oh, it'll look OK when it's on", and, amazingly, they usually did as long as I kept my left shoulder raised all night, or tugged my skirt down at the back every time I stood up.

Jenny had left school and was working as a telephonist, so we both had a bit of cash to spare. We went dancing at the Royal several times each week. Our jive routine was perfect. It was so smooth that others would just stand and watch our moves. Every now and then, though, the DJ would put on a slow number. That was the boys' cue to leap away from the wall they'd been holding up and find a girl to dance with. I didn't look forward to these moments. All I really wanted to do was to be showing off with Jenny, making confident progress through our routine, in perfect harmony with each other and the music.

Still, it had to be done. It was expected. So every now and then throughout the evening I would consent to dance with some bloke, who would spend the next three minutes trying to touch my bum as I constantly moved his hands further up my back, where they would try to inch round to the sides of my breasts. Then there would be the erection pushing into my leg or belly. Sometimes, it has to be said, I would be particularly cruel by rubbing myself against the hard protrusion, then at the end of the number walking swiftly away, leaving my partner on the dancefloor, dealing with his problem as best he could. Ah! Revenge was sweet!

Another friend, Pam, was going out with a bloke, Paul, from Shoreditch. Jenny and I bumped into them one night at the Royal when Paul's mate Tony was with them. Tony was cute. He had blonde hair, high cheekbones and wore a very sharp, grey mohair suit. And he was short. I liked that in a man. I told Pam that I quite fancied him. Sure enough, the message got back to Tony in record time. Before the evening ended, we'd had several dances, without either wandering hands or erections, and he'd taken me home, where we indulged in a lengthy snogging session on my doorstep. We arranged to meet again later in the week.

I worried that he would have heard of my reputation, but realised that coming from a different part of London, even if it was only a few miles down the road in the East End, he would not be part of the local gossip chain. This was proven over the next few months, as he took our courtship very slowly. He was respectful and never tried to go beyond the boundaries I set.

Eventually, of course, we found ourselves about to Do It.

"Have you ever done it before?" I asked him.

"Yeah. Of course. Loads of times."

I didn't believe him, but made no comment.

"What about you? Have you done it before?" he said.

"Just a couple of times." I crossed my fingers behind my back.

He produced a condom and put it on with shaking hands. Well, that was another gold star for him. I'd rarely known of other boys using a condom.

When he came he called out, "I love you!"

What? Did he say what I thought he said? He loves me! He said he loves me. Oh. My. God. This is it. This is my real, proper, genuine, authentic, actual Boyfriend. No one had ever said that to me before, and I'd been longing to be loved.

"I love you, too," I managed. In my head I was already arranging the wedding.

Poor Tony. He never knew what had hit him. We'd met at sixteen, and were engaged at seventeen. He bought me a second hand ('antique') gold ring with a small sapphire surrounded by teeny-weeny diamonds, with one missing. I loved it. We decided not to tell our respective families just yet. They were bound to say that we were too young.

In fact, the problem turned out to be something quite different. We'd been seeing each other for about two years when he told me that his parents thought we should stop seeing each other. They were worried that we were getting too serious and, although they liked me, they were not happy about mixed relationships. In other words, because I was Jewish, albeit non-practising, who wouldn't know one end of the Talmud from the other, who ate pork pies with abandon and who hadn't been to a synagogue since the last wedding. And Tony, being an obedient child, agreed to stop seeing me.

I cried as if my heart would break, which I thought it would. We found a compromise. He would tell them that he had stopped seeing me, but we would meet in secret. My family had no problems with our relationship. The new arrangement meant that we would only be able to see each other a couple of times each week, at least until we turned twenty-one and could do what we chose.

Since we continued to have sex, he probably didn't want to lose that particular pleasure. I'd actually introduced him to some pretty wild games. Dressing up, fantasy, different positions – and I did it all in the guise of 'Shall we try this?'

I must say that over the years I'd learnt how to be good in bed. During the wild year there had been a stunning boy that I'd met when I was out with Pam one evening. He couldn't decide which of us he wanted, so we both went with him to his home, which turned out to be a mansion in Chelsea. He didn't want a threesome, so took Pam to bed first, and then came for me. It was only when he said, "Can you move around a bit, like your friend?" that I realised this was a preferred requirement.

Another lesson was learnt when Tony and I went away to a holiday camp. We'd made friends with some other young people there, and one afternoon as I passed by a certain couple's chalet, I heard the girl grunting and screaming. Eaten up with curiosity, I asked her later what had been happening.

"Well, we were having it off," she said.

I didn't get the connection.

"So what?"

"Um. Well. I almost always pretend to come," she explained. "It keeps him happy if he thinks I've had a good time, too."

This was a revelation. I'd been enjoying sex up to a point, getting aroused, but I never knew there should be something else. It was the first time I'd realised that women could also have an orgasm and also that they were expected to make a noise about it.

I don't know if Tony noticed the difference, but from that very day I gradually started to incorporate more sound effects into my performance. What with the hip grinding, the ever-changing positions, imaginative practices and now a sound track, I like to think that I made him a very happy bunny. And if he was happy, I knew that he'd come back for more, regardless of what his parents wanted.

I turned seventeen in 1964. The Swinging Sixties were well under way and we'd still never had it so good. The contraceptive pill had become widely available by then, although I'd taken myself to the Marie Stopes Clinic and been fitted for a Dutch cap. It was easy to put in and take out, apart from the times when I'd overdone the spermicidal jelly and it would whizz out of my hand and across the bathroom floor. How I'd never become pregnant was a mystery to me. Of all the boys I'd had sex with, only Tony had consistently used a condom.

It was around this time that I had my first experience of using drugs – sort of.

We were hearing a lot about purple hearts – amphetamines used particularly by the mods to stay up clubbing all night – but I was too scared to use them. Instead, when Tony and I went to an all night club (well, it was actually the Old Bug 'Ole cinema, which had been transformed into an R&B venue), I dosed myself up with ProPlus, bought at the local branch of Boots the Chemist. I must have taken about twelve of the tablets and did manage to stay awake all night. However, the first thing I did upon arriving home was to throw up in the kitchen sink. Very cool.

Clearly drugs were not for me (well, not yet). I never even drank alcohol. I was still asking for milk or cola at the Royal when we went dancing. On one occasion we were invited to a party. I thought that at seventeen I really ought to try to be a bit more grown up in my choice of beverage, so got stuck into the gin and orange squash in a big way.

All went well until there came a point when I had to lie down on the coats in the bedroom, which was a big mistake. The bed seemed to be spinning, and I knew I should hold onto the sides to stop myself from falling off. Finally, Tony appeared, to take me home. I can't remember how we got home, but I do remember that he rang the front doorbell and then scuttled off, leaving me standing there with my shoes on the wrong feet. I haven't touched gin since.

The Baby, with my sister Sheila

The five year old, with Mum and Dad

Scruffy Sisters

The Mod

On leaving Pitmans College I found a job in the City with an insurance company. I was supposed to be a shorthand typist, but they soon found out that the quality of my shorthand rendered me unsuitable for that post, and introduced me to the newfangled audio typing.

What a relief to be able to throw the shorthand notebooks into the bin. The salary was £20 per month. By the time I'd given Mum something for housekeeping and paid for my fares and lunches, there wasn't a huge amount left over, but I managed to spend what there was on clothes, clubs and dancing.

We still went to the Royal, but Tony had introduced me to rhythm and blues. We'd go to sweaty, crowded clubs to see Ike and Tina Turner, Georgie Fame, Long John Baldry. I loved those rhythms, the wailing guitars and the songs of pain, love, happiness, anger and sex.

As the beat hit my solar plexus, it would take over so that a state of euphoria would be experienced, and I would give myself over to the music, swaying and moving my hips in time to the persistent sound.

Discovery

We were having a night off from the boyfriends, me and Jenny. We'd gone to the Royal, after a long telephone conversation about what to wear.

"How about that new sweater, the pink one? If you wear that, I'll wear my blue one," I suggested.

"No. I've gone off it. It makes me look fat."

"Oh. OK. Can I have it then?"

"Well, I might wear it. Tell you what, let's both wear blue."

It was some time before we both decided on short-sleeved, baggy sweaters, hers in pale green and mine in pale pink. We teamed them with pencil skirts and Hush Puppies brogues. Our faces were very pale, with white lipstick, masses of dark eye make-up and pretend lashes drawn under our eyes. We both looked rather ill, but so, so trendy.

My hair was worn like Cathy McGowan's, presenter of Ready Steady Go! A dead straight bob, which had to be ironed to get the bushiness out of it. Then I'd sellotape the side curls to my face when I went to bed, otherwise it just wouldn't go into the right shape.

We went to the Royal at every opportunity, with its huge dance hall and glittering, many-mirrored cylinder in its centre, slowly revolving, reflecting coloured lights onto the dancefloor. It was the epitome of glamour.

We would twist and jive and do the hitchhike all night long. When we danced, I felt that we were not two people, but one, as we whirled, dipped and twirled in perfect harmony. I sometimes danced with other people, but could never get the same beautiful symmetry I had with Jenny.

There was a ritual in our preparation for these nights. At home we bathed, put our hair in rollers or ironed it, put our make-up on and decided what to wear, via lengthy phone calls to each other. When we arrived at the Royal we'd head straight for the ladies' cloakroom. This was a vast area, which not only held the toilets, cloakroom and perfume machines, but also had about a hundred mirrors, each with its own individual shelf.

We'd spend another twenty minutes or so here, finishing our hairdos, putting on another layer of mascara and chatting about our preoccupations: boys, appearance, work, parents and boys – in that order. We told our secrets only to each other.

"Oh gawd, this eye shadow looks terrible. I should have come on last Tuesday. I'm dead worried," said Jenny.

"You ought to get a Dutch cap, like I have. It's a bit of a palaver getting it in, but at least you don't have the argument every time about them putting on a rubber johnny. D'ya wanna borrow my Max Factor?"

On this particular evening, we were standing close to each other. Jenny leant back to consider the rather startling image of silver eye shadow, while I went on fiddling with my hair. As I raised my arm to have another go at back-combing, my right arm brushed Jenny's breast.

It was like an electric shock. I gasped and trembled. She didn't notice my reaction as I took stock of the softness of her body, its proximity, the smell of her perfume. If I felt like this when I stroked her breast with my arm, how might I feel if I stroked other parts of her with other bits of me?

It was amazing, delicious. I felt drunk and reckless. I wanted that feeling again.

It's not that I was a lesbian. Oh no. I knew a lesbian, or thought I did. She worked in the park and wore a dark uniform, with sharp creases in her trousers and a crisp white shirt with a black tie. She was about forty, stocky with short, greying hair. She didn't look or behave anything like me, so it stood to reason that I wasn't one of those.

I just wanted to experience that delightful sensation again, the smooth yielding of a rounded body, wanted to kiss a silky cheek and wrap myself around a compliant and welcoming girl. But lesbian? Queer? Dyke? No, absolutely not.

And Jenny was not the one that I wanted, in spite of her being the bearer of a defining moment. She was my best friend and I loved her, but not in that way. It would have felt like incest.

So I became a woman with a mission. I had to find a girl, who was not a lesbian either, but who would come on this adventure with me.

I had absolutely no idea how to do that.

Desperately Seeking Susan, Jane or Daphne

So there I was in Tottenham, which, let's face it, was not exactly a metropolis, wanting to find a girl to kiss. It was 1964 and Gay Pride was still a twinkle in some queen's eye.

How on earth would I find someone? Hmm. How about

the armed forces… now there's a thought. Surely with all those women working together, there would be the odd one or two who would be up for an exciting activity, apart from travelling, synchronised marching and wearing a quite attractive uniform.

I sent off for recruitment brochures for all three services and read them very carefully, looking particularly hard at the photos of women in them. There were several likely looking candidates, appearing a little severe, it must be said, with hair pulled back into tight buns or cut shorter than I would like.

Occasionally, I saw one that showed the officers at a formal do. Now, that was more like it. The women wore lovely dresses, with loose hair, and definitely had on lipstick and mascara.

I decided that the army had too much square bashing. I'd never been keen on exercise, and thought that I would be expected to run. Not my thing at all. And I didn't like the uniform.

The air force really had very little to offer women, so it came down to the navy, which had the added attraction of seeing the world. Two of my brothers had been in the Merchant Navy, and had come home on leave with interesting stories of Argentina, New Zealand and Singapore. Yes, that would do.

However, upon making further enquiries it emerged that women in the navy were never assigned to a ship and never went abroad. They were expected to work in the UK, doing something with signals and dit dit dah. Or dah dah dit. Whatever. It was not what I had in mind, although they did have the best uniform.

Back to the drawing board.

I did not know of any helplines, clubs, pubs or societies for girls like me, who were not lesbians, but who were kind of interested. I longed to see something in *Honey* magazine that might point me in the right direction, but they were determinedly tight-lipped about anything other than heterosexuality in its many forms of clothes, make-up and boys. Mary Quant's mini-skirt fashions were being replicated everywhere and if my skirt came below my fingertips, I knew it was too long, so the magazine was useful for that kind of essential information.

I kept my eyes and ears open for any kind of hint, but these longings seemed destined to be a pipe dream.

By the time I was nineteen, I'd had a number of jobs as a secretary. I kept getting sacked for poor time-keeping. I'd write in my diary 'Must be on time for work', but only rarely managed to do it. It was never difficult, though, to get another job. I'd be sacked on a Friday, go to an agency on Monday, get an interview for Tuesday and be in the new workplace by Wednesday. In 1966 I was working for ABC Cinemas, in their head office at Golden Square.

I really liked it there. My boss was Alan, a senior architect, who was easygoing and fun, although he would insist on giving dictation with his pipe in his mouth, which meant I had to guess what he was saying quite a lot of the time. A challenge when it came to typing it, as shorthand was never my strong suit at the best of times. I shared an office with Melia, a sweet girl of Greek origin.

The secretaries were managed by a woman, who seemed very old. She was probably only fifty or so, but to me she seemed ancient. She had been with the company for a long time. Her name was Miss Sugarman, although she was married. Apparently, she had got married late in life, so had kept her maiden name. That's not unusual now, but at the time was pretty radical. The senior staff called her 'Sugar', but us whippersnappers would not dare to call her anything but her full title.

The term 'firm, but fair' must have been invented for Miss Sugarman. She ruled with a rod of iron, but flashes of humour would appear now and then. As secretary to the Head of Architecture, she had a huge office all to herself. She sat behind a long leather-topped desk, queen of all she surveyed.

When I was called in to see her for some misdemeanour (probably being late for work), I used to think to myself, "One day I'll be on the other side of that desk."

One of the perks of the job was getting two free tickets every week for any ABC cinema, so going to the pictures was a regular feature.

I was still engaged to Tony (although his parents remained unaware of our proposed nuptials), even if it was getting less and less romantic, as he would sometimes not turn up for dates, or would playfully slap me or twist my wrist in a Chinese burn. When we talked, it would mostly be about the film of the day or one of the R&B clubs we were planning to go to, or about his job as a printer's apprentice.

"What d'you want to see on Wednesday? *Eldorado* or *Batman?*" he'd ask.

"Oh great. Cowboys or comic books. Can't we see something I'd like, for a change? What about *Georgy Girl?*"

"Nah. I'm not going to see that rubbish. We'll go to see *Eldorado*. My boss gave me a job today, making up a hardback book. I had to talk to the guv'nor about what paper to use."

"Oh. What did he say?"

"Medium."

We never talked about feelings, thoughts or dreams. Those were the conversations I had with Jenny, still my best friend, although I never told her about my new attraction to girls.

Debbie, my sister, and I were close, although we rarely went out together. There was a day, though, when we were going somewhere in her car, driving through central London and had just negotiated Hyde Park Corner.

"I went to an interesting party," she said.

"What do you mean?"

"Well, um, it was a bit different to usual parties."

"How different?" I asked, my curiosity aroused.

"Well, um, they're called swinging parties… it's like an orgy."

"What, you mean that it's full of people having sex?"

"Well, um, yes."

I immediately spotted an opportunity arising, one that I had been awaiting for two years now. Taking a deep breath, I asked, "And do women ever go with other women there?" trying to sound casual.

"Oh, yes," she replied breezily. "Anything goes."

Oh, yes. This was it. A way in, at last.

"Can you take me to one of these parties?" I asked in a nonchalant sort of way, hoping she wouldn't notice my sudden shortness of breath.

It turned out that my brother Charles had started going to a naturist club in Hertfordshire. He kept this quiet within the family, but it came out (as it were) one day when Debbie was at home, not feeling well. Charles had been preparing to go out for the day and Debbie, in need of cheering up, had asked if she could go with him.

He explained that he was going to a country club and that she might not like it, but Debbie (a game girl) insisted that she would. Well, she went, she saw, she dropped her drawers and took off her bra... and was liberated. Not long after this, my sister Sheila also started going to the club, taking to naturism like a duck to water.

The club was set in several acres of parkland, with a winding path going through it. No cars were allowed beyond the car park at the entrance, and then members had to go through a wooden gate, set in a high fence. Once past this barrier, the members were free to walk around without clothes.

Set back from the path were caravans, mobile homes, wooden chalets and tents, all in their own piece of land rented from the club, and surrounded by leafy woods. It was very idyllic and rustic.

There was a swimming pool, surrounded by gardens and lawns, and a clubhouse for social events, with a bar serving drinks and snacks. The ambience was congenial and country club in every sense, except that everyone was naked. So they swam naked, ate naked, played badminton naked, cooked at the camping stove naked (always a bit dangerous) and sat reading the Sunday papers naked.

When Debbie and Sheila started going there, it wasn't long before a certain male contingent hit upon these two young, attractive women, inviting them to a special party, kept secret from most members. They both went, but good girl Sheila decided it wasn't her cup of tea, while Debbie (the adventurous one) wanted to explore the possibilities.

And now it was my turn to check out the swinging scene.

I decided to wear my new mini-skirted dress. This was made of a floaty chiffon material, white with tiny navy polka dots. The sleeves were bell shaped; the bodice fitted snugly and was cut into a low square shape, revealing my considerable cleavage. The skirt flared and came to about five inches above my knees.

I wore my hair long and loose, freshly washed and ironed, so that it hung straight down my back. I'd carefully done my make-up, drawing the eyelashes below my eyes with a steady hand, and securing the false eyelashes on my eyelids with the special glue.

Turning this way and that to check my reflection in the full-length mirror, I decided that I looked every inch the modern girl – sexy but cute with it. Debbie was all ready to go, also looking suitably glamorous in a black, halterneck mini-dress.

"We're off to a party," I said to Mum. "See you later."

"What time will you be home?" she asked.

"Don't know. Late, I expect."

Exiting quickly before she could ask any more questions, we were out of the house and into Debbie's car in moments.

"How many people do you think will be there?" I asked her.

"Don't know. There's usually around twenty."

"Blimey. That's a lot of car keys." I'd read all about these parties in the *News of the World*, so had an idea of what to expect.

Debbie laughed. She thought I was joking.

I tried not to bite my nails; I didn't want to chew off all the pale pink nail varnish. I was getting palpitations, but trying to keep calm.

Was it too late to change my mind, I wondered? What if no one fancied me? Maybe I wasn't wearing the right clothes? Would there be any other girls there who weren't lesbians? Perhaps I should just join the army after all.

We arrived at a large house on the outskirts of Hampstead,

surrounded by a sturdy fence and an iron gate, beyond which was a landscaped garden. Ringing the doorbell, we were ushered in by a slim, blonde woman wearing a long, multi-coloured silk dress.

"Debbie, dahling," she gushed, giving Debbie a kiss on both cheeks. "So pleased you could come. And this must be your sister."

She smiled as she looked me over, then put her hand in mine and drew me into the house, giving me similar continental kisses. I was immediately charmed and my nerves almost disappeared. I hoped that she wouldn't notice how clammy my paw was.

Going down a wide corridor we were ushered into a huge room. It was furnished with the kind of décor I'd only seen in films. A deep shag pile carpet, soft sofas, real paintings on the wall, heavy drapes that were already drawn, shutting out the summer evening. The lighting was discreet, with wall and standard lamps creating a glow, and was enough to see but not too bright. Music was being played softly on the stereogram. Frank Sinatra told us that Chicago was his kind of town. Debbie was immediately taken off elsewhere by an attractive bloke, who told her he wanted her to meet someone or other.

People stood around in couples and groups, the women in fashionable clothes and the men in suits. All had a drink, and snacks were being offered around. Their accents were either foreign or pure cut-glass English. Some were clearly The Beautiful People, but others were middle aged and rotund. This latter category was mostly men, although there were a few older women too. As I stood alone on the edges of the group, gazing wide-eyed at my surroundings, I found myself also holding a glass of wine, although I didn't notice it being put there. There wasn't a car key in sight.

Then my chin hit the floor. A couple had taken over one of the sofas, where they were enthusiastically having sex, the woman sitting astride the man. She wore stockings and suspenders, with elbow-length gloves and not much else.

Her partner appeared to be naked. I stared until I realised that I might look uncool, but then noticed that several other people were looking at them. Not only that, but these other people were clearly getting turned on, removing bits of clothing, and starting to kiss and fondle each other.

Sometime later, I was sandwiched between a good-looking man of about thirty-five and a stunning woman of around the same age. We were all undressed by then. The woman put her hand around my waist and declared, "Look at her tiny waist. Isn't she gorgeous?"

The man nuzzled my neck, murmuring his agreement. "Delightful."

I couldn't work out how to get this woman alone, but it didn't really matter, as I was able to stroke and caress her in the way I'd been longing for, while she fondled me. It was everything I'd thought it would be… and more, but it was like having a taster. Absolutely delicious, but nowhere near enough to satisfy my appetite.

Unfortunately, it became clear that there's no such thing as a free lunch (or a free taster even), and the price for being able to make love to a woman, was to also have sex with several men.

Being nineteen, attractive and new to the scene meant that I was a very popular party guest. By the end of the evening I'd been well and truly had and, although it was not what I'd been dreaming of, I thought that I'd maybe found the passport to another way of life.

This was just the beginning. All I had to do now was to work out what came next. I'd had the appetiser, now I wanted the main course.

I started going to these parties regularly, maybe once or twice a month. My eyes were opened to all sorts of mild sexual kinks: bondage, spanking, golden showers. None of it was very serious, although occasionally there would be a partygoer whose whole sexual pleasure revolved around a particular perversion. Those people could be a bit scary, especially one who was dressed head to toe in rubber, with his face concealed, apart from his eyes, mouth and nose. I managed to avoid that one by scuttling out of whatever room he appeared in.

I found that I was meeting people from all sorts of professions: lawyers, psychiatrists and doctors. There were creative types: people who worked in advertising or were well-known actors. They all seemed to have been privately educated, and were articulate and confident. Just being in the same room with these people was such a new experience, never mind socialising with them and shagging them.

I think that Debbie and I were a bit of a novelty, too. Quite apart from being siblings, we were clearly not of the same class as these other partygoers. Debbie had a definite London accent, although people sometimes thought she was Australian!

My accent was less pronounced, probably due to being tutored in 'proper' English by a speech therapist when I was a child. I'd had a lisp and although Mum, in her usual dramatic fashion, had wanted me to have surgery to make my tongue shorter, she was persuaded by the school nurse to let me have speech therapy instead. This meant that, not only was I taught to lose my lisp, but also how to pronounce 'th' so that I now said 'thank you' instead of 'fank you'. My accent was not quite posh, but not cockney either.

I found that I was in constant demand. For the first time in my short life, I was aware of being reasonably attractive. It was a heady experience and my confidence soared. I found that I could walk into a room and people would stop their conversations to look at me. I would almost immediately be surrounded by men… and sometimes women.

The confidence translated itself into an uninhibited, sexy, bold girl. It was a fantastic feeling. I felt that I could do anything, be anyone, and go anywhere. I was hot and it was 1968. The world was different now. We had the pill, we had groovy music, we could wear clothes designed to let you move freely, we could wear flowers in our hair, and there was I, right at the centre of it all.

There was even a film out with lesbians as the central characters. My mum went to see it and said that we should go, too. "It's all about those Lizabethans," she said. "You need to know about life." The film, *The Killing of Sister George* did come as a revelation to me. Apart from anything else, I learnt that there were clubs for lesbians. Not that I was a lesbian. But the club looked, erm, interesting.

I was still living at home and seeing Tony, although this had now dwindled to just once or twice a week. I justified holding onto the relationship by telling myself that I was going through a phase. At some point, I would give up on this yearning for another woman and settle down to marriage with Tony as we'd planned.

In my fantasy I never got further than the wedding day, seeing myself in a confection of lace and satin, being the centre of attention, and loved to distraction by my new husband. Naturally, I did not tell him about the parties or my suspicion that I was not a lesbian.

It was, therefore, something of a surprise when I got a phone call one day from a girl I didn't know, who said her name was Pat.

"I'm pregnant," she announced. "Tony's the dad and we're getting married. He's not going to see you anymore. I hope that you find another boyfriend one day."

Blimey. I had no idea that he'd been seeing someone else, although all the clues were there. I was shocked, yet felt strangely relieved. I could stop making plans, keeping secrets and living such a schizophrenic lifestyle. I did shed a few tears, though. It was the end of something that had been very important to me, and we'd lasted (heaven knows how) for five years, during which time we had both grown up and changed.

He didn't have the balls to tell me himself that it was over, and I never saw or spoke to him again.

Later that summer I went to a party at the naturist club – a formal affair in the clubhouse, which was closed to the members that evening. An old hand by now, I wore a long cotton dress, blue, with shoestring straps and a sweetheart neckline. Under it, I wore a strapless bra and stockings held up with suspenders, and tiny knickers. Yes, I definitely had the hang of these parties now.

There was to be a proper sit down meal prior to the main event. The guests started the evening with an aperitif, and we were then seated at a long refectory table in the clubhouse.

The first course was served: artichokes with a buttery sauce. Now, I'd never had artichokes before. I'd never seen an artichoke. I didn't even know it was called an artichoke. Instead of waiting to see what everyone else did, I took up my knife and fork and dug in.

Well, the wretched thing shot off my plate and right down the long table before falling on the floor. No one said anything, or acknowledged my now lost vegetable. I giggled, but then had to sit and wait while the others spent an interminable time chewing through the leaves until they finally got to the choke and we could move on to the next course.

The host that evening was John. He owned the club. He was around forty-five years old, balding, with a hooked nose, and had a belly that arrived in the room before the rest of him. He homed in on me like a starving man. I suppose we had sex, but I can't remember that particularly, because John was the first man who actually talked to me and seemed interested in what I had to say.

"Do you go to work, Janet?" he enquired.

"I'm a secretary."

"Do you like being a secretary?"

Eh? No one had ever asked me that before.

"I don't know. It's OK I suppose."

"If you could do anything you wanted, what would you like to do? What's your dream?"

"Um. I always wanted to travel. I've thought about being an air hostess, but I think you have to be able to speak other languages."

He didn't laugh, or point out that as I was less than five foot tall, I wouldn't be able to reach the overhead lockers. I'd never been on an aeroplane so didn't know about these requirements. John nodded sagely and asked, "What is it about travelling that appeals to you?"

And so it went. He made me think and I liked that. He was interested in me, and that was a novelty. He was clearly well educated and clever, but wasn't talking down to me or being patronising. As the owner of the club, I guessed he was wealthy. He could have anyone, but it was me that he was interested in. I was flattered. It wasn't so much the wealth that impressed me, but the confidence and power that went with it, and which John had in spades. When he asked to see me again, just the two of us, I did not hesitate. I wanted more of his single-minded attention.

So we started a relationship of sorts. He'd meet me in town on a Friday evening, usually at Baker Street station, as I was working nearby. We'd go for a meal, and then he would drive us to Hertfordshire. I would stay the weekend with him, and we would make love, eat out and, best of all, talk into the small hours.

John lived in the grounds of the club. He had a wooden chalet deep within the woods surrounding the more public areas. It had a rustic charm, with all mod cons. A kitchen, sitting room, bedroom and bathroom were all contained in his log cabin. The bedroom and sitting room were full of interesting ethnic, esoteric or mystical bits and pieces. There was a Navaho rug on one wall, a painted, framed pentacle on another. The shelf held a model of Ganesh, made of silver, with a human's body and an elephant's head. On the bed was a hand-sewn patchwork quilt, its intricate pattern and colours endlessly fascinating.

He would tell me the story of each piece, explain them to me, taught me words like 'esoteric'. I was fascinated by it all, so different from anything and anyone I had met before.

I found that I was gaining confidence in my intellect. I'd always been an avid reader. Now John would suggest books for me to read, and we'd discuss them. And what books they were! Authors I'd never heard of: Solzhenitsyn, Hermann Hesse, André Gide.

I did not always understand the finer points of these books, but it was stretching and challenging me. I was an enthusiastic pupil. Eliza Doolittle to his Doctor Higgins, Trilby to his Svengali.

I wasn't in love with John, but he excited something in me that had been dormant until then: a delight in learning. Our lovemaking was nothing special, truth to tell. I saw it as the price to be paid for the good bit… the talking.

It was during one of these talks that I confessed to him.

"I think I might be bisexual."

"What makes you think that?" he asked.

"I'm attracted to women. I just want to hold them, kiss them and stroke them. I don't know why, but I know that's what I want. I tried to get something going at the parties, but it never really took off. I don't know any other way of meeting women, but I really want to. Do you think I'm a pervert?"

He smiled. "No, not at all. Actually, I have another girlfriend who is also bisexual. Would you like to meet her? See how she goes about getting partners? You could compare notes."

So an arrangement was made. The next weekend we were to meet up, he would bring Rose with him and we would all go out for a meal. I was excited about it, but a bit worried about meeting this woman. What if she was a really mannish lesbian? Or dead kinky? What on earth would we have in common?

I'm Not a Lesbian, But…

It was October and the evenings became dark early, the street lights coming on and casting an eerie orange glow over London. The city streets had that smoky smell, redolent of autumn in England.

John met me at the station as usual. I could see the shadowy figure of a woman in the back seat, but could not make out her features.

"Meet Rose," John said. "Rose, Janet. Janet, Rose."

We said hello to each other quietly. I tried to twist around from the front seat to look at her, but still could not get a sense of what she looked like. I felt nervous and ill at ease, my newly found confidence leaving me stranded. I couldn't think of anything to say. My stomach felt knotted and I wondered if I would be able to eat at all in the presence of a real, live, experienced bisexual woman.

John kept up a barrage of small talk as he sped along the busy road until we reached the Indian restaurant we always went to on Edgware Road. The waiter greeted him by name, and nodded at me. As we entered the brightly lit room, another waiter offered to take our coats.

Rose was wearing a heavy woollen garment, similar to a duffel coat. I was not impressed by her fashion sense, as I slipped out of my Biba copied coat, picked up on Petticoat Lane for a fiver.

I now got an opportunity, though, to have a really good look at her. Slim, but nicely rounded breasts and hips, mid-height, long, dark hair worn loose, a full mouth and hazel eyes. She wore a blue, cotton shirt tucked into tailored trousers, with a silver-buckled belt threaded through the loops. She should have looked butch, but somehow didn't. I sensed a softness, a vulnerability, which I found attractive.

As we perused the menu, I kept peeking over the top of it to sneak a look at her. I was fascinated. She caught my eye and smiled. Oh no! Was I obvious in my interest in her? I wanted to come over as all cool and laid back, but I felt my face get hot.

When we ordered our meal her voice was low, husky even. She was clearly middle class, speaking with one of those unmistakable accents.

"So, Janet," she said, "John tells me that you're also bisexual."

I choked on my poppadom and managed a "Mmmff" in reply, her directness throwing me into even more of a panic.

"How long have you been interested in women?" she asked.

I took a big gulp of the wine that had arrived on our table before answering.

"Um. Well. Er. I've been interested for a while now. Two years, actually."

"Have you had a girlfriend?"

OK. Here we go… time to admit my lack of experience.

"Well, I haven't actually had a girlfriend, although I have met some girls at parties… oh! Do you know about that, the parties, I mean?"

I took another swig of wine, wishing that I'd worn something I could remove, like a cardigan. I was sweating.

"Yes, yes. Of course. John and I are old friends and we have no secrets. Did you like any of these girls in particular?"

I said that I'd liked all of them, but couldn't find a way to develop any sort of relationship with them. I told her how I'd first become aware of my attraction to women, how I'd tried to think of ways of meeting them, and how it had come to nothing.

As the food arrived, and we began to eat, she listened attentively, asking questions now and then. John seemed content to let us talk and was uncharacteristically quiet.

By the time we'd had kulfi and coffee, I was feeling more relaxed, partly due, no doubt, to the wine I'd consumed by then. We left the restaurant and John suggested that Rose and I both sit in the back of the car for the ride back to Hertfordshire, where they both lived.

By the time we reached the M1, Rose had leant over to kiss me, little fluttery kisses, her tongue darting around my lips like a butterfly. She let me stroke her and I began unbuttoning her shirt, melting, almost swooning, with desire when I felt her hand straying to my thigh, up under my skirt. I wanted her there and then in the car, on the motorway, but she teased me saying, "Let's wait until we can be more comfortable."

Once or twice, I saw John looking in his rear view mirror, so guessed that he would want to be part of any action. I wished we could be rid of him, but knew that the system demanded that he would want his percentage. Walking to his cottage, Rose held my hand, sometimes stopping to caress and kiss me, until I felt like a walking, talking beacon of electricity.

Rose and I undressed each other, John watching every move as we began to make love. Although it was still fairly uncharted territory for me, I knew what to do, my hands and lips making their way around her body like they were coming home. Her softness, her curves, the silkiness of her skin and the way her long hair stroked me made me shiver with desire. High on wine and scented joss sticks, when she touched me I felt like I was having an out-of-body experience.

I suppose at some point John joined us, but I was hardly aware of him. All that existed for me that night was Rose and me, glowing in the candlelight, as we discovered each other's bodies.

It didn't happen that night, but soon, a few lovemaking sessions later, I found the Holy Grail, the pot of gold at the end of the rainbow, the never before experienced, but often faked, ultimate goal. I wasn't ready for it, but it was ready for me. My whole being, from my toes to the top of my head, went into a level of pleasure so intense that I lost all sense of where I was for those few moments.

Finally. So that's what it's all about.

Rose lived nearby with her husband. Oh yes. She was married and had several children. She lived in the family home and had an arrangement, she told me, with her husband. She was ten years older than me. What she didn't tell me, but what became clear in time, was that she was deeply in love with John.

She was working part time as a life model at an art school, where a foundation course was the main focus, but they also had adult education classes in painting, drawing and sculpture. Rose also modelled at some of the London schools of art.

She had a history of mental illness. After the birth of her first child she had such severe postnatal depression that she was sectioned. Although that was some years ago – her eldest daughter was now nine years old – Rose was still prescribed Mandrax for depression. She also saw a psychotherapist every week.

She painted as a form of therapy and self-expression. Her paintings were all abstract, and largely consisted of wetting a large piece of paper, then using coloured inks to form shapes on the wet paper. Sometimes this resulted in an outline or silhouette that was quite lovely, a fluid pattern that flowed in jewel colours. However, at other times it just appeared to me to be a jumble, a mess that a five year old could lay claim to.

Rose explained her painting in a blurb for an exhibition she'd had. The psychobabble of her wording made little sense to me. She stated that her paintings were a reflection of her inner life, a way of making her thoughts and feelings tangible, with the aim of the viewer asking what the painting meant to them, not of interpreting them

Oh. OK. What was it again…?

What I really came to hate was when she would ask me what I could see in the paintings. Then, having squeezed out of me that a part of it looked like a wolf (or a cat, or a cow – I wasn't very imaginative on this score) she would want to analyse my response.

"You see a wolf. What does that mean to you? How do you feel about wolves? Who is the wolf in your life?"

Although our relationship went on including John for some time, there came a point when it became clear that he was surplus to requirements, at least for me. Rose was as keen as I was for us to meet independently of him, although she still continued to see him. John and I came to a mutually agreed, amicable parting. No problem for either of us.

Rose had friends at the club who had a chalet, which they had told her she could use at any time. I saw her at weekends and we would stay there, making love for hours, playing music, the strains of Pink Floyd or Simon and Garfunkel floating over us as we explored each other, slowly stroking and caressing. It was so far removed from real life that it felt like we were living in a film, or characters in a book. It was a blissful and joyful time for both of us, I think.

Even now, whenever I hear the opening chords of 'Knights in White Satin' I am immediately transported back to being naked in the hazy sunshine, idyllic and dream-like.

I stopped going to the swinging parties. There was no need now that I had achieved my goal. I did not miss the frenetic coupling, or the old men who often had pretty young women as their partners, or the mixing with the middle and upper class professionals.

Debbie had continued going to the parties, realising that this kind of company could open up a different kind of lifestyle to the one she was expecting as a working class girl from Tottenham. She had become aware, though, that she was the only woman at parties without a regular partner, which made her feel awkward.

She advertised in a swingers' magazine and, having met a number of men, found one she felt comfortable with, who was interesting and good company. He was very posh and much older than her, but she did not mind that. He said he was a journalist and that his name was John Armitage.

She had been seeing him for two years before she found out that his name was actually Evelyn King, and that he was a married Conservative Member of Parliament. They continued their affair, although Debbie was still living at home. Evelyn occasionally came to Tottenham, where we all felt he expected the women to curtsey and the men to tug their forelock. That's how autocratic he was.

Meanwhile, my own affair with Rose was blossoming, although she had another female lover, Jackie, who was married to Bill, a wealthy industrialist. They had a semi-open marriage, where he was tolerant of Jackie's bisexuality. So that was alright.

Given the way that we met, I was sanguine about these other relationships Rose had. It was all part of the swinging scene, and there seemed to be an unspoken agreement that monogamy was old hat, that we could all be free to make love to multiple partners, if we so wished.

So Rose was a busy woman. As well as seeing me, she was

also having sexual relationships with John and Jackie. Oh, and she was still living with her husband, too, but I didn't know whether they were still sleeping together. All this was as well as looking after her children, and doing her part-time modelling work.

In spite of the new sexual openness, Jackie was very discreet in her relationship with Rose. It was only a couple of years before, in 1967, that homosexual acts between two men had become decriminalised, providing they were both over twenty-one. While homosexuality had been illegal for men, it had never been against the law for women.

The story was that when Queen Victoria was presented with the proposed legislation to make male homosexuality illegal, someone suggested it should also apply to women. Queen Victoria's response (Gawd bless 'er) was "But surely it's not possible between women." None of her advisors liked to explain that it surely was.

Anyway, Jackie had introduced Rose to the only lesbian (and perfectly legal) club in Britain, The Gateways in Bramerton Street, off the King's Road. When Rose suggested that we go there one Saturday, I was beside myself with excitement. The club had appeared in the 'Lizabethan' film *The Killing of Sister George*, so had a certain notoriety, which was very appealing.

An early spring evening saw us travelling into London on Rose's motorbike. It was unseasonably warm, so we didn't need too many layers to protect us from the weather. Riding slowly along the King's Road in 1969 was such fun. The cool and the kooky were in evidence and I had to keep turning my head to keep pace with all the sights.

We'd dressed for the occasion, with Rose in jeans, a flowery shirt and a matching tie. She wore her hair long and loose, and had just a hint of lipstick and mascara. I, on the other hand, had gone to town with full make-up. I wore white plastic, knee-length boots and a blue mini-skirted dress. My hair was also worn down, all glossy and held back with a thin white headband.

Rose had been to The Gateways before so she knew where

to park. In a side street, she led us through the tall wooden gate into a kind of tiny courtyard, filled with crates of empty bottles. The next step was to ring the bell attached to a door, which had a sliding visor. Suddenly, the visor snapped back and a deep, but obviously female, voice demanded to know if we were members. Rose, just a little nervously, admitted that we were not but could we come in as guests?

The door inched open enough to let us through and the voice (which we could now see was attached to a short, stocky woman in jeans and shirt) instructed us to talk to Gina.

We carefully negotiated the steep stairs into the basement area. At the foot of the stairs we found a middle-aged woman, dark-haired, hatchet-faced, and smoking from a long cigarette holder. I smiled at her in what I hoped was a beguiling fashion, all the while shaking in my plastic boots. I left it to Rose to do the talking.

Gina was husky-voiced, and looked and sounded very stern. She gave us some forms to fill in and said we could come in tonight as her guests, but if we came again, we would need to become members. Rose and I nodded enthusiastically in agreement. Anything!

Rose grabbed my hand and dragged me into the cloakroom. My mouth had fallen open as I gazed, fascinated, at the writhing, dancing, smooching, snogging mass of people on the dancefloor. I tried to distinguish which of these were men and which were women, until I realised that they were all women!

The air was thick with smoke and music emanated from the jukebox in the corner. Smokey Robinson warbling 'Heard it Through the Grapevine' and Dusty Springfield, rumoured to be one of us, singing somewhat ironically that she could only love 'The Son of a Preacher Man'.

The walls were painted with murals, and tables and chairs lined the edges of the room. Down one end of the small, crowded space was a bar, managed by a chunky, handsome woman with an American accent. I later learnt that this was Smithy – any other name was unknown – who was rumoured to be Gina's lover.

On that first night, Rose and I danced for the first time. What absolute joy to be able to hold each other in a slow dance, where I could rest my face in the space between her neck and shoulder, and she could run her hand along my back. We soon noticed another move among the women in the room, where they placed one of their legs between those of their partner, and they both sort of ground against each other on the spot. We found ourselves trying this out and, yes, it was well worth the effort.

The only low point came when one of the very butch women, dressed entirely in a man's three-piece suit with all the extras (shirt, tie, cufflinks) and a short back and sides haircut, looked disparagingly at Rose and said, "She needs to make up her mind whether she's butch or femme."

There was certainly an informal dress code, with the butch girls being very mannish. This was sometimes inadvertently comic, particularly if they happened to be very short or quite buxom. Not that anyone ever commented. It was just accepted as their choice. The femmes, by contrast, were done up to the nines in make-up, skirts (always skirts) and high heels. Sometimes a couple would defy convention by both being dressed in trousers and shirts, but closer inspection always revealed that one had slightly longer hair – aha! She was the femme, then.

By ten o'clock the small room was heaving with women, their personal dancing space having decreased to about twelve square inches per individual. But it didn't matter that we got bumped from all sides. We were being bumped by breasts, rounded bottoms – soft bits and pieces that were beautifully female, familiar and friendly. The room was thrillingly alive with the elation of an open enjoyment of sexuality.

The club kept pub hours, so closed at 11pm. I was so high, so turned on by it all, I did not want to go home, but there was nowhere else for us at that time, so we roared back to the chalet in double quick time, far too elated to sleep, making love until the early hours, and planning our next trip to this newly discovered nirvana.

Going to 'The Gates', as we came to know it, became a regular outing, maybe every other weekend. The club finished early, and we would be reluctant to make our way home, being high with the music and dancing. There were very few places lesbian women could go for entertainment, although I think there were more venues for gay men.

We discovered a mixed nightclub behind the famous Windmill Club in Soho. It was called The Rehearsal and featured drag acts, overseen by a dragged-up compere. It had a nice atmosphere, in spite of occasional straight couples who would be there to sightsee. The Rehearsal would stay open until around one in the morning, when all those still standing would be encouraged to join in and sing the following, set to the tune of 'Sunday Sweet Sunday', a popular song from the sixties musical *The Flower Drum Song*.

Sunday, on Sunday, if you're feeling blue,
Down The Rehearsal, it's swinging for you.
Letting your hair down with everyone gay,
Camping the night away.
And there's a cabaret for those who like a happy song,
A welcome if you want to bring a friend along.
Fun for the ladies and fun for a gent,
If they're bent.
Butches and bitches, we're short and we're tall.
Down The Rehearsal, we come one and all.
Sunday at seven, we'll meet everyone
At Archer Street, West One.
While all the other people go to places dull and drear,
Come to The Rehearsal where the crowd is queer.
Dancing and drinking we'll never be blue,
Me and You.

Given that this was way before Gay Pride, and homosexuality had only been legalised for a couple of years, this was pretty saucy stuff.

After a while we got to know some of the other women at The Gates, a group of whom had been in the army, but had to leave as their sexuality had been discovered, sometimes by very underhand means. It meant a dishonourable discharge for them. Now in Civvy Street, they made new careers for themselves as bus conductors, park attendants, or any job where they could wear a uniform to work. All the ex-army girls were butch, with very femme girlfriends.

One night, someone acquired some hash, which they rolled into a tight little cigarette. We gathered around in someone's back garden and took turns at smoking it. It did nothing for me, except make me cough. I couldn't understand why anyone would bother with it.

My look was femme, which made me very popular with this new crowd. It wasn't long before I found myself attracted to Dot, who was around my age, but with much more experience. She was funny, short and gamine. I wanted her, and wanted to widen my lesbian horizons. After all, Rose had been my only lesbian girlfriend, and who knew what I might be missing if I just stuck with her?

Rose was dumped.

Dot and I eventually went to bed, but I was still learning. What I learnt on that first night was that Dot was a 'stone butch'. She wanted to make love to me, but did not want me to touch her.

Now this was not my cup of tea at all. I might look femme, but I wanted mutual action in the bedroom. That might have been something of a surprise to Dot.

We had a couple of sessions of struggling with each other, as she would not explain that she did not want to be made love to. So I would stroke her, and she would remove my hand. I would lie on top of her, and she would push me off. It was all very exhausting, and not much fun.

I dumped Dot.

By now it was summer 1969. Debbie told me that she was going off to the Isle du Levant in the South of France for a six-week holiday with the old swinging crowd. This island had a naturist beach, and not many clothes were worn elsewhere.

A new adventure was called for, and I decided to join her. Why not?

Sun, Sea and Shocks

1969 was an eventful year: the Beatles gave their last ever performance on the roof of Apple Records; a heavily pregnant film star, Sharon Tate, was murdered by the Charles Manson gang; colour television made its first appearance in the UK… and I went abroad for the first time.

Debbie and I planned to travel in her brand new car, purchased with her share of the profits from the hairdressing salon, now sold. We loaded it up to the gills with whatever we thought we might need. A few clothes, but not many given that we were going to a naturist resort. A two-person tent, with camp beds and sleeping bags, a tiny kettle, a saucepan and a frying pan. We'd cook on the one-ring Camping Gaz cooker we had, and so took a gas cylinder for that too.

As I did not drive, Debbie advertised for a travelling companion to share driving and petrol costs. She found a young man, Bob, a schoolteacher, who was going to the South of France to visit his elderly relative. He was good humoured, chatty and easy-going. We met several times in London to plan the trip. We thought he'd be perfect and looked forward to sharing his company.

We went on the ferry to Calais and then set off on the long drive to the south, stopping overnight at a youth hostel. None of us had a great deal of money, so we decided to have a picnic for supper, with Bob offering to drive to the nearest village for a baguette, cheese and tomatoes. Debbie was hesitant in giving him the keys to the car, but felt that we knew him well enough by now. It was fine, and he soon returned with the goodies for our meal.

Arriving in Le Lavandou on the French Riviera, I saw the Mediterranean Sea for the first time. I was stunned by the intense blue of the ocean. When I ran into it to paddle, the water was so clear that I could see little fish nibbling at my toes. It was warm, too. The whole experience was a bit different from going in the sea at Southend. I was enchanted.

Bob was concerned that the car had a slow puncture in one of the tyres. He offered to take it to a garage for us, as he spoke good French and could discuss it better with the mechanics. We'd told him our plans, and he said that he would like to join us on the island for a few days, after he had visited his aunt, who lived a little way down the coast.

He asked if he could borrow the car for this journey, saying that he would only stay overnight with Aunty Edna, then come to Levant. He would have to leave the car on the mainland, as no motor vehicles were allowed on the island. By now, he felt like a friend, someone we had known for ages, so we agreed to see him in a couple of days.

Debbie was concerned that she would not have anywhere safe to leave her travellers cheques in the tent, so had decided to leave them, concealed, in the car.

We had to take a little ferry to Levant. We said goodbye to Bob, who was planning to go to his aunt later that day, and we boarded the ferry for the short trip. It was blisteringly hot and the breeze from sailing was a welcome relief from the heat.

Arriving and disembarking at the dockside of Levant, my first sight was of men and women walking around, all very tanned, and wearing a triangle of cloth over their genitals, a bit like a thong. I later learnt that this was called a 'minimum' and was worn whenever the nudists were away from the beach. But this was all they wore, whether shopping or in a café, certainly during the day, although people tended to wear clothes in the evening. Well, it could get a little chilly then.

Of course I was used to public nudity, having been involved in the naturist club in Hertfordshire, but these people all looked so glamorous. It must have been the deep tan, or just their confidence, as they strolled around with their naked children, chatting to this or that acquaintance.

By the time Debbie and I found our campsite, stripped off, and set about putting up our tent, it was around midday. Neither of us were expert tent-putter-uppers, so it took a few false starts before we were convinced that it would stay up.

A couple of hours later, standing back to survey our work, I realised that I had become badly sunburnt on my breasts. By the time we went to bed, I had huge, painful blisters on both boobs. We just weren't used to that level of sun, and the current received wisdom was to apply olive oil and vinegar as a sun tan lotion. A bit of salt and pepper and we'd have a ready-made salad dressing.

We went to see the island doctor next morning, an elderly Frenchman, who examined my breasts lovingly for a long time, before announcing that I should apply diluted bleach. Eh? I don't think so. I managed to acquire some calamine lotion, and made sure that my boobs were covered when the sun was at its hottest, usually by positioning a silk scarf over them when on the beach.

There was an expectation on the island that the naturist values would be embraced by everyone staying there. It wasn't a formal rule, but if anyone came onto the beach and did not disrobe, they would get a slow handclap. It was, I must say, a bit intimidating. I just about got away with the draped scarf, which I would let fall as I went swimming in the sea.

We'd met up with some of the old swinging crowd, but thankfully they had their children with them, so there was little partying on the agenda. I really did not want to swing anymore, and I think that word had got around that I was now playing for the other side. Instead, we just socialised over the occasional meal or on the beach. It was all very civilised and friendly.

By our third day on the island, we were getting worried that Bob had not yet arrived. After some discussion, we thought that we should go to the mainland and talk to the local police. The last ferry for Le Lavandou had left at five in the afternoon, and we would have to wait until the next morning, which also gave Bob one last chance to arrive.

Next day there was still no sign of him, and so we sailed over to Le Lavandou and found the *gendarmerie*. As we tried to explain our plight and concern in schoolgirl French and Pidgin English, the policemen clearly thought it all a great joke. They barely took any details of Bob, the car or the traveller's cheques. They were more interested in ogling these two young female tourists in our shorts and T-shirts. In spite of all that, it all seemed to take forever, and then we found that we had missed the last ferry back to the island.

We did not have enough money on us for a hotel, so found a campsite, hoping that we would be able to hire a tent for the night. There was nothing doing, but two young French girls heard us trying to arrange something and kindly let us stay in their tent. They cooked us a meal with *'corn-ed bif'*.

The next morning we returned to the island, but were very low in spirit. We had little money and no car. Fortunately, we still had our return tickets for the ferry, but would have to somehow make our way across France to Calais.

We explained our predicament to our friends on the island, but none of them offered any help. I guess as we were not screwing, they did not feel under any obligation to get their wallets out, and we were too naïve to directly ask for financial help.

Debbie thought about calling Evelyn at the House of Commons, but was worried that this would lead to all sorts of complications for him. It wasn't that long since the Profumo affair in 1963, and the newspaper hacks were always on the lookout for a new scandal.

We went to see the British Consul, who was arrogant and

patronising, stating, "Oh, I've met people like you before." He gave us a £5 note and said, "I don't suppose I'll ever see that again." Yeah, right. Thanks a bunch.

Although the whole debacle must have been devastating for Debbie, and she would have been worried about how we would manage, she kept her cool so as not to frighten me. We did some calculations and decided that the money we had on us would last for a few weeks if we were very careful. We thought that we could save money if we hitchhiked back to Calais. After all, the worst case scenario had happened, so we might as well stay and enjoy the summer for as long as our cash lasted.

So that's what we did. We ate fried eggs cooked over our little camping stove, pinched leftover bread rolls from restaurant tables, ducked and dived and coped. We made a game of it to see how well we could manage, and it was actually quite fun at times.

Debbie acquired a holiday romance, Casey, who took us out for dinner now and then, so that helped, too.

A few weeks later, we packed everything up. One of our 'friends' agreed to take our tent home for us, but did not offer any other help. We had a suitcase and a sleeping bag each, and so made our way to the nearest main road on the mainland with a large piece of cardboard, upon which was written 'Calais'.

We did get lifts, but it soon became clear that having a suitcase each was an impediment to hitchhiking. We decided to spend some of our precious cash on shipping these back home, which left us with just the sleeping bags, a small rucksack and a handbag apiece. We just about had enough space for a change of clothes, a jumper and the minimum of toiletries.

We stayed in youth hostels and occasionally tried to save money by sleeping rough. There was one night when we settled ourselves down late at night in a virtually deserted train station. We were just dropping off, when the police arrived and moved us along. It was too late by then to find a hostel, so we mooched about until we found a train in a siding that looked like it wasn't going anywhere. Some boys had spotted us, though, and followed us onto the train, wanting sex. We had a tussle with them and they eventually left us alone.

We were finally, exhaustedly, thankfully slipping into sleep when the wretched train started moving. We leapt up, gathering our belongings in a moment and jumped off the train. I think that was the last time we tried economising on accommodation. We had no choice but to carry on staying in hostels and hitchhiking.

Standing by the side of the road, each of us with a tightly rolled sleeping bag and a small rucksack, with a handbag slung across our respective chests, I held up our handwritten sign to let drivers know that we were headed for Calais. We both stood with arms outstretched, thumbs pointing upward. The cars and trucks roared past us, each with a 'Whoosh', spraying us with dust.

Sometimes we'd catch a glimpse of a driver or passenger looking at us, with curiosity or hostility. We'd been standing at this spot for almost an hour and now the sky was darkening, threatening rain.

Then an open truck stopped and the driver leaned over in his cab to enquire, "Calais?"

"Oui, s'il vous plaît."

He opened the passenger door and I scrambled up the high step, using the dashboard to haul myself onto the bench seat next to him. Debbie came up after me, and we both stuffed our luggage wherever we could in the small space.

Our driver was a thick-set man of about forty, with dark greasy-looking hair and numerous tattoos on his arms. As we set off, conversation was limited.

"Vous êtes anglaises?"

"Oui. Vacances."

He nodded. We had a few more rather tortured attempts at being sociable before lapsing into silence. The road stretched before us, as he put his foot down on the gas, passing the signs by the side of the busy road very quickly. My eyes grew heavy and I found myself nodding off, until Debbie gave me a sharp nudge in the ribs.

"Where are we going?" she hissed. "He's gone off the main road."

"Où est, où est…" I struggled with the question; I couldn't remember how to ask where we were going. Fear took hold and my heart was hammering against my ribs. Adrenaline kicked in and now fully awake I could see that he had turned off down a side road, really more of a dirt track than a proper road. He didn't respond to the question or even look at us, but just kept driving further and further into the countryside.

Eventually he stopped. We seemed to be in a stone quarry. He jumped out of the cab at the same time as we slid out of our seats. He was quicker and, before I knew it, he had one arm around my throat and held a large metal wrench in the other hand. He was using this hand to rub my body while forcing me to walk backwards.

I wonder if I can scream? I thought, very calmly, considering. I took a deep breath and opened my mouth. I did scream, loud and piercing it was, too. Unfortunately, there did not seem to be a soul around for miles. We were in a completely isolated place.

Almost at the same moment I became aware of Debbie in front of us. She was in a semi-crouching position, holding a small pointed knife in her hand. I didn't know she had that. It looked like our vegetable knife. She inched towards us.

"Let her go," she demanded in a quiet but determined voice.

I felt his hold on me loosen slightly. She'd taken him by surprise.

She said again, "Let her go. Let her go." All the while slowly getting nearer to him.

His grip on me loosened a little more, and I managed to twist out of his grasp.

Still aiming the knife in his direction, and not taking her eyes off him, she told me to grab whatever I could of our possessions, and then run. "I'll catch you up," she said quietly. Reaching into the cab I got everything: sleeping bags, rucksack and handbags.

"Got it!" I yelled.

With that we both ran down the dirt track while our attacker picked up rocks lying about the place and threw them at us. To one side of the dirt track was a wooded area. Without stopping to check with each other, we tore into the wood, tripping over fallen branches and tumbling down a hill, but not pausing until we came to a clearing.

Catching our breath for a moment, we became aware of a group of people – women and children – sitting around a brazier. They looked at us with mistrust, as two men appeared out of a nearby shack and started to walk towards us. As they got nearer, I could see that they were carrying rifles.

We held up our arms in true western film fashion. It was an automatic reaction to the sight of those guns. At the same time we were gabbling "S'il vous plaît, s'il vous plaît… nous sommes…" Oh shit, what is it? Herdu? Lerdu? Perdu? Is that the word for lost? Oh, bugger. Yes. "Nous sommes perdues, s'il vous plaît."

They did not smile, but at least lowered their guns.

"Erm… Où est grande rue, s'il vous plaît?" I asked, very, very politely.

They pointed to their right and we scuttled off, calling our thanks. It was about half a mile through a copse before we found ourselves on a busy main road. There was even a bar a short way along, which we fell into before splashing out with our meagre resources and ordering a brandy and coffee.

We then cautiously continued our journey, still hitchhiking, getting ever nearer to Calais and ultimately Tottenham. I never thought that I would miss that North London parish, but now I longed to be there.

When we finally saw the white cliffs of Dover, I knew how Vera Lynn must have felt when she sang about them.

Be Careful What You Wish For

Back home I was broke, and had to find a job quickly. Looking in the *London Evening Standard,* I spotted an advert for the Playboy

Club, which was seeking Bunny Girls. They were offering a good wage of around £40 per week, plus something like £200 in tips. This was far more than I could earn as a secretary.

My newly found confidence and deep tan encouraged me to phone up and make an appointment with the Playboy Club in Park Lane, almost next door to the Dorchester Hotel.

Having arrived on time, with freshly washed hair and full make-up, I was taken to meet a woman, who was clearly no teenager, but who was so beautifully coiffed and dressed, it was impossible to guess her age. She asked me a number of questions.

"Why do you want to be a Bunny?"

"Well, I like meeting people and I don't like early mornings. I'm guessing that the work here is mostly in the evenings and at night."

"Hmm. We have a rule that Bunnies cannot date the customers. How do you feel about that?"

"Fine. I have a boyfriend," I lied. "I'm not looking for anyone else."

"Hmm. What experience do you have of waitressing?"

"None at all, but I am a quick learner."

"Hmm. Have you ever mixed cocktails or worked in a bar?"

"Not really. But I'm sure I could do it."

"Hmm. Do you like a drink yourself? We discourage Bunnies from unladylike behaviour."

"I'm practically teetotal. I hardly ever drink alcohol, and would never drink until I was drunk. It's so undignified." I pursed my lips and tried to look disapproving. Really, I should have had an award for this performance.

Having established that I was a practically a nun in my private life, I was then taken to meet another impossibly glamorous woman, who was introduced as the 'Bunny Mother'. I was asked to take all my clothes off, except my knickers (thank goodness I'd worn ones without any holes). Then I was measured by a seamstress and helped into the Bunny costume.

This resembled a one-piece swimming costume, made of

black velvet, with a fluffy tail on the bottom. It was strapless, boned, with high-cut legs and had a long zip up the back. It felt like wearing a very restrictive, tight corset.

However, when I looked in the full-length mirror, I saw that my already generous bust was emphasised, my waist looked tiny and my bottom had a life of its own. Very high-heeled shoes and a hairband with two rabbit ears completed the outfit. I looked fantastic.

I was shown how to do the 'Bunny Dip' and asked to demonstrate this way of serving the customers. Apparently, Bunnies never, ever bend over to serve drinks or whatever, presumably in case their breasts pop out of their costumes. Instead, they carry the tray on one hand, and bend from the knees to place coasters and glasses on the low tables in the club.

I managed to achieve this several times without dropping the tray or tripping over the shoes. I even kept a smile on my face and my boobs in the costume.

"OK, darling, you can get back into your own clothes now," the Bunny Mother told me. "We like you, but you need to lose 5lb. Then come back to us."

I went home walking on air, promising myself that I would lose the required weight. However, by the time I got home, all resolve had disappeared, particularly as Mum had made sausage and mash for dinner. Oh, well, back to the job drawing board.

Looking for a secretarial job, I registered with an employment agency, where I had to fill in a long questionnaire, including one question on religion. I wrote 'atheist' in the space provided.

There followed a typing test, and then I was seen by an interviewer. She looked at my form, looked at me and asked, "How can a Jewish girl be an atheist?" I laughed and said, "Oh, quite easily." She looked very disappointed, but nevertheless sent me to several interviews.

My confidence was sky-high. I looked good with a deep tan and sun-streaked hair. I smiled a lot, gave good answers and could offer a typing speed of sixty words per minute. That's fast. I got offers of jobs at all of them, but picked the one that sounded most interesting at an advertising agency.

On the first weekend after getting back from France, I went to The Gateways on my own. I wore a half-lined white lace mini-dress, so that my white bra was showing through the top half. The outfit set off my tan to perfection. On my feet were strappy little sandals, gold and silver leather framing my toes. My hair was loose in a glossy pageboy cut.

Lord, were those butches round me like bees to a honey pot. Even Smithy smiled at me when she was collecting the glasses. I danced all night with this one and that, all of them giving me the glad eye, telling me I was sexy and holding me tight. I could have had my pick, but then at the end of the evening found that I just wanted to go home, alone.

I'd had a card in the post from Rose saying that she was having a private view of her paintings and would I like to come? My heart sank a little at the thought of all those wolves, or horses, or whatever I was meant to see in them, but I found that I wanted to see her.

I wore the same white lacy dress when I went to the private view in St Albans. Rose did a double-take when she saw me, and was clearly nervous.

"I didn't think you'd come," she said.

"Well, of course I came. I wouldn't miss this, would I?"

"You look wonderful," she told me. I told her where I'd been for the summer, and explained that I'd only got back recently.

"Look, I've got to go and mingle, but don't leave without saying goodbye, will you?"

I sipped my glass of warm white wine and wandered around looking at the paintings, many of which looked very similar. There is, after all, only so much you can do with wet paper and coloured ink. But, hey ho, what did I know about art?

The crowd had started to thin out a bit and I was thinking that I ought to make a move if I wanted to catch the train back to London. Rose came over to me.

"Don't go home. Come and stay with me tonight. We can go back to the chalet. I want to catch up with all your news."

There was something about her voice, her eyes, that vulnerability that had touched me before. I found that I wanted to hold her, I wanted to talk into the night with her, wanted to play some music that had a special meaning for us. 'Lay Lady Lay' perhaps. I had a momentary flashback to when we last made love, when we shared mutual pleasures, with none of this stone butch business. We understood each other's desires.

Oh, sod it… I just wanted to be with her.

So I went back to the chalet, and that was the real start of our relationship. My experiences since breaking up with her had only served to fuel my old yearning to be loved, to be held, and to be needed. She offered me all of that as we fell in love.

Rose was intense, passionate, erudite and obsessed with her inner life and psyche. She was obsessed with my psyche, too. She could also be funny, spontaneous, cultured and sensual. And, later, possessive and unreasonable.

She was a Buddhist, another revelation for me. I had never met anyone who was involved in Eastern religion or philosophy. I was interested in how it worked and she taught me to meditate. Later in our relationship, I would go with her to a Tibetan Buddhist retreat in Scotland. I liked the peacefulness of that place, the calm and quiet of the centre and the countryside surrounding it.

She had studied ballet as a young woman, and still had an enthusiasm for classical music and dance. She introduced me to those pleasures, and we would go to see the Royal Ballet at Covent Garden. I learnt to share her excitement, seeing a very young Wayne Sleep in *Les Patineurs*, effortlessly appearing to ice skate across the stage. I thrilled to the music of the ballet, becoming absorbed by its emotions and grace. We went to see modern dance, too, with its exuberance and overt sexuality. It was all uncharted territory for me, all a learning curve.

She had taught horse riding, and still rode, exercising horses for friends. This became another activity she shared, finding a stocky little pony for me to hack through the Hertfordshire countryside. I found that I loved the animals, their warmth and solidness, their strength and gentleness. I even loved my enforced riding lessons.

"Keep your heels down," Rose would tell me.

"Don't let him eat!" she'd yell as my steed found a particularly tasty bit of hedgerow.

"Keep his head up and don't pull on the reins." That one was a bit tricky.

And what did I give her? I made her laugh. I was eager to absorb all the new experiences she presented to me. Rose continued my intellectual education where John had left off, suggesting books for me to read, and I continued to be an enthusiastic pupil, which must have been gratifying for her. I was a tender, ardent, adventurous lover. What more could a girl ask for?

So I started to spend every weekend with her at the chalet. Sometimes we'd go out to the ballet or to The Gates (chalk and cheese) and sometimes we'd go for a hack. We'd spend time with her children, of whom I became increasingly fond.

Rose was still living with her husband during the week, and I was still living in Tottenham and working as a secretary in the West End. She was an artists' life model for the Slade and Central Schools of Art, and would take me into London on Monday mornings on the back of her motorbike.

Somehow Sheila, my sister, had cottoned on to the fact that I was having a lesbian relationship with Rose. She told my mum. There was no need to tell her, but Sheila was the good daughter and so spilt the beans. I was very angry with her. Mum didn't really understand and asked, "Why can't you find a nice boy? He wouldn't have to be Jewish. Don't do this."

"Mum, just be glad that I'm happy. This is what I want."

"It's because of Tony, isn't it? Because of the way he treated you."

"No, it's got nothing to do with him. I don't want to get married, don't want a boyfriend. It's just the way I am."

I had wanted to leave home for some time. The magazines of the day, *Honey* and *Petticoat*, regularly ran articles about young people who shared flats, while television programmes like *The Liver Birds* showed two girls having a wonderful time, living together away from their family, having fun and being naughty with no one to tell them off.

I began to make plans. Mum had never taught me to cook. The kitchen was her domain, and to enter it while she was cooking was at your peril. She'd say, "This kitchen's too small for two people."

So I went to adult education cookery classes and learnt how to make toad in the hole, macaroni cheese and shepherd's pie. All good, basic stuff. Oh, and Christmas cake, which took hours to bake and which I never attempted again.

Then each pay day, I bought any essentials I thought would be useful for a girl sharing a flat: bedding, two plates, two bowls, two sets of cutlery and a saucepan. Everything got stowed away and hidden at the bottom of my wardrobe. I did not discuss my plans with anyone, except Rose, Debbie and my old school friend, Jenny, although I did not see so much of her these days.

I had told Jenny that I was in a new relationship, with a woman. To her credit, Jenny barely blinked. Although lesbians and gay men were viewed with suspicion by the media and the public, Jenny was totally accepting of my sexuality, only asking the questions she might have about any new relationship.

"How did you meet her?"

"How old is she?"

"What's her job?"

Jenny and I continued our friendship for some years, until distance and new lifestyles got in the way. We lost touch for thirty-five years, but eventually met up again through Friends Reunited. She hadn't changed a bit, and was still the scatty, affectionate chatterbox I'd known as a young woman.

In 1970, about six months after Rose and I resumed our relationship, I knew it was time to leave home. I wanted to be nearer to her, so chose St Albans as my new base and found a house in York Road, a leafy avenue with terraces of large houses. There was a shared bathroom, kitchen and lounge, with several spacious bedrooms rented out to three young women.

Rose arranged to use her husband's car to help me move my stuff. I took the coward's way out and did not announce my intentions until the night before I was leaving. All hell broke loose. At that time young working class women only left home to get married – or go on the game.

When Rose turned up, my mum stood on the doorstep and told her in a wavering voice, "You're taking my baby away." As this was the most demonstrative she'd ever been, I hardened my heart and told Rose to just drive.

Sharing a house wasn't quite the way it appeared in the magazines and on telly. For a start, the landlord, a middle-aged bachelor who had lived in the large 1930s house with his mum until she died, was a bit creepy. The shared lounge had the only television and, although he did not live on the premises, he was often there. Watching TV usually meant having to share the sofa with him. Not a relaxing experience.

The other thing was that he had chosen my housemates. We were all strangers to each other, and I actually saw very little of these girls. Sometimes our paths would cross to and from the kitchen or bathroom, and we would politely say "Hello", but there was no socialising, no parties and not many laughs to be had with them.

Never mind. I was so much nearer to Rose now and it made life easier, particularly when I found a job locally, too, with the pharmaceutical company Smith & Nephew. It was a bit boring and not what I'd been used to as it was in a very large typing pool. Still, it beat having to deal with commuting in and out of London. And Rose was spending more and more time with me, rather than being at the chalet or at home.

She suffered badly from asthma. On one occasion she was having a particularly bad attack and, although she was with her family that night, I was so worried about her that I called out her GP, a very sympathetic man, who was aware of our relationship. She ended up going into hospital for some time.

When I next saw our doctor, we discussed Rose's health generally and he said that he thought she would always have psychiatric problems and did I feel able to cope with that? I was so in love with her that I was convinced I could do it all, although I was having trouble sleeping. He gave me a prescription for Mogadon and commented that I had been very calm when I'd called him during Rose's asthma attack, and had I ever thought of going into nursing?

Well, no, I had not until then. Now the seed was sown, I started to think about it and to make some enquiries. At the same time, Rose announced that she could no longer live with her husband, that things had become impossible at home, and that she felt we should find a place where we could live together.

It would be painful for her to leave her children, but she said that her husband would contest any application she made for custody, citing her sexuality to stop her having contact. That would, for sure, make the newspapers, resulting in difficulty for her children, whom she adored.

Talk about all change. I was very excited by both the thought of a new career, and of living full time with my love. I set about finding us a flat to rent in St Albans, and viewed one in a huge Victorian house, with gothic gables, surrounded by tall trees in the front garden and a large back garden, which housed a block of old, disused stables. It had a winding wrought iron staircase leading to a room with a dusty upright piano.

The rooms in the house were large and airy, spacious with high ceilings and lots of windows. These properties had been divided into flats, but were not entirely self-contained, as the tenants shared a hallway with a stained glass front door and stairwell, and there was a shared bathroom for two of the flats and a bedsit.

The ground floor had the largest flat, with a young family

living there. The middle flat comprised a kitchen and two rooms, while the third floor contained a bedsit and another smaller flat.

The landlord used to live in this house with his family but, now the children had grown up, they had downsized and moved to Yorkshire. He was a nice man, a classical musician, with a gentle approach. He told me that it was the middle flat that was vacant. I explained to him that I would be sharing the flat with a friend who was currently ill in hospital and mentioned that she had studied ballet and music. I said that I was a secretary, currently thinking about becoming a nurse. We liked each other, I think, because he said that he was happy to rent the flat to us, although he had not met Rose.

I moved in summer 1971. It was a lovely house, in spite of the temperamental water heater in the bathroom. We decided to each have a bedroom, as Rose would want to use her space as a studio. The two large rooms were divided by a box room, which had a big old-fashioned folding bed, housed in a wooden cabinet. We called it 'The Coffin Room'. The landlord said we could use it for the occasional guest, usually one of Rose's children.

The bedsit on the top floor was occupied by Mick, an art therapist of about twenty-six, with long hair and a nice smile, short of stature and a bit scruffy. He was easy to talk to and seemed a likeable bloke.

Julie was a thirty-something single woman who had the flat on that floor. She was a librarian who dressed the part. Rather prim and proper, she and Rose got on like a house on fire, united by their class and a love of literature and music.

The ground floor was taken by a couple, Annie and Tim, both in their twenties, who had a small child. They were friendly enough, but kept themselves to themselves.

When Rose came out of hospital, she joined me at Lemsford Road and we soon made a home of the place. At the time, she and her husband had started divorce proceedings and she had, of course, had to leave her children with him. It must have been a very difficult time for her, but I was so thrilled to be finally living with someone who loved me, that I may not always have been as sensitive as I might have been to her situation.

At twenty-three my own happiness was paramount and, while I tried to put myself in her shoes, it sometimes felt that it had no relevance to my life. I couldn't see what the problem was: she and her husband no longer loved each other, she would be able to see the children whenever she wanted, and she would be living with someone she adored, with whom she could make passionate love, who was happy to cook for her and who got on well with the kids.

Rose continued to see John and Jackie. While this had not been an issue for me earlier in our relationship, since I had fallen in love with her, I now hated it. I hated having to share Rose with another woman. I hated thinking about her and John making love. Knowing that scenario as intimately as I did, I could visualise almost every move.

It was the only thing we ever rowed about.

"I'm seeing John on Friday, so I won't be back until Saturday morning."

"Don't go. Please."

"I've told him that I will and, anyway, I want to. I haven't been with him for a long time. At least three weeks. You've had me to yourself all that time."

"Apart from when you went to see Jackie."

"Yes. Apart from that time."

"Why do you have to see him? Aren't you happy with what we do? I know you are. I can tell that you are satisfied. Why can't that be enough for you? It's enough for me. If you really loved me you wouldn't go."

Rose sighed. We'd had this conversation so many times.

"I do love you. You do satisfy me, but I have needs that you can't help me with. We all have a variety of needs, and just one person can't fill all of those different parts of me."

"Well, what needs are not being met? What's he got that I haven't? Apart from the obvious."

"Look, I want a man. It's that simple."

"Oh, go on then. Just fuck off and leave me alone."

Then I'd storm out of the room, slamming the door, and go and weep in my own room until she came in to lie on the bed with me, and we would make up with kisses and sex.

She'd still go and see John on Friday though.

Getting Me Kit Off and a Rude Awakening

One night, coming back on her motorbike from an evening out in London, Rose ran into the back of a car. She broke her hand and had to wear a plaster cast. This meant that she was unable to keep her commitment to modelling at St Albans School of Art for the rest of that term. I was sick to death of the tedium of the typing pool at Smith & Nephew, and was more than happy to give a week's notice so I could cover the remainder of Rose's life modelling contract.

Rose briefed me, explaining that I would need to be able to sit very still for about an hour, after which there would be a break. She said that I should take a robe of some sort, so that I could cover up when not modelling, and that it was probably more convenient to take a flask of coffee for the short breaks. Otherwise I would have to get dressed, go to the refectory, drink coffee, get back to studio and undress, all in fifteen minutes.

My first class was with a group of foundation course students. The tutor suggested a pose for me, sitting on a chair on which velvet drapes had been arranged. My hands were in my lap, with my feet firmly on the ground. It was very comfortable and, if I did find my nose was itching, I would employ the meditation techniques taught to me by Rose. They usually worked and I could rise above the discomfort.

When the tutor told the class, "We've a lovely model today", it made me smile. I was still so hungry to hear that I was attractive.

He carefully arranged two electric bar heaters either side of me, and regularly checked whether I was too hot or too cold. As the year went on and the studio's temperature lowered, I would often find myself burning on one side of my body, and freezing on the other, but I rarely complained.

As time went on, I found that I was in demand for a number of classes, not just life classes, but also the portrait course where I wore clothes, a large hat and several rows of beads around my neck. My favourite class was the one I called 'The Mothers'. This consisted entirely of ladies of a certain age, all solicitous about my welfare, checking whether I was comfortable, whether I wanted something from the refectory and so on. I sat for them in both life drawing and sculpture.

There was one pose in sculpture where I was lying down, and each and every 'mother' in the room modelled me as looking at a bird bath. There may still be bird baths all over Hertfordshire, with a comely, naked maiden gazing at the robins and starlings, covered in bird shit.

Sculpture, being three-dimensional, required the model to be placed on a revolving dais, which was turned slightly every now and then, so that the students could get all perspectives. This was fine when I was sitting or lying down, but when I was standing, I would get a bit nervous as the platform was moved, feeling a little dizzy. There was one occasion when I had a slight stomach upset, and my nerves got the better of me. In the peaceful atmosphere of the studio, the dais was turned, and I got anxious and farted quite loudly. No one said anything.

Sometimes when I went for lunch I would see Quentin Crisp in the canteen, surrounded by adoring acolytes. This was around the time that his book *The Naked Civil Servant* had been published so there was a great deal of interest in him, although he already had celebrity status in the art school circuit, partly due to his wonderful acerbic commentary and partly to the impossible poses he took up. We occasionally said hello to each other, but I was too shy to impose any further conversation on him. I did once try to emulate his poses, by twisting my body so that all my weight was on one leg. It was incredibly painful, and I did not repeat the experiment.

Most of the poses I was asked to take up were very comfortable. There was one where I was positioned on a draped mattress on the floor. I had one arm under my head, with the other arm by my side. The heaters were blazing away and I drifted off. Well, actually, I fell deeply asleep.

I woke when I sensed movement around me and found that the students were going for a break, which was my cue to put on my robe and retire to the dressing room.

Unfortunately, the arm that had been placed under my head had gone to sleep, too. I had absolutely no feeling or control of it. Trying to get that limb into my robe was a challenge, as it flopped about and refused to behave.

I'd applied to St Albans City Hospital to enter their State Registered Nurse course. Not having any GCEs, I had to sit an entrance exam, which wasn't too difficult. A few weeks later I had an interview, where the only problem was being told that I would be expected to live in the nurses' home. I countered this by explaining that I was in a relationship and living with my partner. I was suitably discreet when talking about this, finding ways to avoid indicating gender of said partner.

Shortly afterwards I had a letter telling me I had gained a place on the course and was due to start in January 1972. I was thrilled and nervous. I hoped that I'd be able to cope with all the bodily fluids, but looked forward to wearing the uniform.

Rose and I decided to have a holiday before I started and we agreed on a fortnight in Brighton, known to have several mixed gay clubs. She found us a self-catering flat very near to the seafront at the Kemptown end of the area.

The late September sun shone weakly through the net curtains of our rented apartment. The weather had been good until now and we had taken a ride on Rose's little motorbike to Devil's Dyke. I hadn't worn any knickers and our lovemaking started on the way there, probably very dangerously. Once in the park we found a secluded place and, spreading a blanket, carried on… Oh, how we carried on.

It was exciting being outdoors in a public place, but when I glimpsed a man behind a nearby bush, I jumped up.

"What's the matter?" Rose asked.

"There's someone there. A man…"

Then she saw him, too. We were on our feet and out of there in a matter of moments. It wasn't until we were well away that we relaxed, giggling about the incident.

In the evening we found one of the gay clubs we'd heard about. It was reminiscent of The Gateways in that it was also in a basement – would we ever see daylight as lesbians, we wondered. A tiny room, packed with lesbians and gay men, all battling for a space to dance the night away. It would appear that this was a closed community, as everyone seemed to know each other. We were aware of a few curious glances at us. It didn't feel very friendly. Perhaps they thought we were tourists, out to see the sights. I remembered one girl I chatted to at The Gates who told me, "I'm not a lesbian. I'm just here to do research." Well, weren't we all?

After that, we barely left our apartment, except for a bit of shopping here and there, and an evening meal. We indulged, instead, in a kind of sex-fest, making love for hours on end, stopping for a glass of wine and to catch our breath. Our world for the rest of that fortnight became eat, drink, make love, night, day, sleep, make love, drink, make love, day, sleep…

The bedroom took on a kind of otherworldliness, being the sole centre of our tiny universe. I started to feel quite strange, like there were nothing else in the cosmos, just me, Rose and this slightly clinical bedroom, with its white walls and flat prints in frames. The heavy, permanently drawn curtains only served to emphasise the isolation of our highly charged time there.

We were having sex again when Rose's usual tenderness suddenly became very rough. I heard her say, "Is this how you liked it with John?"

I wasn't sure that I'd heard her right. "Eh? What do you mean?"

"Like this, was it?" she said aggressively and started tearing into me.

I didn't know what was going on. Was this a new sex game? Or was it real? Whatever, I didn't like it and pushed her off me.

"Don't do that, Rose, you're hurting me."

"I bet you didn't say that to John, did you? I bet you screamed with delight, didn't you?"

It was as if there was another person in bed with me, a hostile stranger I'd never seen before. I felt frightened and confused.

"What's the matter? Why are you saying this stuff? I don't understand."

"Of course you understand. You liked it with him, didn't you? You didn't mind when he was rough with you, did you?"

She talked on and on and on. Accusing, angry, frightening. I wanted her to stop. I wanted to go to sleep and find this had been a bad dream. I took a Mogadon, my prescribed sleeping tablet.

She carried on for what felt like hours. She would not let me sleep. Every time I started to drift off, another diatribe would start.

"What do you do when I'm not at home? Eh? Who are you seeing behind my back? You seem very friendly with Mick? Are you fucking him? You are, aren't you? You say you love me, but what do you get up to when I'm not around. Eh? Talk to me. Tell me the truth, Janet, because I will find out."

I took another Mogadon. I just wanted it to stop. I felt so very tired. My eyes were itchy with fatigue and my brain felt like it was wrapped in cotton wool. I wanted to be unconscious. I had a further two tablets. And still I could not sleep, and still she talked on.

Eventually she went out of the room. I think she went out of the flat. Blissful silence. I took two more Mogadon. Please God let me sleep let me sleep let me close my eyes and be quiet and sleep and be asleep and this to be a dream a nightmare that will all be over when I wake.

And then I slept, with the bottle of tablets clutched in my hand.

That's how Rose found me when she came back into the bedroom. She shook me. "How many have you taken? Answer me."

"Dunno. Siii or se'ern."

"Are you sure?"

"Yeah. No. Dunno."

Later she told me she'd rung a doctor who said that I was not in any danger, and I should just be allowed to sleep it off. We never talked about the mad drama that had led to my apparent overdose.

But the honeymoon was well and truly over.

Immediately after this episode, Rose arranged for me to go and stay for a few days with Jackie and Bill. It was a strange choice, seeing as Jackie was my rival in her affections.

Rose was convinced that I was now disturbed, needed help and should not be left alone. There was little discussion about these arrangements, and I felt like a wrung-out dishcloth, so went along with all of it.

As it turned out, Jackie was a nice woman. Very efficient and matter of fact, she made me comfortable in their spare room. The house was in an exclusive part of London and, while not particularly grand, it was warm, welcoming and cosy. Her husband, Bill, was a genial kind of bloke, good humoured and talkative. They had three little blonde boys who were polite and sweet.

I had no idea what I was doing there, but it seemed as good a place as any to be feeling washed out, and Jackie did look after me, bringing tea in the morning to my bed, cooking healthy and delicious meals in the evening.

Once I got back to Lemsford Road, Rose convinced me to find a psychotherapist, having got a contact name and number from her own shrink. I went to see a woman in Harley Street who asked me a number of questions. I think I was still shocked by recent events because I felt muddle-headed and vague, although this may have been due to the Mogadon. This woman advised me that I should not enter psychotherapy, but instead needed a psychiatrist.

Rose insisted that I report back to her and then set about finding me a psychiatrist. As for me, I felt that my life was spinning out of control, but seemed unable to get a handle on it. Everything I had held true, Rose's love and the meaningfulness of our relationship, was being shaken and questioned.

I saw a man to begin with who asked me questions like "Do you use a dildo?" and "Who is the man in your relationship?" Instead of telling him to mind his own fucking business, I was so submissive that I actually answered these very intrusive questions, although I suspected he got off on them.

Once again, Rose wanted details about these sessions and, this time, it was a good thing because she found a woman for me to see. Except this woman appeared to fall asleep whenever I saw her. She'd be alert for the first ten minutes of our time together but would then seem to nod off. Sometimes, I'd just sit there and not be able to think of anything to say in which case we'd be in a not uncomfortable, companionable silence for forty minutes. I never had any great insights during this time.

Fortunately, over the course of several months, I found my own self once more. With hindsight I can see that Rose was manipulative and controlling, and the mental health issues were more hers than mine. I was just a very young woman, trying to find her way in the world, being influenced by an older woman, who I believed to have the answers to all life's questions. But I never quite trusted her again after that, and our relationship was different. I would be far more defensive and quick to anger. Although I was still in love with her, I sensed I needed protective armour to keep me safe from her more extreme emotions.

Help was at hand, though, as the New Year brought a new challenge. Nurse Green was about to make her first appearance.

3

Carry On Nurse Green

My first day at the St Albans School of Nursing was a confusing torrent of information about all sorts of practical things: security lockers, which wards were medical, which were surgical, geriatric and so on. There were forms to fill in about next of kin, our contact details and National Insurance numbers.

We were told when we would be paid, and given a schedule for the next three years of when we would be working on the wards, when we were in study blocks and when we would have annual leave.

Then there were the rules about uniform: no aprons worn outside the wards; navy raincoats to be worn over uniforms when not at the hospital; cloaks not to be worn outside the hospital; hair should not be loose or touching our collars; tan tights only – no black ones; mufti (what on earth was that?) to be worn in school; no jewellery on the wards, apart from wedding rings; no make-up (everyone groaned at that, quietly resolving to carry on wearing subtle mascara, at least); belt colours that denoted the year to which students had progressed; navy uniforms denoted ward sisters; light blue ones for staff nurses… it seemed to go on and on.

Later in the week, we were measured up for our uniforms, which I thought were rather attractive. A mauve and white small check, loosely fitted dress, held in at the waist by a stiff Petersham belt – purple for first year students. Attached by studs was a starched white collar, worn open at the neck, so that it formed a V-shape. On top of the dress, we were to wear a stiff white linen apron, its bib secured to our dresses by safety pins on the underside so that they did not show. We were also issued with a rather dashing red-lined cloak for covering up when outside the ward. The only let-down was the cap, which was made of white cardboard until we qualified, when we could have linen ones. On the plus side it formed a rather cute shape when pinned pertly onto our hair.

Almost all of the other new students were to live in the nurses' home, a short distance from the main part of the hospital. Fortunately, the hospital wasn't that far from Lemsford Road and, once I got a bike, I could get there in about ten minutes if I pedalled like the clappers, but I couldn't seem to break my old habit of always being late for work.

At twenty-three, I was a little older than most of my classmates, although there were a couple of others in their twenties. The majority, however, were about eighteen years old.

A large contingent were from Malaysia, a couple from Hong Kong, and the rest were mostly white British females, with three young men who stood out like awkward sore thumbs.

We spent several weeks in school, learning how to make beds (the corners were particularly important apparently), how to lift a patient, how to move them from bed to chair and vice versa, how to change a dressing and give a bed bath. Some of these activities were fun, particularly when one of us was required to volunteer to act the part of the patient. Other times we would practise resuscitation on a dummy known as Resussie Annie – cue for much giggling. We were shown how to give injections, and practised on oranges in the classroom.

I did well with these practical tasks, but found that I struggled with the more academic side of learning biology and physiology. I'd done so little formal studying in the past that it was a new activity for me, and I had to work hard to get to grips with it.

We were in school for six weeks and, as I got to know my new colleagues, I found them to be delightful. They were, on the whole, friendly and funny. There was Dayang, one of the

Malaysian girls, who was short and skinny, with a pudding basin haircut and who had the dirtiest sense of humour imaginable.

Karima was also Malaysian, a little doll of a girl, absolutely beautiful with doe eyes and a full mouth, who wore her long, black, glossy hair loose while we were in school. I just wanted to spend every hour of every day gazing at her.

I became good friends with Val. She described herself as Eurasian, and I learnt that this meant her background was mixed race of Indian and white British. Val was stunning, very attractive with wide eyes and long, dark hair and skin the colour of milk chocolate. She was a curvy girl who seemed to be completely at ease with her full body. She was engaged to Gerry, a childhood sweetheart. While Val was outgoing and exuberant, Gerry was quiet, thin and completely besotted by her.

I was friendly, too, with Juliet, whose British family had gone to Australia under the post-war £10 emigration programme. She had decided to complete her nursing training in England so that she could 'do' Europe and visit her family in Ireland. Juliet was tall and thin, with that typical Irish colouring of blue eyes and dark hair. She had terrible dress sense, and often wore strange and mismatched outfits when off duty.

Louise was a tall British girl, the daughter of nurses, and from a large Irish-origin family. She had umpteen siblings, several of whom were nurses and most of whom played a musical instrument.

Actually, I had already met Louise in other circumstances. I'd been coming home one evening from the art college when I saw a young woman on her hands and knees looking under a parked car. My curiosity was roused and I asked what she was doing.

"There's a cat under the car, and I think it's hurt," she said.

I joined her on the ground and peered under the car. I could see a cat, but when I reached out to try to coax it out, it shot out from beneath the vehicle into a nearby garden.

"Well," I said, "there's gratitude for you."

The girl laughed. "If it can run like that, there can't be much wrong with it."

She looked down at her dirty knees and shredded tights and said, "I'm meant to be going to a party."

"Why don't you come back to my place?" I suggested. "I only live across the road and I can give you some tights."

"Really? Oh, wow! That would be great."

So she came home with me, washed her knees and put on a new pair of tights. She went on her way with a cheery "See you around... and thanks!"

And that was that, until I bumped into her again a few weeks later at the DSS when I was signing on, my contract at the art college having ended. We had a brief chat, and then went on our respective ways.

So when I saw her in the nursing school, it was like kismet. We had to be friends. And she turned out to be great fun, naughty and a bit of a hippie. I liked Louise a lot.

The principal of the School of Nursing, Miss Flagg, was a terrifying woman of about six foot, built like a tank, with a short and sharp haircut. We discovered that she had trained in the army, which made her look and sergeant major manner completely understandable.

Someone also discovered that her deputy, Miss Gray, had also trained in the army and they now shared a flat. Miss Gray was rather softer than the principal, wore her hair longer and usually had a dash of pink lipstick. Hmm. Well, I had my suspicions about their relationship but kept it to myself.

I was very careful not to disclose my own sexuality, and took to avoiding being specific about the gender of my partner, which is less easy than you might think, always having to refer to 'them' and 'their' rather than 'he' or 'she'. I became quite an expert at this, but if I had to mention my partner's name, I would call them 'Robin' rather than 'Rose'.

Miss Flagg and Miss Gray were churchgoing, evangelical Christians. On one occasion I was summoned to see Miss Flagg.

"Nurse Green, I am very concerned about your timekeeping. Why are you always late?"

"Um. Well. I sometimes have trouble getting to sleep and then I can't get up in the morning." I didn't explain that the trouble getting to sleep was often due to lengthy lovemaking sessions or fiery arguments with Rose.

"Do you have troubling thoughts when you are trying to get to sleep?" she asked in an uncharacteristically caring manner.

Oh blimey. Now what had I started? I had to think quickly to get out of this one.

"Yes, sometimes. I worry about whether I am making the right choices and whether my family are alright."

"Oh dear," she said, still gentle, leaning towards me. "Do you have any religious faith, Nurse Green?"

I was a bit thrown by this development and couldn't think of a lie quickly enough.

"Well, I come from a Jewish background, but I'm really an atheist," I told her, like a lamb to the slaughter.

Her whole demeanour changed, and she sat up straighter, the caring smile disappeared and her voice was back on the parade ground when she said, "I see. Well, you had better buy yourself a good alarm clock and make sure you are on time in future, otherwise you will find yourself in serious trouble. Do you understand?"

"Yes, Miss Flagg. I'm sorry, Miss Flagg. I promise it won't happen again."

"That is correct, Nurse Green. It definitely will not happen again."

I'm not sure whether it was my Semitic background or the fact that I was clearly no candidate for evangelical conversion, but I had lost my chance of getting on the good side of Miss Flagg.

Over the course of that first six weeks in school, we were told that we would have to give a talk to the rest of the class on a medical or nursing subject, assigned by the tutors. I had never had to do anything like this before and was, frankly, terrified. The thought of standing up in front of everyone and reading out words that I might not be able to pronounce, or that would reactivate my childhood lisp, was scary.

I was relieved when I found that my subject was 'The Common Cold' – it was not a difficult subject; in fact it was pretty straightforward. Unlike Val's subject, which was 'Emphysema – Signs and Symptoms'. Or Louise, who got 'Treatment of Fractures'.

I got stuck into the research and found that a cold was an acute respiratory tract infection, and that its Latin name was *Coryza*. It was caused by an organism and the symptoms were rhinorrhoea (runny nose), nasal obstructions and sneezing. There was quite a lot more, but by the time I finished writing I felt reasonably well prepared, although still nervous.

The day came to present my seminar to the class and I stood up with knocking knees.

"The Common Cold," I began, "is caused by an orgasm...".

As soon as I'd said it, I realised my mistake and just wanted the ground to open up and swallow me whole. No one giggled, no one spoke. You could hear a pin drop. After a millisecond's hesitation, I continued. I knew that the show must go on! Afterwards, Val said to me, "Did you mean to...?"

"No, no. I was just so nervous, I got muddled up."

"Did you see Miss Flagg's face? She looked like thunder."

"Oh, no! Now she'll think I'm taking the piss, on top of everything else."

"You rebel. Still it was bloody funny, wasn't it?"

Towards the end of our first block in school, we were assigned a ward on which to shadow an experienced, third year student nurse. I was to go onto Men's Surgical. This would be the first time that I had worn my uniform, which was now completed by red and black pens in the breast pocket, a small notebook in the side pocket of my dress and a fob watch pinned onto the top of my apron, together with a badge announcing that I was 'Nurse Green, Student'.

The dress and apron were held in at the waist by a tight purple belt, and I'd arranged my long hair into a thick plait, which was then pinned up, with my cap secured on top of it. My tights were the official American tan, and I wore black, flat, lace-up shoes, which would prove a blessing as the day wore on. Looking into the full-length mirror before I left the changing room, I threw my black and red cloak over my shoulders, admiring the whole effect. I liked what I saw, although looked more confident than I felt.

I arrived on the ward at 7.30am. This may be the only occasion that I was on time. I was greeted by a staff nurse, who was slim and pretty in her blue uniform. She was friendly and told me that I would be shadowing Student Nurse Walker, who turned out to be an unsmiling, mousy-haired and skinny young woman. There was no question of exchanging first names, so we formally addressed each other as 'Nurse Walker' and 'Nurse Green' respectively. Actually, this was standard protocol, but I wasn't that familiar yet with the formalities.

The first job of the day was to take the breakfast trays round to the patients, asking them if they wanted porridge or cornflakes. The hot meals were waiting to be distributed and every patient had the option of a cooked breakfast.

Next on the agenda was a handover meeting, where the nurses all squeezed into the Sister's office, and we were brought up to date with the events of the previous night, each patient's current condition and plans for the coming day. The nurses were each given particular responsibility for looking after specific patients. Much of this discussion went over my head, of course.

The next activity was to get patients washed and out of bed, wherever possible. This involved a blanket bath for many patients, something I had learnt in school and felt confident about. As each patient was washed, they would be helped into their dressing gowns and slippers, and then sat in a chair. Pairs of nurses would then make their bed. Nurse Walker turned out to be a tartar, with a particular obsession for the corners of the bed linen to be geometrically neat and in line.

"That won't do, Nurse Green," she admonished me. "That corner is not tight enough. Do it again."

After several of these comments, I was swearing blue murder under my breath.

"Oh, for Christ's sake, shut up you fucking cow of a bitch."

"What did you say?"

"I said that I was sorry it wasn't up to scratch."

We worked our way all along one side of the long ward, until we got to Mr Black. He didn't have a pyjama top on, so I washed his upper half before turning down the sheets to deal with the rest of him. I was momentarily halted as a fetid smell hit me. Taking a step backwards, I saw that Mr Black appeared to have a hole in his belly, around which was secured a clear, plastic bag. This was filled with shit, which was oozing out of the top of the bag.

"Oh, did I tell you that Mr Black has a colostomy?" the nurse bitch from hell asked.

I never knew there was such a thing as a colostomy, or what it entailed. I stood and gazed at the disgusting mess in abject horror, the putrid smell reaching me even as I inched away from it.

"You'll have to change and clean it," Nurse Walker said to me.

With this, she handed me some plastic gloves and went out of the closed curtains, leaving me with the patient.

I managed to raise my eyes from the awful wound on his abdomen to Mr Black's face. He said, "I'm so sorry, dear. I don't know why that's happened. It's not very nice for you."

I felt tears prick my eyes at his obvious concern, and I felt ashamed that my response had been apparent to him. I managed a weak smile, and a lie. "It's OK, Mr Black. Not a problem. Let's get you cleaned up."

It was baptism by fire, but I never again had a problem with dealing with any kind of bodily fluid. Snot, mucus, urine, faeces, blood, vomit, pus. Nothing, but nothing, disgusted me, and I could clean up, apply dressings, dispose of any of them.

Oddly, the only thing I had problems with was false teeth.

Moving On and Tripping Over

At home things were relatively OK, although there was no doubt that the dynamics of my relationship with Rose had changed since the events in Brighton. I felt that I could never really trust her again. I had seen a side of her that was destructive and a little mad perhaps, and I was wary of meeting this person again.

We were having more arguments, which often went on into the small hours, when I would be all too aware of having to get up next morning, and begging her to stop talking and let me go to sleep.

It was Rose's *modus operandi* to peck away, going on and on, almost with a stream of consciousness, which accused or berated me, and whatever I said in my defence was turned against me.

She would use psychobabble, or bits and pieces of this or that psychoanalytical theory, to illustrate just how sick I was, or what I needed to pay attention to in order to become a better person. I was in awe of her knowledge of these things and usually unquestioning of her 'diagnosis'.

Every row would be resolved by lovemaking, and so we would enter a peaceful, loving period when we would be affectionate, have fun, talk about both important and frivolous things.

Every day I would tell her about what had happened at work. She would prompt me to share the minute detail of every conversation, every interaction of the day, and I was having such a good time, I wanted to share the excitement of this new career.

Then I was assigned my first ward. It was to be the Gynaecological Ward. When I told Rose, her response was: "Did you ask for that ward?"

"No. We don't get a choice. They just tell us where we are going to work."

"Well, that's a bit of a coincidence, isn't it?"

"What do you mean?"

"Are you telling me that you won't enjoy looking at women's vaginas all day, every day? Because some schools of thought suggest that there is no such thing as coincidence."

"Oh, for Christ's sake. I hadn't even thought about it that way. Is that what *you'd* be doing?"

"It doesn't matter what I'd be doing, because it's not me that will be working there. Go on. Admit it. Just say it. You'll get an erotic buzz from it. You know it's true."

And on and on it went, until I lost my rag and hit her. I think this was the first time I slapped her face. I'd swung my arm back and forward again with the palm open, until it made contact with her cheek. She looked shocked, and I was also taken aback.

I hadn't planned to do it, and immediately felt ashamed that I had lost control to that extent, but… oh, my goodness, I'd enjoyed it, too. Not only did it shut her up, but it had made me feel powerful and in control for that moment.

I apologised, of course, and we fell into bed as usual, having a session of violent sex, rather than our usual gentle lovemaking. It was passionate and wild, and we were even more inventive than usual.

This may have been the first time I hit Rose, but it would prove not to be the last. And she reciprocated in kind. Our relationship had taken yet another turn into ever darker avenues.

Rose had taken an 'A' Level the previous year, and had applied to, and been accepted onto, the foundation course at St Albans College of Art. Her work started to move away from her usual abstract forms (thank goodness – I was running out of images that her inky pictures supposedly conjured up for me). She was now producing very good life drawings and paintings, including a portrait of me. She was applying to art colleges in and around London for the next step: a degree in fine art.

Rose had found yet another lover from among the foundation course tutors. This was in addition to me, John and Jackie. As usual, I kicked off about it. It just hurt so much that she would do this and it felt like a betrayal.

She must have felt restricted by my longing for a monogamous relationship because she told me that I should move out of the Lemsford Road flat, that we needed to change the basis of our relationship, although she still loved me. She suggested that I move into the nurses' home. I was so tired of all the extreme emotions, the rows and the making up, that I could only agree.

Consequently, I moved out of that beautiful house and into one of the nurses' hostels. Actually, it turned out to be a really good decision because I loved it. It felt like living in a boarding school, and I'd always had a yen to do that since reading all those books in my childhood. What were they called? Mary of Grey Gables? Something like that. Those girls really had adventures and fun, with midnight feasts and best friends. Whenever my mum threatened to send me to a boarding school, I would think, "Oh, yes, please!"

In the nurses' home we each had our own room, with a single bed, a wardrobe, a chest of drawers, a desk and a chair. Each room had a basin, and there were several bathrooms on each floor.

Downstairs was a shared kitchen with cubbyholes for keeping our respective groceries, one cooker, a sink and a large fridge. There was a shared sitting room with a television, along with a sewing room – lots of girls still made their own clothes at that time.

The warden's office was also on the ground floor, opposite a payphone. The warden, a cheerful woman called Mrs Wicks, did not live in the home, but worked a nine-to-five shift for five days of each week. I think she was meant to ensure that no boyfriends were staying over, but she turned a blind eye to the many boyfriends who did sleep there regularly.

The L-shaped building was also home for the minority of male student nurses, who fitted along one corridor on the ground floor. Apart from their bedrooms and bathrooms, we shared the other spaces with them.

I started off keeping my groceries in the shared kitchen, but soon realised that my food was being used by A.N. Other. I thought that I'd hit on the perfect solution by writing labels to put on my milk, saying 'I've spat in this' and another on my butter, 'I've licked this'. It actually seemed to work for a while, but I ended up keeping as much as possible in my room, just like all the other nurses.

Val, Julie and I discussed the problem of food going missing, agreeing that it really wasn't fair of this anonymous person to help themselves to whatever they found. We came up with a dastardly, but ingenious plan. We bought a pack of Ex-Lax, a very efficient laxative, but which looks and tastes like chocolate.

We also bought a pack of Cadbury's Bourneville Miniatures, which really is chocolate, but tiny little bars of it. After carefully unwrapping (and eating) the Bourneville, we took the covering off the Ex-Lax and re-wrapped it in the real chocolate packaging. We then left the box of 'chocolates' in the shared sitting room… and waited.

I know, I know. It was so mean and underhand, but very effective. A day later we found out that Pam, snooty Pam with the rich boyfriend, had taken two days off sick with awful diarrhoea, which had come out of the blue. She did recover, but never got to the bottom of it. As it were.

I'd become fairly friendly with one of the male nurses, Craig, who was tall, slim and very attractive in a craggy sort of way. He was about twenty, so a little older than most of the student nurses, and a bit younger than me. We would talk about the meaning of life, in that pretentious way that only the young, who have an opinion on everything, will do. I was flattered that he was interested in me, and that this did not appear to be sexual.

On a sunny spring day, we were both off duty and had the sitting room to ourselves, when he announced that he was off to see some friends in St Albans city centre.

"They've got some acid. I'm going to drop a tab with them. Have you ever tried it?"

"No. Have you? What's it like?"

"It's, like, far out. Really blows your mind, but in a good way. Do you want to come with me and try some?"

"I don't know. I've never taken drugs and you hear such scary things about LSD. What if I try to fly out of the window?"

"They live on the ground floor." Craig grinned at me. "Come on, Janet. Take a risk. You'll like it. It's a fantastic buzz and you'll see the world differently."

It felt like an ordinary social visit to a young couple. When Craig and I arrived we were offered tea and biscuits, which we accepted. I played with their black kitten as we talked of this and that.

"Listen to this. It's Deep Purple. They rock, man."

"Yeah, that's solid. Really groovy."

"I've got some Thai stick. D'ya want a blow?"

"No, thanks, man. I'll stick with the acid today. What about you, Janet. Do you want a joint?"

"Oh. Um. No, thanks. I think I'll just have the acid, too."

"OK. Craig said this is your first trip, yeah? You just put it on your tongue and let it dissolve."

I took the miniscule tablet and put it in my mouth, as did the others. Then we all sat and listened to the music. Nothing happened. I wondered if we'd been given a dummy tab. You read about suchlike in the *News of the World*.

I was still playing with the kitten, when I noticed that I could see every minute strand of fur. It made the little cat look electric, with all its hair standing on end. As I gazed at it, the same thing happened to the carpet. I could see every loop, and the blue colour was the brightest jewel ever seen. It shone and shimmered. I was fascinated by both the carpet and the kitten.

I was vaguely aware of Craig getting up and going out of the room, saying he'd see us later. It may have been ten minutes later or two hours, but when I finally looked up, I saw the young couple laughing and I immediately knew that they were laughing at me.

I didn't want to stay there and be mocked, so I left the house, although I remember the girl saying, "Don't go. I'll make more tea. Stay here." I wouldn't stay though, and wandered off to the nearby park. I sat on the grass, which I could see growing. I got frightened when a dog passed by; spittle was drooling from its mouth, and its teeth were yellow fangs.

I looked at my hands, and they were red, veins standing out, thin. They looked like the hands of an old, old crone. I knew that I had aged a hundred years and that I could die at any time.

I felt that I had to get to somewhere familiar, somewhere safe. I walked and walked until I found myself at Lemsford Road. Someone let me in and I went into Rose's room, only to find the flat empty. I wrote her a note, or tried to, but my hand wouldn't write the words properly. The pen seemed to have its own life and skittered about the piece of paper.

I left Lemsford Road and went to the nurses' home. By then it was early evening. The place seemed empty so I found some coins and rang the Samaritans from the public phone in the hallway. The volunteer who answered asked me quite soon if I'd been taking drugs. Maybe my speech was slurred.

While I was on the phone, Craig came in, but I felt so angry with him for leaving me with those strangers that I wouldn't acknowledge him, turning my back. I hung up, after assuring the Samaritan that I felt better and, in fact, I was starting to feel more normal.

I went to my room but it wasn't long before Craig came and called my name. I wouldn't let him in at first, but he persisted and I opened the door.

"Are you OK? I went to look for you, but Mo and Mike said you'd gone off on your own. Why did you do that? Were you having a bad trip?"

"You bastard. You shouldn't have left me there with those people. They were laughing at me."

"No, no. They weren't laughing at you. That's the drugs talking. Acid can make you paranoid."

"Well, why the fuck didn't you tell me that? I was really scared. It was all horrible," I said, my voice wobbling, and tears starting to fill my eyes.

"It'll be better next time. You'll know what to expect," Craig said.

"Next time? What next time? I'm never having that stuff again." Ahh. Well, we'll see.

Death, Diatribes and Debt

It was on the gynae ward that I had my first experience of working with a terminally ill patient, Mrs L.

She was an elderly woman who had cancer of the vulva. This had developed into an open, suppurating wound, which had to be cleaned and dressed daily.

The wound smelt of rotting flesh once the dirty dressing was taken off, and the patient would whimper in pain, although we nurses tried to be as gentle as we could.

Mrs L drifted in and out of consciousness. This may have been due to her illness or to the very strong cocktail of morphine-based drugs being given to her for pain relief. She had very few visitors, although a son would come in from time to time.

I was frequently part of her daily care. Mrs L was tiny, very thin and frail, with little strength. She could not get out of bed so, with another student, I would give her a blanket bath, change her sheets and her nightdress, comb her thin hair to look neat, then arrange her pillows so that she was relatively comfortable.

A more experienced student showed me how to change her daily dressings, ensuring that all instruments and lint remained sterile. I soon graduated to being allowed to complete this on my own.

I fed Mrs L liquids from a cup with a spout, and spooned liquidised mush into her mouth at meal times, learning how to pace the feeding so that she had time to swallow. She was like a baby bird, and would open her mouth once the previous spoonful had gone. As I fed her, I would talk to her.

"Here we go, then, Mrs L. You're hungry today, aren't you?

That's it – you tell me when you're ready. It's a lovely day out there. The sun is shining and the daffs are coming up. Spring is here and the trees are getting green…"

Just nonsense really, but I wanted to talk to her, to make conversation as I would with anyone else. I've no idea if this was comforting to her or whether it was bloody irritating to have some twit chuntering on when all she wanted to do was die in peace.

There came a time, though, when she could no longer be fed and was hooked up to a saline drip to keep her hydrated. Other than this, her care continued as before.

It was just a matter of days before she died. It was at 2.30pm, shortly after I'd come back from lunch and before the afternoon round of tea for the patients. A quiet time of day. I'd glanced through the window of her side room and there was something about her colour that wasn't quite right.

Going in and touching her hand, I found her to be very cold and still. It was the first time I had seen a dead body and, although shocked to find myself touching a deceased person, I was calm and sort of glad for her. She had been in pain for a long time, suffering not only from the symptoms of cancer and her awful wound, but the indignities of being dependent on others for her most basic needs, and having her body exposed to many people.

I went to the sister of the ward to say that Mrs L had died. This particular sister was one of the older members of staff, who was gentle and caring about the patients and the students. After checking for herself that Mrs L had, indeed, passed away, she closed the curtains of the side room and placed a call to the junior doctor to come and confirm the death. She told me that I should help Nurse Dunn, a third year student, to lay out Mrs L.

"Nurse Green," she said, "have you ever experienced someone dying before?"

"No, Sister. This is the first time."

"Well, my dear, it's nothing to be frightened of. Death is just the natural end to life. I don't know if you are religious at all, but I always think that the body is just a shell. Their spirit is gone, and what is left is an empty vessel. Does that make sense to you?"

It did, and I was so grateful that she had taken a few minutes to reassure me. It was to be the first of many more deaths I would witness as a nurse, but I always remembered her words and felt comfortable in dealing with the end of life.

Once the doctor had confirmed the death and completed the death certificate, I followed Nurse Dunn into the side room to start the laying out process. Nurse Dunn was coming to the end of her training. She had a calmness about her, which transmitted itself to me. I had been feeling anxious about the laying out and not sure what to expect. I couldn't remember any information being given to us in nursing school about this situation. I hadn't realised that it was part of my nursing duties.

We started by giving Mrs L a blanket bath, exactly as we would have if she had still been alive, being as gentle and discreet as when we washed a living patient.

When washing a patient's back, they would be rolled onto their side and held close by one of the nurses to ensure they did not fall out of bed. Nurse Dunn rolled Mrs L towards me and, as she did so, Mrs L sighed. I was taken aback and gave a little squeal. I thought she was dead! My more experienced colleague explained that sometimes there was a little air left in the deceased's lungs, and that this would be expelled as the lungs pushed against each other, sounding like a moan. It had given me quite a turn.

The only thing that was different from a usual bed bath was that we put swabs into all orifices. Nurse Dunn explained that this was to stop any bodily fluids from seeping out. We cleaned her mouth with cotton buds and a mild mouthwash solution, and Nurse Dunn put Mrs L's false teeth into the dead woman's mouth, telling me that this needed to be done before rigor mortis set in.

Mrs L was then dressed in a plain, white cotton shroud and I combed her hair. Lastly, we positioned her so that her arms and legs were straight, and covered her with a clean sheet. She was ready for her journey to the mortuary.

I found, to my surprise, that I rather liked the process of laying out. It felt like one last kindness, a caring act that I could provide for the patient. It was always done with another student, and I found that some nurses talked to the deceased throughout, or held their hand, or even gave them a kiss on their cold cheek at the end of the procedure.

★

I was seeing Rose at weekends, going to Lemsford Road, if I was off duty for Saturday and Sunday. Sometimes she would come and stay over with me at the nurses' home and we would squeeze into my single bed, spooning against each other.

She had sub-let the second bedroom in the flat to another student on the art foundation course. I rarely saw this innocent usurper, and life with Rose continued, albeit within a different framework.

We cooked and ate together, made love, occasionally went for a hack on the ponies at her disposal, saw her children and still had the most vicious arguments, which often descended into violence from both of us. When not having a row, we would be affectionate, passionate and laugh together, but the conflicts were now a regular aspect of our life.

Rose still saw her many lovers, as well as me, and the knowledge of this continued to tear my heart out. To her credit, she never made a secret of these liaisons. Perhaps it would have been less painful if she had. At the same time, she would continually accuse me of wanting to have sex with virtually everyone – except next door's dog, and that was only a matter of time.

She wrote to me saying that she loved and needed me, but could not allow herself the indulgence of me, because that would lead to her being consumed. It would, she said, lead to tension and agony for us both.

She could not stand, she wrote, the strain of persistent harassing from inside herself of who was I with, who was I talking to, what was I doing, what did we say? She acknowledged that it made her bitchy, anxious and fearful, and also made me unhappy. She wrote that both of us would experience mutual anger, resentment and suffocation.

She was right, of course. In the same letter she told me that she could not give up having sexual relationships with men, or with Jackie. Yet neither of us seemed to be able to back off from the monster that our love had created.

And so we continued, hurting and being hurt.

★

The process of being a student nurse dictated that we had to work our way around the hospital, experiencing all the different wards and departments for about three months on each specialism.

I was moving around the hospital now, getting experience on Men's Surgical, Orthopaedics, Geriatrics and so on. On each ward we were required to complete a period of night duty. Being more of a night owl than a morning lark, I quite enjoyed these hours, the only downside being finishing night duty and then finding oneself back on days within a twenty-four-hour period. It was hard to get my body clock into a new zone that quickly.

St Albans City Hospital was housed within Victorian buildings – dark and oppressive. The wards were long rooms, with beds placed either side, with a couple of side rooms and a day room for patients to watch television and smoke. (In those days patients were not discouraged from smoking; in fact, many of the nurses and doctors lit up at every opportunity!)

Doing night duty could be particularly eerie. There were usually two students on duty, with a matron making regular rounds during the night. We would sit at the nurses' station in the middle of the ward, which was only lit by one lamp, and whatever kind of moon it was that night.

When one student went for her break, the other would be on her own for forty-five minutes or so... in the dark, with just one light, the moonlight shining through the windows, the patients appearing as silhouettes, if they were sleeping sitting up in bed... And it was very, very quiet. As quiet as the grave...

It was during one of these solitary moments that I became aware of someone watching me. I froze, turned slowly in my chair, trying to make out if there was an intruder in the shadows of the ward. My heart bumped in my chest and my breathing became rapid.

"Who's there?" I asked.

There was no reply.

"I know someone's there. Who is it?"

The silence became ever deeper, and I felt the hairs on the back of my neck stand up.

Then I saw him. Mr M in Bed 8 was staring at me, unblinking. Well, one eye was. That was his glass eye. The other one was closed and he was snoring gently.

It was on day duty on Men's Medical that I worked with Karima, the beautiful, tiny Malaysian student nurse. She was about my height, but whereas I was curvy, she had the body of an adolescent, with breasts that seemed to be just developing and a tiny waist. For work she would arrange her long, black hair into a thick plait, which was then pinned up under her cap. She had almond-shaped eyes and a mouth that looked permanently bruised, as if she had been kissed for a very long time, just moments ago. As I said, beautiful, and so softly spoken.

After the patients had lunch, the routine was to give them some bedrest time, while we nurses quietly went from bed to bed, taking temperatures, blood pressure, pulse and asking whether they had had a bowel movement that day. I did one side of the long room while Karima looked after those on the other side.

We finished at more or less the same time, but as we went to put away the blood pressure machines, Karima exclaimed that she had forgotten to ask Mr P whether he'd had a bowel movement. Mr P's bed was right down the far end of the ward and we had been on duty since 7.30am, barely stopping work except for a coffee break, and we were due to go to lunch now.

Karima sighed and, clearly trying to save her aching feet, called out in her soft voice, along the length of the ward, "Mr P… have you had a bowel movement today?"

Mr P, being eighty years old and hard of hearing did not catch what she said, but his neighbour told him that the nurse was asking him a question.

"What did you say?" he asked.

"Have you had a bowel movement?"

"What was that, dear?"

"Have you moved your bowels today?"

"Towels? No, dear. I don't need any towels."

"Have you had a shit?" she bellowed down the room.

There was a shocked silence as all the patients fell quiet, and then the room erupted with belly laughs. I swear that this profanity, coming so unexpectedly from such a dainty girl, did them more good than twenty milligrams of Valium.

And it turned out that Mr P's bowels were in fine working order.

When we were in school, which we were every nine months or so, our hours were from nine o'clock until five o'clock, Monday to Friday. It was great in terms of being able to live an ordinary life, but my salary was affected, as extra money for working weekends and nights was not included. I only had £13 per week after tax, National Insurance and superannuation contributions. A deduction was also taken out of my salary for accommodation in the nurses' home. There wasn't much left to pay for the necessities of life or for entertainment.

I was never much good with managing a budget and when sterling decimalisation was introduced in February 1971, I completely lost the plot. It was difficult enough to keep a check on my spending without the confusion of having to convert pounds, shillings and pence into something else.

I started to get into debt, living off an unofficial overdraft. I would be in credit for about a week after pay day, then the overspend from the previous month, plus the bank charges, would mount up and I'd go overdrawn again. The debt was growing ever bigger by the month and I never seemed to catch up, no matter how much I tightened my belt. I stopped opening letters from the bank and just hoped for the best, without having any real strategy for dealing with it.

All of the student nurses were, of course, earning the same pittance, but many of the younger ones had some financial help from their families, which helped keep the wolf from the door. I never felt that I could ask my mum or siblings to help out. I'd opted to live independently from them and had to lie on the bed I'd made.

I tried, I really did, to live within my means. I ate in the nurses' canteen, which was cheap, but often consisted of heavy, stodgy dishes – although I loved the pies served with chips, followed by puddings of syrup roll and custard.

I started to put on weight. I thought that if I started smoking it might help reduce hunger pangs. We all believed that kind of thing about the special powers of tobacco. I wasn't alone. Going into the nurses' lounge at break time, one could barely see through the clouds of scented vapour emanating from all those fags.

I used to get fruit and vegetables from St Albans market. I remembered one of Mum's ploys was to go to the market just as the stallholders were packing up. They would discard any bruised and slightly damaged food, just chucking it on the road to be cleared up by street cleaners, or the local bag lady, or me. All it needed was a wash and to cut out the spoilt bits and, hey presto, free food.

I also discovered that if I went shopping in the market wearing my red and navy cloak (which was against the hospital rules), with my uniform underneath, the stall holders would often throw in a couple more tomatoes, cut a slightly larger slice of cheese, or even refuse payment saying, "No, that's alright, darlin'. You angels did a good job of looking after my old man." They were very kind, and I have to admit that I exploited that benevolence whenever I could.

I finally faced the bank manager and got an official overdraft, which most of the time I managed to live on. But sometimes I went over my limit and the bank would refuse to let me have any cash. At those times I survived on food stolen from the ward, or the spare meals sent for patients who had been discharged, stuffing my pockets with wrapped cheddar cheese portions, rolls and boiled eggs.

I tried to cook more at the nurses' home, but as ingredients frequently disappeared within hours from the shared fridge, it didn't make cooking from scratch easy. Val showed me how to cook a chicken curry – exotic fare, indeed. She also showed me how to make rice cooked in the oven with onions and turmeric. We shared meals if we were on the same shift, but it was less easy if we were working at opposite ends of the day, or on night duty.

Entertainment for all of us was largely limited to what was cheap or free. We had picnics in Verulamium Park, or parties where we drank the cheapest cider, creating hangovers that lasted all the next day. We would go on blind dates, set up by those nurses who had a boyfriend with unattached friends. The lads would usually pay for us to get into the disco and buy drinks. Or we would just get together in the lounge of the nurses' home for a night in front of the telly, watching clever sketches from *The Two Ronnies*, or the exploits of young women sharing a flat in *The Liver Birds*.

Living in the nurses' home was fun. I liked it. I enjoyed the camaraderie and the similarities with my childhood fantasy of being in a girls' boarding school.

It also gave me respite from Rose's more excessive accusations of infidelity in thought or deed. Or her constant analysis of my psychological state of mind. Or the criticisms of how I dressed to attract the nurses, doctors, patients or next door's dog. We seemed to have more violent arguments than peaceful and loving times. It was very wearing, particularly if these rows happened at night, when she seemed to be able to harangue me all night while I could barely keep my eyes open, and worried about being able to get up for work in the morning.

I have a collection of very bad poetry that I wrote around this time. My mature self can see how dreadful they were, but even more shocking is the level of sadness and depression they express.

Still we continued, neither of us able to stop the ever-escalating cycle of unhappiness.

Turn and Face the Change

In May of 1972, I went on holiday with Julie, my Australian nursing friend. We travelled overland with a group of young people and a couple of driver/guides in a minibus, camping en route. The drivers were Colin, a short guy with mousy hair, who was the quieter of the two, and Ricky, who was blonde, bronzed and confident.

Our ultimate destination was mainland Greece, where we pitched our tents in a tourist complex. Once there, various trips and excursions were arranged for the travellers. On one occasion I stayed behind. I just wanted a day of lazing on the beach. Everyone else, except Ricky, went off for the day.

Sitting and chatting to him in the beach bar, we were joined by a group of American GIs. They introduced us to a drinking game and, before too long, I was absolutely smashed, barely able to stand up. Ricky kindly offered to take me back to my tent. Oh, you're ahead of me, are you?

Yes, that's right. The next thing I remember is that we were both naked and I managed to get sober enough to say, "Have you got a rubber?"

"Nah. Never use 'em, darlin'. I don't like the way they feel. Don't worry, I'll get out in time."

As soon as he'd finished, I had a premonition, a feeling that my luck had run out. I staggered to the shower block and tried to fashion a crude douche... and crossed my fingers. What else could I do? There was no morning after pill then, even if it had been available in Greece.

Ricky studiously avoided any further communication or contact with me for the rest of the holiday. He'd linked up with the most attractive girl in the group, a tall, willowy teenager, who was beautiful and knew it.

I hadn't had sex with a man for a long time, and I wasn't expecting to have sex with anyone on holiday, so I wasn't on the pill, didn't have a Dutch cap and hadn't brought any condoms.

Two weeks after we got home, I missed a period. I knew that I was pregnant, and knew that I could not cope with having a baby at this time of my life. I was also concerned that I would be the same kind of mother as my own mum. Hadn't I already demonstrated a tendency towards violence in my relationship with Rose?

It wasn't long before she noticed that I was regularly throwing up and that my breasts had become swollen almost overnight.

"Well, I might have known that you'd find some man to fuck while you had the opportunity."

"No, honestly, it wasn't like that. I got drunk and..."

"Oh, that old chestnut. Drunk and forced to have sex? Or drunk and lost your inhibitions? Or drunk and didn't know what you were doing? Which was it?"

"Oh, God. I'm really sorry. What shall I do?" I asked, tears welling up.

"Do you want to get rid of it? You'll have to see two doctors. You'd better make an appointment for this week."

"Will you come with me, Rose? Please?"

"Look, you made your bed, now you can lie on it... on your own. No, I won't hold your hand on this one."

"What do you mean 'on this one'? When have I asked you for your support before?"

"Janet, you know that I have supported you countless times in the past. You must have wanted to get pregnant."

"No, don't be ridiculous. Of course I didn't."

"Yes. In your subconscious you wanted to get pregnant, and that's why you got drunk and had unprotected sex."

"Oh, for Christ's sake. I got drunk because I was on holiday and got carried away with the fun of a drinking game."

"Well, maybe you wanted to fuck this bloke in your subconscious, and you had to get drunk in order to allow that to happen. So was it good sex? I bet you enjoyed it, didn't you? Did you come? How many times did you fuck? Did you approach him, was it, or the other way round?"

And so started a diatribe that went on until the early hours.

It was actually all quite straightforward. I saw my GP, who referred me to a psychiatrist. They both agreed that this pregnancy should not continue as I was in no fit state, emotionally or financially, to have a child.

I had a termination at a hospital in another town at eight weeks. The foetus would have been a speck, barely developed, but I found myself imagining how it would have been to have a baby to hold, a downy head to kiss, inhaling that lovely milky smell that only small babies exude. A sense of loss hung about me for a while, but it passed eventually and I moved on, with only the occasional lapse into quiet grief, early morning tears waking me up.

The surgery completed, I took a week off work. My GP was diplomatic and just wrote the reason on my sickness certificate as 'minor surgery'. Then it was back to work, and back to the usual constant swing of pain and pleasure with Rose.

That September she started her degree in fine art, having gained a place at Kingston Polytechnic. She'd found a bedsit in Teddington, and we agreed that she would come back to the St Albans flat every other weekend, partly to spend time with me, but mostly to see her children. She would continue to sub-let the other bedroom, but would keep her room there.

She had moved away, and we were moving on. David Bowie sang of 'Changes' and the lyrics had never seemed so relevant as they did that summer of 1973.

A Variety of Bills

Out of the blue, I got a note from Bill, the industrialist husband of Jackie, Rose's bisexual lover. He invited me to meet him for dinner, giving me a phone number to contact him. He said that he had enjoyed my company and would welcome the opportunity to get to know me better.

Well, I was flattered by his interest. A free dinner, in a great restaurant, with a rich bloke! It was an offer few student nurses would be able to resist. So I didn't. Resist, that is.

I only had a vague memory of what he looked like. He was not particularly attractive, of average height and build with heavy features and a large nose, but I remembered that he had that easy charm and confidence that comes with being successful and wealthy. And that is attractive, although I wasn't anticipating any sexual involvement, so it wasn't an issue.

Getting ready to go to town, I had a long bath and shaved my legs cautiously. The last thing I wanted was to nick myself with the razor. I took special care with my make-up and hair, which was fairly long at that time. I wore it loose, caught up at the sides with tortoiseshell combs (actually plastic, but they looked alright as long as you weren't too close). My best dress was lilac, printed with tiny white flowers. It was fitted at the waist, and the skirt ended just above my knees. I wore it with wedge-heeled sandals.

Meeting with him in the early evening of the following week, he took me to his place of work. Being after six in the evening, all the staff had left for the day. It consisted of a floor of office space and a warehouse where the items he dealt in were stored. He clearly wanted to impress me with his wealth and the range of his business, so I made all the right noises and, in truth,

I did find myself interested in the details of how the business was run, how many people he employed and so on.

He then retrieved his large saloon car from a garage under the building. The seats were cream leather and the dashboard had row upon row of buttons and dials. I leant back against the cushioned interior and enjoyed the sensation of my bare legs against the soft upholstery. Blimey. This was the life!

He had booked a table at a restaurant in Soho, the Gay Hussar, which served Hungarian food. He told me that it was extremely difficult to get a table there, but he had 'contacts'. The restaurant was certainly full. Every table, covered with the whitest of cloths, seemed to be taken. The walls were lined with framed pictures, photos and cartoons of the great and the good, theatricals and politicians, artists and poets.

The buzz of conversation was just within the levels of comfort, and the waiters darted about between the tables almost, but never quite, bumping into each other. The menu was a confusing list of dishes that were quite unknown to me, some of which sounded very strange. I was in a foreign country and wanted to experience as much of it as possible that evening.

I started with a cold, cherry soup. The first mouthful exploded with a medley of flavours. Sweet, sour, salty all together. How did they do that? I wished I could lick the bowl, and had to force myself not to run my finger around the drops that were left.

Next I had veal goulash. Unaware, as I was, of the cruel farming methods used to produce veal, I just delighted in the way the meat melted in my mouth, the spicy, creamy sauce coating my tongue with tastes unknown to me.

The portions were generous and I was getting full but Bill encouraged me to have dessert, and I was too delighted and too greedy to resist. Tiny pancakes filled with sweet cream cheese were brought to the table, to be eaten a nibble at a time.

We'd shared a bottle of wine with our meal, which helped conversation to flow easily. Bill was a good listener, asking questions, drawing me out of any shyness. All the usual ones, of course, like did I have siblings, where was I brought up, what work had I done, but more interesting queries, too.

"Is nursing ever upsetting?"

"When did you discover you were a lesbian?"

"How do you get on with your family?"

He told me about himself, too. That as a young man, he had graduated but without any plans. He had fallen into manufacturing and the import/export business almost by default, due to working for a distant relative who had been based here in London.

He made it clear that he was now very wealthy and had two homes: one in Knightsbridge and another by the sea. He had met Jackie through mutual friends. They had both been unaware of her bisexuality until quite recently, and he was happy that she had found a lover in Rose, who he got on with. He was confident that Rose did not pose any threat to their marriage.

At the end of the evening he told me that he had enjoyed our time together, and asked if we could meet again. From my point of view, the evening had been a great success: interesting conversation, a wonderful meal and no expectation of sex. If that wasn't enough, he had arranged for a chauffeur-driven car to take me home to St Albans, and had given me two £10 notes, saying that I should buy myself something nice. Yes, of course, I would meet him again.

I got another message from him about a fortnight later, asking me to meet him again in London. Once more, I took a lot of trouble with my appearance, this time wearing a new dress, bought with his present to me. It was a red, silky material, fitted at the waist with a flared skirt. Actually, it was a similar shape to my nurse's uniform, which so flattered my figure.

This time he took me to the Playboy Club on Park Lane. There were a couple of burly blokes in tuxedos on the door who let us in with a nod as Bill showed his membership card.

Upstairs was a darkened bar, tables illuminated by pools of light. There seemed to be a lot of red velvet seating, some in private booths. There were waitresses dressed in the very tight costumes, which I remembered from my interview there. They sported a fluffy pom-pom on their bottoms and a headband with pink and black ears. Some were very slim, whilst others were nicely curvy. All looked confident and efficient.

I didn't know what to ask for when Bill suggested a pre-dinner drink. He asked if I liked vodka, which I did, mainly because it didn't have any taste. He ordered a Bloody Mary for me. The Bunny Girl who served us asked if I wanted "ice and spice with that?".

I had no idea what she meant, but Bill murmured that she wanted to know if I wanted Worcestershire Sauce in my drink. She delivered our drinks by bending her knees and placing paper coasters, our drinks and a bowl of nuts on the table. I remembered this posture, known as the 'Bunny Dip', from my job application.

We went to dinner in the restaurant there. This time the menu was more familiar to me, but still luxurious for a very poor nursing student. I started with prawn cocktail, the epitome of sophistication in 1973, followed by a steak with peppercorns, flavoursome and tender. It came with a bowl of thick chips, all crispy outside and floury inside. I was in heaven. I barely had room for pudding, but forced myself to have Black Forest Gâteau, another measure of elegance.

Bill told me that since Jackie had discovered her bisexuality, he found that he also wanted to experiment. He wondered what it would be like to have a homosexual experience. Like many boys, he'd had encounters with school friends as a teenager and, as an adult, found that he liked looking at men's bodies on the beach.

We talked about how he could go about meeting gay men. I suggested a pub, popular with gay men, that I knew of in the King's Road, or The Rehearsal club in Soho. Or he could advertise, perhaps, in one of the swinging magazines. I don't think I was much help, really, as the world of gay men was largely unknown to me, but he decided that he would try a few of the avenues we'd talked about.

Once again, he had arranged for a chauffeur-driven car to take me back to the nurses' home in St Albans, and once again gave me £20 to spend on myself.

I couldn't believe my luck. I'd really fallen on my feet with Bill – not only wealthy, but I also liked him. He was funny and interesting – a good dinner companion who made me feel valued. Generous, too. His presents were almost making a huge difference to my strapped finances. And he did not, apparently, expect me to have sex with him. A bonus.

When we next met at the Dorchester Hotel, he reported that he'd gone to the pub in the King's Road, and had a good evening chatting with a number of gay men. At the end of the evening, he'd gone home with one of them, but when push came to shove (as it were) he'd been unable to perform. I didn't ask for too many details and he didn't provide them. Suffice to say that Bill had decided that particular road was not for him.

However... he'd seen some transvestites at the pub and was now curious as to how it might feel to dress in women's clothes. He wanted to know how it felt to wear make-up, have long hair and what tights felt like. Was it nice to feel a skirt swishing around your legs, and were breasts heavy to carry around?

"I don't want to look like a parody of a woman," he said. "I want to look like an ordinary woman, like Jackie or you."

He asked me to buy him some clothes in a size that would fit him, and to bring some make-up for him on our next date. He also wanted a blonde, shoulder-length wig, and asked me to buy this for him, too. He gave me £100 in cash, and said that I should use that to shop for him, and to keep whatever was left over. He said that he would book a hotel room for our next date so that he could dress up.

It was quite a challenge for me; I had to estimate what size he might be, as well as speculate about what sort of clothes he wanted.

I made an educated guess that Marks and Spencer would be a good source of wardrobe for 'an ordinary woman', so bought a pretty bra (40B cup), lace-edged knickers, American tan tights (extra large), a flower-sprigged blouse and a plain black skirt in size eighteen.

I even got some falsies for him to put in the bra, although the shop assistant had looked askance when I bought them, as I clearly needed no help in that department. I decided that Bill would have to make his own arrangements for shoes (I had no idea where to buy size ten stilettos), or go barefoot. I purchased a wig from the market, in glossy honey-coloured nylon, styled into a long bob. He could use my make-up.

He'd booked a room at the Connaught Hotel in central London. We ate in their restaurant and then went to the reserved room. I had money left over from the shopping trip, which I'd offered to give him earlier, but that he had refused, saying, "No, that's alright. I appreciate you going shopping for my lovely things." I didn't argue with him.

We agreed that I would do Bill's make-up and then leave him to get dressed in the bathroom. We talked about how the rest of the evening might pan out, and the understanding was that we would act out a fantasy where we were platonic girlfriends, and where I would tell him/her how lovely s/he looked. Then we'd just sit in the hotel room and gossip... like girls did. He'd decided that he would like to be called Stella.

He had a final shave, and then I set to work with foundation, powder, blusher, eye shadow, mascara (two layers) and lipstick in Candyfloss Pink. Finally, standing back to look at my work, I had to admit to myself that I really wasn't sure about the end effect. I'd tried to keep the look fresh and underplayed, but there was something that was missing. Never mind. There was no more that I could do, so I left Bill to put on his wig and new clothes.

After what seemed an age, he called out from the bathroom that he was ready and was coming out. The door opened slowly and then, making a grand entrance, Stella emerged into the bedroom. I looked long and hard, struggled to keep a straight face, and said, "Oh, you look gorgeous!" Unfortunately, at this point my self-control shattered and I snorted with laughter, rolling on the bed, crossing my legs to stop myself weeing.

Stella was, quite simply, the ugliest-looking woman I had ever seen. She looked like a butch bull dyke, done up for a fancy dress party.

"I'm sorry," I gasped. "You do look amazing. Just not what I'd expected. Now why don't you sit down and we can talk about boys."

Stella/Bill was very upset at my reaction.

"I've taken a lot of trouble, you know. You could at least appreciate the effort I've made."

"I do, I do. I'm sorry. Please come and sit down."

"No. I'm going home."

"Not like that, I hope," I managed to say without giggling.

He stalked back into the bathroom, in a huff worthy of any drag queen, slammed the door, and did not emerge until he'd washed off every speck of make-up and was dressed again in his usual Savile Row suit.

"You might as well stay the night. I've booked the room on my account, so if you want to order room service, go ahead. I'm very disappointed in you, Janet."

"Oh dear. I am sorry, Bill, I don't know what came over me. I hope we can still be friends." And I was sorry. I knew by now that Bill was a sensitive soul and that he was genuinely hurt.

He left without making any further arrangements, but did kiss me on the cheek as usual. I got into the king size bed, turned on the TV and ordered a hot chocolate from room service. I'd never stayed overnight in a hotel before so it all felt like an adventure and very glamorous. If this was to be the last time I had the opportunity to live the dolce vita, I wanted to make the most of it, so ordered breakfast from room service for the morning.

I didn't hear from Bill for a few weeks after that. I thought that I'd burnt my bridges, and that episode of being wined and dined had come to an end. The other nurses also noticed that I wasn't getting all dolled up on a regular basis and asked if I was still going out with my boyfriend. I don't think they knew that Rose and I were lovers, only that we were friends.

When I next saw Bill he told me that for his next adventure he'd like to have a heterosexual extra-marital affair. I knew what was coming, of course.

"Will you take our friendship to the next level, Janet?" he asked. "I feel comfortable with you. And I've talked it over with Jackie. She says that, if I'm going to have an affair, then she would rather it was you, who she knows and trusts. What do you think?"

Well, it seemed rude to refuse him, and easier to go along with it. I have to say, though, that Bill was not a great lover, but I did my thing of performing to Oscar levels, and he seemed happy enough.

The first time, he used a condom, but I wasn't going to get caught again and took myself off to the Family Planning Association to be fitted with a coil. The procedure was agony. I clenched my teeth and told myself it would be worth it not to have to worry about pregnancy.

Seeing Bill became a regular, three-weekly arrangement. We'd meet at the Connaught Hotel, where he would have booked a room. We'd have dinner there, then go for the main event, which was always very straightforward and without any complications. Shortly after this, he would shower and leave me to spend the night in the hotel. Each time he gave me £40 "to buy yourself something nice".

Now, £40 was a lot of money to me. Almost three weeks' wages, and it helped me to get out of the vicious circle of being permanently overdrawn. Bill's gifts were very useful, and I did not think of what I was doing with him as prostitution. My reasoning was uncomplicated: He was rich, I was poor. He wanted to give me presents. I wanted to accept them. Job done.

And since Rose was still seeing a variety of lovers, plus adding a new one here and there, I didn't feel guilty about seeing Bill. In fact, Rose knew about our relationship and, oddly, accepted it. Perhaps she felt that it was keeping it all in the family as she still saw Jackie.

Banged Up, Babies and Butchness

Rose and I continued with our mad, bad and dangerous relationship. We argued constantly, frequently going on for hours into the night, sometimes resorting to violence, and then making up passionately… until the next time.

One weekend when she was in St Albans, we had one of those rows, one of the worst kind, which ended with her going back to her bedsit in Teddington, with much shouting, tears and slamming of doors. As she left, I told her that it was over, she'd gone too far and I hated her.

Of course the moment she'd gone, I felt bereft. I couldn't imagine life without her. Gathering up my handbag and throwing on a jacket, I tore down the road to see if her car was still in sight. It wasn't, so I caught several buses and trains to Teddington. By the time I got there, it was dark. I went to her house and rang the doorbell to the bedsit, but there was no reply. I wanted to say that I was sorry for whatever it was, that I still loved her, that I wanted us to try again to make this thing work.

The house was in a respectable residential area, without many passers-by, so I sat on a wall opposite for some time, waiting for her to get back from wherever she'd gone. Now and then I tried ringing the bell again, just in case she'd been in the bath or on the phone when I'd tried before. There was still no response.

I must have waited for about two hours, by which time it was gone eleven o'clock and I was cold and tired. I'd missed public transport back to St Albans and, looking in my purse, realised that I would not have enough money to pay for a hotel. A passing policeman stopped.

"Are you alright, Miss?" he asked.

I think that he thought I was an amateur working girl, with a very quiet pitch.

"Oh, yes, thank you," I replied. "I've come to visit my friend in that house over there, but she's out and now I've missed the last train home."

"I see. Well, you can't stay here, you know. Where will you go?"

"I'm not sure. I haven't got enough money for a hotel. Do you know of any hostels by any chance? I could go to one of those."

The policeman gave me a steady look, taking in my cheap jacket and plastic handbag. He shook his head.

"No, I can't say I do. Not around here." He paused. "Tell you what. How about you come back to the station with me and we'll put you up for the night in one of the cells? It's not luxurious, but it'll be better and warmer than spending the night on the street. Safer, too."

I was so grateful I could have hugged him.

He was right, though, it wasn't the Hilton. A small bare room, with a kind of metal shelf with a thin, plastic-covered mattress. A tiny basin and a toilet bowl in the corner, all visible from the door, which had a spy hole in it. I didn't care.

It was a safe roof over my head. The officer brought me a pillow and a rough blanket, together with a mug of hot, sweet, strong tea. The bed was hard, the cell was cold, but I slept like a log until about 6.00am when another policeman woke me up with more tea.

"You need to be on your way now," he said.

And, thanking him all the way out of the building, off I went to Rose's lodgings once more. I got there by about quarter to seven, and this time she answered the door.

"Oh, Janet," she sighed. "What are you doing here?"

I told her of events the previous evening and where I'd spent the night. I told her I was sorry, I loved her and that I was really cold and hungry.

She let me in and made me some breakfast, then we made love and we fell asleep.

I rang work to say I was sick. Teddington to St Albans was a fair old way, and I couldn't do that and a full day's graft on so little sleep.

I was actually quite sorry to miss a day because by then I was on the Obstetrics Ward to learn about midwifery. It was a happy experience, partly because Val and I were there at the same time, so we had fun together, but could also compare notes on what we were learning.

The midwives were a lovely lot. Very relaxed most of the time, friendly and welcoming. We received a very comprehensive training during the ten weeks or so that we experienced the department. As well as being on the Labour Ward, we also did a stint on the Special Care Baby Unit, Ante- and Post-Natal Clinics, and some domiciliary visits after mother and baby had gone back home.

Although we were not qualified to deliver a baby on our own, we did help with deliveries, and were allowed to be very hands-on. No matter how many babies I saw being born, it was almost always a wonderful experience – quite magical to see this small, bloody, screaming person come into the world.

I got used to seeing the mothers, mostly having been foul-mouthed banshees during labour, smile and cry as they held their babies for the first time. Some fathers were present at the births by 1974, although it was still a new idea. They would often have this glazed expression, grinning or tearful, but dazed by the whole event.

We saw natural births, induced ones and caesareans. Some women had every drug available and some had none at all. Some labours went on for hours on end, while other babies just popped out, like peas from a pod.

Of course, not every labour led to a happy event. One very young woman had been found at home by her mum, sitting on the toilet, with the baby suspended from the still attached cord, head down in the lavatory bowl. Her family had not known that she was pregnant. The cord was cut by nursing staff when she came onto the ward. The baby did not survive.

Another woman, the daughter of a consultant at St Albans, had a seemingly normal pregnancy and went into labour without any complications. However, at the moment she put her legs into the stirrups in the delivery suite, she went completely rigid, then started to shake, having a fit. The midwife called for the doctor immediately, although she had already diagnosed pre-eclampsia, due to high blood pressure.

She told me to help her get the patient's feet out of the stirrups, as she was in danger of her legs breaking due to the seizures she was experiencing. It was a frightening experience, although the patient was not aware of the ensuing drama. Her condition was stabilised and her baby was safely delivered via a caesarean.

Most women stayed in hospital for a week or so following the birth. The first-time mothers would learn how to breastfeed, if possible, or bottle feed if that was their choice.

They also learnt how to bath baby. The student nurses were given the task of demonstrating this. I had my own training of one practical demonstration by a midwife, then had to show the new mums how it was done. My heart was in my mouth the whole time as I bathed this soft, slippery mite, loaned to me by his trusting mother for the occasion. There were no mishaps on that or other occasions, but I suspect this was due to good luck.

I observed one complicated delivery, being carried out by a very posh, scary obstetrician consultant. He was in surgical scrubs, his mouth covered by a mask. The midwives were in the same garb. I was instructed by one of them to get 'uhuhuh forceps'.

I didn't actually hear the first word, but picked up on the urgency of the situation, and tore off to the instrument room. All the instruments were in white sterile packs, labelled with their name, stored on shelves. There were dozens of these packs, and I found myself wildly looking up and down the shelves trying to find the right one. There were packs labelled Haematic Forceps, Uterine Forceps, Biopsy Forceps, Peritoneal Forceps to name just a few.

"Oh blimey. Which one is it? When she said 'uhuhuh forceps', what did it sound like?" I muttered to myself.

Panic set in. I grabbed the nearest pack that had 'forceps' in the title and hoped for the best.

Back in the delivery room, the midwife took the sterile package and opened it onto the instrument trolley by the side of the consultant. My heart sank as they both looked with widened eyes at the tool that slid out.

"Nurse!" the doctor bellowed. "I cannot deliver a baby with these."

The midwife signalled for me to follow her to the instrument room, where she snorted with laughter.

"Oh dear. You gave him the forceps we use to fish toilet paper out of the bedpans."

Early in 1974, I started work on the Children's Ward – a mostly enjoyable experience, although some of the senior staff were mired in the values of the past. I remember picking up a distressed toddler to give her a cuddle, and the sister shouting at me to "Put that child down, Nurse Green." And she was one of those sisters you did not argue with.

There was one little boy of about eight years old, called Graham, who had hydrocephalous. It meant that his head was very big and out of proportion to his body. He also had problems with mobility, although he had his own little motorised wheelchair, which he used to scoot around the ward. In spite of his illness, he was bright and funny. I would hear him calling me, usually when I was right down the other end of a very long ward.

"Nurse Green, Nurse Green!" I'd hear and, knowing that he was in his bed and unable to mobilise, I'd tear down the room to get to him (not running though – that was not allowed).

"What is it, Graham?" I'd puff.

"I love you, Nurse Green."

Then there was Samantha, a five year old, with the dulcet tones of a mini Joanna Lumley. She came into the ward with a plaster cast on her leg, having been transferred from Casualty.

"Hello," I said. "What happened to you, then?"

"Well," she said. "I was in bed, fast asleep, and the next thing I knew was that I'd fallen out of bed. It really hurt, so I called for my mummy, and when she came in I said 'I think I've broken my fucking leg'."

Somehow it didn't sound so bad coming from a very well-spoken five year old. I burst out laughing, which prompted Samantha to comment, "It's not fucking funny, you know."

Some of the children were very poorly. There was one, Sharon, who had been born with severe brain damage, and was now six years old. She came in to give her family some respite from caring for her. It must have been very difficult for them as they had other children.

Sharon needed care twenty-four hours a day. She was not able to do anything for herself, not even sit up in bed. She could not speak or hear and could not communicate in any way. She needed to be bathed, fed, nappy changed. Because of her inability to move independently, she also needed to have her pressure areas tended to throughout the day.

It was very sad. Sharon had no quality of life, and I wondered if allowing her to live had been the best option for her. Thankfully it was not my decision and I cared for her as best I could, although sometimes found myself welling up with tears as I did so.

It was at times like this that I found living in the nurses' home to be such a support. Yes, we had great laughs together but we could also talk about the difficult points of the job.

I wrote a poem:

There's an advert I've seen,
Night nurse sits serenely at desk,
Lightbulb shining on her, halo-like.
Ministering angel, assisting her child patients
Calmly, kindly – cap straight, apron uncreased.
Man, she ain't got nothing on us.
We dispense sedative drugs to calm frightened kids.
'Don't pick that child up. She's only wanting her mum'

Says change-of-life unmarried SEN, and
'Why are you holding that baby?
Just change the nappy and put him down.
Let him cry – he'll soon drop off.'
Our advert nurse avidly studies child psychology
Under her lightbulb of all pervading knowledge.
Whilst I flounder – fish out of water – between
The orders of the two contestant Senior Nurses,
And I can never get it right.
'Feed the babies when they cry.'
Says change-of-life SEN.
'Feed the babies at 10 pm.'
Says pretty Staff Nurse Foo.
Compromising, I craftily jab the kids
Awake at 10.15 pm. They yell.
Feeding time is now.
'Nurse Green (lowest creature, student) –
See who is crying, vomiting, has a wet bed.
And who is that arguing, talking, singing?'
Night drags on, intermittent with supper break.
(Three quarters of an hour.)
Tea break (half an hour).
Soggy sandwiches, stale tea.
In between, illicit black coffee in ward kitchen.
Morning dawns.
Grey light on grey rooms.
Final rush –
Bottles in steriliser and put away.
Temperatures.
Orally for over five years old,
Rectally for under five years old.
So it's 'under tongue' and 'roll over', respectively.
Get them washed, teeth brushed, however perfunctorily.
A urine specimen from diabetic child to test –
'Can you do a wee-wee, dear? Quickly then.'

And don't forget to feed the babies.
Pump them full of Ostermilk and wind.
Tidy up, put away washing bowls, tooth mugs.
Make beds, sit children tidily on top.
Finished.
Done for.
Eleven and a quarter hours
The night shift is.
I bear little resemblance to advert nurse.
Cap askew, apron crumpled and soiled with vomit,
Plus God knows what else.
'Can I go off now, please?' I ask.
Not just hopefully, but despairingly.
Voice tired, legs aching, eyes bloodshot.
Change-of-life, having sat on her fat arse
Throughout the night, replies brightly
'If all the work is done, you may.'
I don't answer. It's the safest way.
Drag myself, body automatically, mind following,
Back to my sunk-in-the-middle bed.
Nurses' Home room.
Sanctuary.
I wonder what it's like to be advert nurse.
Uncrumpled, kindly, serene, responsible.
Sitting on the paper page, through the looking glass.
'People remember nurses' says the blurb
Captioned under that, or some other, enticement.
I hope to God that none of these kids
Remember me or my colleagues in later life.
It might be a traumatic experience.
The reality is that grim.

In spite of the occasional frustrations, illustrated in the above long and not very good poem, I felt that I had found my forte in nursing. I loved looking after people and enjoyed the easy companionship with other nurses. I didn't mind the unsociable hours or the night duty, and even liked the uniform.

What was less enjoyable, though, was the pettiness of some senior staff. I remember being severely reprimanded for wearing black tights when I'd run out of the regulation tan ones. Or the time I had my hair cut, quite short, but was told that it was sitting on my collar, and that I would have to have it cut again.

I ended up with a short back and sides. Looking very butch was no compensation. And it was difficult to pin my cap onto.

All Change

In May of 1974, I went on a pony trekking holiday with Debbie. It was lovely to spend some time with my sister, doing something we both enjoyed in the verdant hills of rural Wales. We had such fun, and it was a short respite from the constant arguing and making-up routine of the now limping relationship with Rose. She was still seeing John and Jackie, and I was still occasionally seeing Bill, although this was now cooling off. It was her liaison with John that I found particularly difficult because I knew that she was in love with him and always had been. If only it could have been a purely physical thing, then I might have been better at accepting it, but it was that emotional investment she made with him that hurt me so much.

In June of that year I had a phone call from my brother Ron. My mum had suffered a stroke and had been admitted to hospital in Hackney. I went to see her there and found her to be cheerful enough, apparently making a reasonable recovery, although her speech was slurred. There wasn't much else I could do, as I was still living in St Albans, but my older siblings were talking about finding her a place in the local Jewish nursing home, which was just down the road, so it all seemed to be in hand.

At work I moved onto my next ward, which was Casualty. It was fun and interesting. The doctors who worked there were less formal than some of those on the longer-term wards, and the Casualty staff had a gallows sense of humour, essential for working in that environment, so I discovered.

The pace was frequently fast and furious, although there could be lulls when nothing seemed to happen and no patients came in, apart from one or two who had "cut meself shaving, didn't I?" or "I've been awake all night with terrible wind."

Saturday nights were always mad, with attempted suicides and young men with wounds from fighting, car or motorbike crashes, or simply dead drunk.

One of these had, his friends told us, been drinking solidly for the past eight hours, and came in completely unconscious. Out cold. The assessing doctor called me over and said, "Watch this." He then gave the patient an injection of multivitamins, whereupon the bloke woke, sat up and said, "Where am I?" It was amazing, like a miracle or a hypnotist's trick.

At the other end of the scale, I saw the most dramatic incident of my nursing career when a toddler was brought in by her distraught parents. She had swallowed some sleeping tablets prescribed to her mother. It was thought that it had only just happened, so the standard practice was a stomach wash out. This involved inserting a tube, via the nose, into the stomach, then flushing it with the use of a funnel and warm saline. The child was conscious and her parents were in the waiting room while the procedure was carried out in a small treatment room.

I was assisting the senior nurse and all seemed to be going well, although the little girl was screaming as the tube was fed down her nose. She suddenly went quiet and, when I looked at her face, I saw that she was turning blue. I had never seen such a change in physical appearance, and I told the staff nurse to look at her face.

"What's happening?" I asked.

The staff nurse turned pale herself and said, "Shit. The tube must have gone into her lungs. Get the doctor now!"

As I tore through the department, the parents were saying,

"What's happening?", their concern etched on their faces and their voices shaky. I couldn't stop at that moment to keep them informed, but just said that I'd be back in a moment.

I found the doctor and followed him into the treatment room and saw that the child had stopped breathing. The doctor and senior nurses started CPR, while all I could do was watch this dreadful drama unfold. I didn't know what to do about her worried parents. What on earth could I say to them?

Fortunately, the CPR was successful and the child started breathing again. It was left to the doctor to talk to her mum and dad. She was admitted for observation and recovered fully from the trauma.

In mid-June I went onto night duty in Casualty. I didn't sleep well in the daytime, though, and resorted to taking Mogadon, my strong sleeping tablets. On top of this, I started a very heavy period, losing a lot of blood and having severe cramps.

I felt disorientated, although was still going to work and getting through the shifts, which were, thankfully, quiet. Then Rose told me she was going to see John and would be staying with him at his chalet in the naturist club.

I couldn't bear it. She was tearing me apart by her continued involvement with John. If only she would stop seeing him, I could cope with the others. If she loved me, as she said she did, she would surely stop seeing this man, stop fucking him. I was so hurt, so angry, so sad that all I could think about was going there and making them stop by the sheer force of my emotions.

Suffering cramps from my heavy period and coming off night duty after several days of not sleeping properly, in spite of taking Mogadon, I felt like my head was wrapped in cotton wool. My body was on autopilot, and my only clear thought was that I should go to John's chalet and confront them both.

Which is what I did. I got there at about eight o'clock in the morning and they were both still in bed, which just added fuel to the fire in my heart. I screamed at them. I hardly knew what I was saying, only that it involved the most awful abusive language. It was a terrible scene.

In the end, John pushed me down the path, telling me to go away. He went back into the chalet and I picked up a handy brick, which I lobbed through the window. I'd never been much good with throwing accurately, but this missile hit the spot perfectly. And hearing Rose scream was sweetly satisfying.

Then I went home and took the rest of the Mogadon.

It was Juliet who found me. I should have been up, having 'breakfast' and getting ready for my night shift, and she knocked on my door to make sure that I was stirring. When there was no reply, she came in and had trouble waking me. I was subsequently carted off to Casualty, although did not go through the staff entrance this time.

I was given a stomach washout. Choking, I pulled out the first tube they put down my throat, pleading with the staff to use a smaller one, which they did. It was horrible, humiliating and felt like a punishment. I knew then that I would never overdose again.

I was admitted onto a ward overnight and was seen the next day by a psychiatrist, who did not recommend any further treatment. Rose came to see me; she'd been informed by the hospital, as she was named as my next of kin. She was clearly impatient with me, but still told me she loved me, wanted me in her life. As for me, I could not imagine life without her.

I pondered what had happened to us. How could the intense love we'd had turn so sour? Maybe it was the very intensity of our passion that was the undoing of the relationship. Our highly charged emotions turning about face frequently. I still believed that it could work for us. If only I could accept her for the way she was. She was very sexual and needed many lovers. She said that no one person could fulfil all her needs, whether sexual or intellectual. Although I longed for a monogamous relationship, I promised her that I would try to accept this, if only she would stay with me. With a sigh, she agreed.

I was signed off sick for a couple of weeks and decided to use the time to go on a kind of retreat at a Tibetan Buddhist centre.

I had been to the Samye Ling Buddhist Centre in Scotland a few times with Rose and, although I had enjoyed the quiet serenity of the place, I associated it with her so I did not want to go there.

I knew of another place, Marpa House in Saffron Walden, so gave them a call, explaining that I was recovering from a crisis in my life and needed to get away to a peaceful place. They had a space available and said I could come straight away.

Arriving at Marpa House, the colourful prayer flags fluttering in the breeze outside, and the sweet smell of incense indoors, I was enveloped by the cool darkness of the house after the sunshine of the day. It was very quiet. I followed my nose into the kitchen where several people were preparing an evening meal. They were mostly young and wearing jeans and T-shirts; some of the girls were in loose cheesecloth skirts. There were a couple of older people, too, dressed casually, but conventionally. It was a cheerful, industrial atmosphere, and I immediately felt comfortable there.

A cup of tea was placed in front of me and a little gnome of a man popped up by my side. He was very short, with long grey hair and a matching beard. He looked like one of Santa's helpers. He told me his name was Frank and that he was studying to be a monk. He lived at the centre full time, earning his keep by acting as administrator. I liked him and found him easy to talk to.

Frank would prove to be a counsellor and mentor for me over the next ten days, and was a great source of comfort. I helped in the kitchen and garden, meditating and learning a little yoga. It was peaceful and restorative, and I went back to St Albans feeling stronger and calmer. They are good people, those Buddhists.

Checking my post back home, I found a letter from the head of the School of Nursing summoning me to a meeting with her. No hint had been given as to what it was about. In her office at the appointed time she did not beat around the bush.

"Following recent events, Nurse Green, I do not think that you are cut out for nursing. I would like you to resign from your post."

On the Ile du Lavant

The Hitchhiker, coming home from France

With Debbie, pony trekking

Early in my
relationship
with Rose

Debbie with Evelyn King MP

"What?" I was astounded. I had not been ready for this at all. "But the 'recent events' as you call them, were to do with completely personal issues. It was nothing to do with work."

"Just the same, Nurse Green, I would like you to resign. You have demonstrated an overly emotional personality, which is not compatible with being a nurse."

"Look, I've only got six months to go before my finals. For the past two and a half years I've worked hard and been a good student nurse. I might have been a bit late on duty now and then, but other than that, I doubt you've had any complaints about me."

"Nevertheless, Nurse Green, you are not the kind of person I would want working for us in the future, and I think it better that you resign now."

"And if I refuse to resign…?"

She gave me a smile. "Then you will be sacked."

"I'll think about it," I said.

And I did think about it. I could see the sense in resigning. It would look better on a future CV. And it would mean that I could take a break from nursing and then re-apply to another hospital to finish my training in, say, six months' time.

The news travelled like wildfire throughout the student nurses in the hospital, and the Union rep asked me if I would like her to take it up with the Union, but I was feeling tired and worn down by then (and also did not realise that I would have a good case), so said that I did not want to go down that route.

Leaving nursing also meant that I would have to leave the nurses' home and find somewhere else to live. Rose had rented out 'my' room at Lemsford Road to a student at the local art college, so that was not an option.

Louise told me that she was living in a bedsit about halfway between the hospital and Lemsford Road, and she thought that there would be an empty room in the same house soon, as she knew of another tenant who was moving out.

I left the hospital without any fanfares, very quietly. There was no cake, no card and no party. I just wasn't in the mood.

I met the landlord of the bedsit and moved my meagre belongings into a room, which was tiny, but that had its own Baby Belling cooker and a sink, together with a single bed, a small table and a kitchen chair. A wardrobe and a small chest of drawers were also squeezed into the bedsit. There were some points in the room where I had to turn sideways to get from A to B. A shower and toilet on the landing were shared with several other tenants.

Still, it was a roof over my head, it was warm and clean – and I had a friend there, as Louise was shacked up in one of the bedsits with her boyfriend. This happened to be Craig, the guy who'd taken me to drop acid. He'd left nursing a few months previously and was now doing this and that. I think that Louise probably supported him financially.

I set about finding a job, thinking that I could always get secretarial work as a stop gap. I went into one of the local agencies, Blue Arrow, to register as a temp. However, before I left the girl who was interviewing me asked if I would be interested in working for them as an interviewer. As luck would have it, I'd done a stint of this type of thing years before, so understood how it worked and had been trained.

I was delighted. It was so much more interesting than being a secretary, the money was better and, best of all, it meant they liked me. I so needed that confidence booster that I could have thrown my arms around her and given her a big wet kiss. Maybe not, though.

Anyway, it made me happier and gave me a renewed energy, probably making me more fun to be with. Perhaps it was this that prompted Rose, a couple of months later, to ask me if I would like to move back into Lemsford Road. She had been there over the summer holidays but would be going back to art college in September. She had a new foundation course student coming to rent her room so needed someone to pay rent for the rest of the flat.

It was lovely to move back into Lemsford Road. Its Victorian gothic splendour, although a little tatty here and there, was beautiful, especially after my short sojourn in the bedsit. The rooms were big, airy and spacious with large windows all around. So what if the heater in the shared bathroom was a little erratic? The bath was enormous and one could fully lie down, completely covered with hot water.

I had my own room and I shared the kitchen with the other tenant in the flat. This turned out to be a delightful girl called Lucy, who was friendly and bubbly. She was neat, took her turn at cleaning and never left dirty pans in the sink.

Mick, the art therapist and all-round nice guy, still lived upstairs in his bedsit. Julie, the archetypical spinster, was still in her flat on the top floor. The big downstairs flat, which had two bedrooms, a huge sitting room, a kitchen with an Aga, a scullery and a shower unit, was now occupied by Dany and Phil and their three small children.

Rose and I settled into a new routine. She came back to St Albans every other weekend, spending time with her children and me. Then, on the alternate weekends she would stay in Kingston, where I would sometimes visit her. I tried not to ask too many questions about who she was seeing or what she did with them, but it was difficult. We still seemed to find things to argue about: her friends, who I saw as intellectual snobs, or my friends, who she saw as potential rivals. Or whatever.

Just as that eventful 1974 was drawing to a close, in November I had another call from my brother in Tottenham. Mum had had another stroke. The following day, he got in touch to say she had died and that she was to be buried the next day, in keeping with Jewish tradition in which the funeral is as soon as possible after the death.

She was buried next to my dad in Rainham Jewish Cemetery, a godforsaken place where it's always cold and windy, with row after row of grey or black tombstones. Jewish people do not leave flowers on graves; instead they place a pebble or stone on top of the grave. This lack of colour only serves to add to the depressing and sombre feel of the place. Visiting a grave there does not allow for happy memories, even if I had any of my mother.

I never cried one tear for this angry woman who had so rarely shown me any affection. I wasn't glad that she had died, but I wasn't sad about it either. I wished that she had been a better parent, that she had cuddled me more, that she had shouted and hit me less, and that she hadn't tried to get through that toilet door with an axe.

4

Getting On With the Neighbours

I settled back into living at Lemsford Road. Coming in from work one night with a big bag of shopping weighing me down, I sat on the lowest stair for a moment to catch my breath and summon up the energy to climb the stairs. Dany came out of her sitting room into the communal hallway.

I'd met her before and we had nodded and smiled at each other, mentioning the weather or whatever, before going about our respective business. She always seemed to have full eye make-up on: heavy mascara, eye shadow and liner. She usually wore tight jeans and a T-shirt, but I'd also seen her in some sort of silky, flowing robe. Her body still carried some post-baby weight, making her curvy and soft.

Her hair was remarkable. Long and straight as a waterfall, the colour of autumn leaves. It was constantly tumbling into her eyes, and she would brush it back with her hand in a gesture that I would come to know as her *leitmotiv*.

"Are you OK?" she asked me now as I started to get up.

"Yeah. Fine. Just knackered from living. You know how it is."

She groaned. "Do I ever! Did you carry that lot home from town? That's a long walk."

"Mmm. I just try to think of the fares I'm saving and that the exercise is good for me."

At that point, her little girl toddled into the hallway. This was Lisa, two years old and wearing a bright yellow knitted coat.

"Hello," I said to her. "What a lovely jacket you're wearing. Did your mummy make that?"

She gazed at me, as Dany laughed and said, "You must be joking. My nan made it. Cute isn't it?"

I agreed that it was cute, but that Lisa was cuter. I asked Lisa if she would give me a hug and she obliged instantly. She was lovely. All cuddly and woolly.

"I'd better get on," I said, reluctantly letting go of the small, yellow-jacketed one.

"You should come down for a coffee one night with me and Phil," Dany said.

I thought that she was just being polite in that way that people casually issue invitations but never intend that they should be taken up. I agreed in that way that convention demands.

"Mmm. Thanks. Yes. That would be nice."

And off I went to my solitary evening of TV and a lamb chop.

It was only two days later, on a Saturday evening, that there was a knock at my door. I opened it to find Dany in her silky, flowing robe thingy.

"You coming down, then?" she asked. "I'm making some real coffee and we've got a cake."

I was taken aback. I never really expected her invitation earlier in the week to come to anything. I was a bit anxious about it, too. What would I talk about? They always seemed so cool and laid back. But there was no way out of it, really. She was standing there, looking all expectant. I could only follow her downstairs and into their living room.

Phil sat in a red leather oversized armchair, which matched their sofa. This guy was seriously good looking, with cheekbones you could cut cheese on and very blue eyes. He was broad-shouldered and narrow-hipped. I later found out that he was the laziest man on this earth, so I don't know how he maintained that physique. He was friendly and seemed pleased to see me.

All along one side of the room was a stereo with huge speakers in each corner of the room. Phil told me this was called quadraphonic sound, immediately demonstrating its appeal by putting on Mike Oldfield's *Tubular Bells* album. I have to say that the effect was astonishing. One moment it was an ensemble piece, and the next moment the various instruments seemed to emanate from different parts of the room.

Two of their three children, Carl and Dain, were lying on the floor playing some sort of game, while Lisa was snuggled up on her dad's lap. After a while, Dany clapped her hands and told them it was time for bed.

"Say goodnight to Janet," she told them, which they all did with a peck on my cheek. They were very sweet and well behaved. Carl was five years old, Dain was three and Lisa, at two years old, was the baby.

When she came back from tucking them in, I said, "What good kids. They're all so sweet."

Phil grunted and said, "Hmm. Well, we're not having any more. I've had the snip. You know, a vasectomy."

I was a bit surprised to be given such an intimate piece of information when I hardly knew him, but made some appropriate comment. At this point, Phil got out some cigarette papers. Well, he might have been rolling a fag, but I'd seen the packets of Silk Cut around, so guessed that a joint was being rolled.

"Do you smoke dope?" Dany asked.

Oh dear. Should I pretend to be well acquainted with the drug, or just own up to being almost a marijuana virgin?

"Umm. Well. I have had it before. Just once. It didn't do much for me."

"Oh. OK. Do you want to try it again?"

Well, why not? When the long cigarette was passed to me, I took a puff and passed it back to Dany.

"People usually take three puffs and then pass it on to the next person, rather than giving it back. Have another puff."

I took another toke and went to pass it to Phil this time. I wasn't getting much from it and didn't know what I was meant to be feeling. I saw Phil and Dany exchange a smile. Phil waved it away saying, "You need to really suck hard on the joint and then keep the smoke down for as long as you can. Try it again."

Blimey. What a palaver. Here we go. I took a big inhale, held my breath, and then choked. I coughed so hard that my eyes were watering, but at the same time was aware of my head going off someplace on its own.

"Oh, wow!" was all I could manage to say at that moment.

Dany and Phil were laughing and, as soon as I stopped coughing, I was laughing too. It was like a whole new world opening up. I felt like Alice going down the rabbit hole to discover a completely different way of looking at everything around me.

My vision was sharper, the colours brighter. The music was clearer, every note was pure and every lyric was meaningful. And the conversations! They were often just very, very funny, but were sometimes deep and esoteric.

The joints seemed to be continuous. As we finished one, Phil would roll another.

A while later (one hour? four hours?) I felt very hungry. I didn't want to be rude but remembered that Dany had mentioned cake earlier. I left it for fifteen minutes (or was it forty-five minutes?) before casually mentioning, "Um, did you say you had some cake? I'm feeling a bit peckish."

Once again, there was that knowing smile between Dany and Phil.

"You've got the munchies," Phil said. "It's a kind of side-effect of the dope."

It was a chocolate sponge cake and the first mouthful tasted like manna from heaven. My taste buds had never been so alive, not only aware of the sweetness, but also of the texture of the springy sponge, the melting chocolate coating my tongue, the combination of the two. The whole experience elicited another "Oh, wow" from me. Not very articulate, but totally heartfelt.

Over the next couple of weeks, I spent a lot of time with

them, but mostly with Dany. We became best friends almost overnight, discovering a similar sense of humour and a directness of manner. We talked so easily, our histories and backgrounds tumbling out as we discovered each other.

Her real name was Sheila but she changed it when she left home at seventeen. Quite right, too. She was meant to be a 'Danielle', although most people called her Dany.

When she laughed, which she did often, her laugh was loud and seemed to inhabit her whole body, as she bent forwards and then back, then forwards again. She stood very straight, entering a room with a dancer's bearing. Dany was a yummy mummy before they had been invented.

She was bright, curious and questioning, although she seemed to accept what life threw at her as karma, kismet, fate. Call it what you will – she was content with her lot. She adored her children and, although she complained bitterly about Phil (who sometimes made her cry), she adored him, too. She had a sunny aspect about her, which was only occasionally dimmed by troubles. Dany exuded warmth, which drew others to her, wanting to be bathed in that comforting, encompassing aura.

She had met Phil when she was sixteen years old and he was twenty. She became pregnant almost immediately. Her father, a ridiculous, bossy little man, cut off all contact with her for many years, although she and her mum communicated in secret.

Phil was her first and only lover. She became mother to his children, but also became his possession. He was muscular, attractive and had an air of danger about him. He wanted to control almost every aspect of her life and Dany seemed unable to challenge or defy him.

Phil certainly had an air of the gangster about him, with his good-looking charisma and stories of derring-do. A swashbuckler who had been around and lived on the wild side. I was never sure how much to believe these tales of his. It also emerged that he had been to one of the lesser public schools and he was certainly well spoken. On the plus side, he could be very funny and generous, and clearly enjoyed his children in a kind of macho, blokey way. I liked him.

During our talk-fest, Dany told me that it was Phil who introduced her to using drugs. There was the dope, of course, but he gave her speed and acid as well. She always said that her children's personalities were reflected in the drugs she was using at the time she was pregnant with them: amphetamines for speedy Carl; marijuana for laid back Dain and nothing at all with balanced, calm Lisa.

I think that I fell in love a little with Dany. She gave my life a brightness that had been missing for such a long time. I found my playfulness again. I wanted to spend as much time as I could with her and, while I did not desire her sexually, I loved those moments when she would give me a hug. I'm not sure why I didn't want to go to bed with her, because she was attractive. Perhaps I didn't want to intrude on our developing closeness – and sex always makes a difference to friendship.

She'd guessed that Rose and I had a lesbian relationship but seemed unfazed by this. It was never an issue or a barrier when we talked about every aspect of our respective relationships. I could be more honest and open with her than I had been with any of the psychotherapists I'd seen early in my attachment with Rose.

Many years later, Dany wrote about her take on our friendship.

I can't recall if Jan introduced herself, or we met in passing in the huge entrance hall.

She was a great source of strength to me, great support and more than anything, on my side, even if I was wrong sometimes!

To my mind, you can always tell a best friend by the way you can insult each other, argue and make up without saying sorry. Jan and I would just get on with it, and laugh. Oh, how we laughed. I don't think Phil approved of our relationship, because up to now I'd only had him to bounce my ideas and thoughts and feelings off. Now, slowly, a bond elsewhere was building.

We not only lived at the same address, we shared lives. As the first place you would walk into was our hallway, we could hear who was coming or going. Jan lived one floor above us; I could hear her footsteps. If I had had a bad day or I needed to get something off my chest, Jan's door would be the one I would knock on.

Sometimes she would have had a bad day and the last thing she would want to hear about was my problems! She knew how to tell me if she didn't want to know, she would just say, "I'll come and see you later, I've got this or that to do." OK, Jan, see you later!

We had so many good happy times there. Jan and I seemed to laugh our way through the days, and nights.

I found out, soon after meeting her, that Dany had epilepsy, which had emerged when she was in her teens. It was largely controlled by medication but occasionally she would have a day when she was feeling 'spaced out' and would recognise that this meant she would probably have a fit at some point.

The first time I became aware of how her diagnosis affected her was on a Sunday, as she had invited me to join the family for a roast dinner. When I arrived downstairs, she told me that she was feeling 'fitty', so I suggested that I take over the cooking and so on, but she wasn't having any of it and insisted on completing the dinner.

We'd not long sat down to eat, with Dany and Phil at either end of the table, me sitting between Dain and Lisa, when I saw Dany pointing up at the ceiling but not saying anything.

"What?" I asked, also looking up.

There was a crash and when I looked down, I saw Dany had fallen onto the floor and was twitching uncontrollably.

I knew from my nursing training that putting something into the mouth was outmoded. Current advice was to stop the person from banging their head on the floor or furniture, so I tried to move her chair out of the way and to hold her head still. Phil and the children seemed unperturbed. I guess they'd seen it all before. Phil came over to the still-twitching Dany, waiting until she stopped. Then he picked her up in his arms and carried her into their bedroom, where he put her into the recovery position.

"She'll be OK. Let's go and finish our dinner," he said.

Well, I was a bit concerned but he seemed to know what to do. We left her on the bed and went back to the dining table to find that one of the kids had managed to spill the gravy boat over their dinner so that their plate now resembled a brown puddle with an island of roast potato.

By the time we'd cleared up the mess, finished our dinner and put an apple pie and custard on the table, Dany emerged from the bedroom, looking vague and saying "Did I have a fit?" She sat down and polished off the pudding. It was only after this that she was persuaded to go back to bed while Phil and I cleared up.

Neither Phil nor Dany had jobs, although Dany told me that she had done some waitressing in the past. But what with the children, her epilepsy and Phil's demands on her time (for housework, meals, snacks, coffee, tea, company and sex), it was difficult to find a job with suitable hours. She had her Child Benefit, of course, but did not have any other income.

Phil refused to sign on, but also refused to find a job. He occasionally did a bit of car spraying in the garage at the end of the garden, but this was not an everyday kind of thing.

He often only got out of bed during the day if he needed to go to the toilet; otherwise he was supine with a little television and regular refreshment or sex from Dany. He had a little bell by the bed, which he would ring when he wanted her attention. Dany and I used to laugh about it but she always responded to that wretched tinkle.

I don't know what they lived on, although I know that his mother used to give them money fairly regularly. They always had food on the table, cigarettes at the ready and dope in the drawer.

Sometimes Dany did get short of money and would ask me if she could borrow some tea bags or a fiver until Monday. She always paid me back when she said she would and, on occasion, would do the same for me if I was broke. I suspect that Phil did a bit of drug dealing to get them by. When I asked Dany whether this was the case, she told me that she didn't want to know what he got up to, and I believed her.

I must say that I was envious of their lifestyle. I was never good in the mornings, but after an evening of smoking dope until the early hours, was finding it harder to get up when the alarm rang at 7.30am. My accounts from that time show that I was earning £26 per week. After paying for my rent, putting aside cash for the electric and gas meters, the week's groceries, cigarettes and fares, I had the grand total of £10 left over, at least in principle. In practice, there was often nothing and I would go into overdraft yet again.

Why was I working? Was it worth it? I wanted to be a hippie too. I wanted to chill out, turn on and get wasted. So in February 1975 I gave up work and went and signed on. The interviewing officer at Social Security looked at my details and said that they might be able to offer me a job. My heart sank. What could I say, except "Oh, yes. That would be great!"

Having given me their application form to complete, I saw that the questions were very personal, down to asking where my parents had been born. I might not have been completely honest elsewhere on the form, but I was scrupulous for that part, as I wrote that my mother had been born in Russia. Then kept my fingers crossed.

Sure enough, I was asked to return a week or so later, when the interviewing officer regretfully informed me that as my mum had come from Russia, and the Cold War was still a major political concern, they would not be able to offer me employment.

Oh dear. What a shame. It was all I could do not to dance

down the steps of the dole office. So it came to pass that I was able to drop out, as long as I appeared at the Social once a fortnight to sign on.

Drop Out and Turn On

By early 1975 I was still seeing Bill now and then, although he'd run out of 'wild' things to do and we no longer had a sexual relationship. We'd formed a friendship of sorts, although he still gave me £20 or so each time I saw him. It helped keep me financially afloat, but I otherwise relied on benefits. I had no complaints; this was my choice, but I did have to tighten my belt a little more. I was quite good at making food last.

For instance, if I had a whole chicken, I would first eat it as a roast, but saving all the bones, even those I'd chewed on. The next day I would eat it cold with a salad. On the third day I would completely strip whatever meat I could find on the carcass and make a risotto with an onion, rice and maybe some mushrooms. On the fourth day, all the remaining carcass and the chewed bones would be cooked up with carrots, onions and a stock cube to make a hearty chicken soup, supplemented with boiled rice. On the fifth day… no, not really. Although I did have the *schmaltz* (that's chicken dripping) on bread for lunch.

So times were hard, apart from the occasional night out on the town with Bill, but I could sleep for as long as I wanted, and I could sit in Dany's cosy kitchen for hours talking and laughing, drinking cup after cup of tea. I could stay up half the night smoking dope and getting stoned. Actually, quite a lot of dope got smoked in the daytime, too.

Just before Easter it emerged that Rose had yet another new lover, a man. I managed not to get into a state about it. I was learning. In one of our many conversations about our respective relationships, Dany had told me that Phil was always unfaithful, always on the lookout for a new fuck. When I asked her if she didn't mind that, she had said, "Well, it's always me he comes home to, so I turn a blind eye." It was so similar to the situation I had with Rose, it made me think that I could take a leaf out of Dany's book.

In April Rose went to France for the academic year as part of an exchange arrangement set up by her art diploma course. She would be gone for several months, and we talked about how I might come and visit her for the odd long weekend while she was away. She would be staying in a town called Angers, which gave rise to a lot of self-analysis for her on how she would be working through her own anger (or something like that).

With my friendship blossoming with Dany and my new lifestyle taking off, I was quite laid back about her going away. I hadn't talked to Rose much about the changes in my life. I guessed that if she knew of how close I'd become to Dany, that would have sparked a third degree with her wanting to know what we talked about, had we had sex, did I fancy her, did I fancy Phil, had I had sex with him? What about their goldfish?

Meanwhile, Phil had a brilliant idea for bringing money into their household. Dany could be a stripper. Yes! It was ideal. The gigs would be in the evening and he could drive her there, so fitting in with his waking hours, and I could be asked to babysit while they were out. It was perfect. Dany was up for it. And I would do anything for Dany.

They had a wide variety of friends who often turned up for a coffee and a smoke, including Roger and Judy. Judy had been a stripper, although now she and Roger worked in an Amsterdam sex club where they performed a live sex act several times a day. Judy was tiny, very slim, but with a generous bust, while I understood that Roger (an unfortunate name given his occupation) was blessed with huge equipment.

Phil and Dany talked at length to Judy to see how to get started. They found out that she needed a set of publicity photos, preferably wearing the costumes she would be using in her act, as well as some nude or semi-nude pictures.

The act itself should have a gimmick (just as Gypsy Rose Lee was advised, 'You Gotta Get a Gimmick', in the film *Gypsy*), as there was a lot of competition out there. Dany would need to get several agents to ensure a steady flow of work. She would need tapes of suitable music for at least two acts, each of which would last about nine minutes.

The gigs themselves would be all over the country, on a circuit of working men's clubs, private parties, pubs and so on. The uninitiated always think that strippers only work in Soho clubs, but that is not the case. The other myth that surrounds the work of strippers is that they are also available for sex, but Judy assured them this was not true. It's true that there are some girls who will push the boundaries but most strippers are there to be looked at, never touched.

So we all set to work thinking about what Dany could do in her act as a gimmick. The more stoned we became, the wilder the ideas.

"I know," I said, "you come on wearing a floor-length dress but under it you're riding a unicycle! You could sort of glide on and around the floor."

"Ooh, yes. That's a good one. D'you think I could juggle at the same time?"

"Hang on. How about this… you come on wearing a white nightie and angel wings…"

"With a halo? Like at the kids' nativity play?"

"If you like… and then underneath, you're wearing a devil's costume!"

"Ooh, yes, but before I get to the devil, I could have a sheep's costume, like the one Dain wore at school."

And so it went on, each suggestion sillier than the one before.

Finally, she decided on a gypsy costume with a shawl, an off-the-shoulder blouse and a full skirt, with her hair tied back with a scarf. Her underwear would be black, sewn with sequins, such as gypsies wear (which is a well-known fact). Her music would be made up of appropriate wild, foot-stomping Spanish songs.

Her second act was the *pièce de résistance*. She put together an American Air Force outfit. It had a tight pencil skirt in a buff colour, which she wore with a fitted shirt in the same hue. She'd sewn onto this a number of vaguely military badges. The shirt was finished off with a slightly darker tie. Her hair was twisted into an up-do, which went under a little hat. When she took the hat off, her marvellous hair would fall down, like a naughty surprise. Under the uniform, she wore a white basque with suspenders and stockings. She looked fabulous. Then there was the music… wait for it… Glenn Miller. Perfect.

We had several dress rehearsals in their sitting room after the children were tucked up in bed.

She started with 'Boogie Woogie Bugle Boy', dancing fast to this tune, then slower to the next track 'Pennsylvania 6–5000' and ending up, even slower, with 'In the Mood'. As she danced, she gradually removed her clothes.

She ended up naked for a couple of seconds at her finale. Dany was attractive and sexy, but there was a sweet innocence and good humour to her that tempered any hint of vulgarity. Damn, she was good.

Phil and Dany found out from Judy which agents would be good to contact, and within a matter of weeks the work started to come in. She quickly became a bit of a star on the circuit and was in demand. Occasionally, I would go with them to a gig, startling the organiser who thought he was getting a second act that he had not asked for.

"Relax. I'm the groupie," I'd tell them.

Hippies and the Long Way Home

I continued to spend a great deal of time with both Dany and Phil, becoming an integral part of their social circle. There were always a great number of people visiting them in the daytime and evening. These were mostly from the local dope-smoking community, but there were others, too – Phil's nephews or Dany's brothers, for instance.

It emerged that they knew Craig (of the acid-dropping incident), who turned up at the house with Louise. There was Black Bob, who was actually from Afghanistan, and his girlfriend – a sweetheart who was quiet and looked very straight. She worked in the British Rail offices – but kept up with the dope smoking with the rest of us. Bob was the locality's main dealer.

Who else? Stan and his grown-up daughter, who we thought were having a consensual sexual relationship since his wife had left. Another visitor was Damean. It turned out that this was not his name, but a nickname given, as every sentence he uttered contained at least one 'D'mean?' I never did find out his real name. And Peter, a northern lad who worked at a factory, drank like a fish and smoked dope like it was going out of fashion. I don't know how he managed to hold down a job.

Simon was an old friend of Dany and Phil's. He was Jewish, with a German girlfriend. I wondered if he had chosen a German partner to upset his parents. He was that kind of guy.

His father owned a factory that made boxer shorts. Simon would sometimes arrive with end bales of material, yards and yards of it. Dany and I, being resourceful kinds of gal, would turn this material into curtains, tablecloths, sheets and kaftans for everyone. I remember one Christmas when me, Dany, Phil and all three kids were wearing kaftans made from boxer shorts material. What's more, we all matched the curtains.

Mick from upstairs was a regular visitor, too. He was a nice man. A long-haired, bushy-moustached hippie who worked as an art therapist. Mick was gentle and quietly spoken, with a gullible nature. He was teased good naturedly by Phil and always took it well, although there must have been times when he was pissed off. Phil never knew when to stop.

Dany had met Sandra at the school gates. She was a very pretty girl – slim with bleached blonde hair. Sandra was married to Patrick, who worked in the newly developing arena of computers. They had two children of similar ages to Dany and Phil's.

Unfortunately, Phil set his sights on Sandra and would charm her into having sex with him whenever possible. Dany knew about this and would get upset about it ("That Sandra's been here again. I can smell her fucking Charley perfume!"), but would still maintain a friendship with her. We both liked Sandra and Patrick. They were a nice couple who had married young and who seemed innocent and unworldly compared to some of the Lemsford Road visitors.

Tom was a regular visitor, too. Sometimes his girlfriend, Mel, would come with him, as would his brother, Mark, who had been, until recently, incarcerated in the local mental hospital. Tom was so laid back as to be practically horizontal. A hippie who usually wore jeans and T-shirt, he also had kaftans made out of boxer shorts material. His brother was very attractive and, when he hit on me, one stoned evening, I took him to bed for unsatisfactory sex. We only did it the once, but Mel told me that it was a long time since he'd had a girl and he would now be my friend for life.

It probably wasn't his fault that I didn't enjoy having sex with him. It wasn't a man that I really wanted. With hindsight, I'm not sure why I went on having these occasional forays into heterosexuality. I suppose it felt familiar. I knew what to do and it reminded me that someone was finding me desirable, even if it wasn't the girl of my dreams.

Well, I didn't really want him as a lifelong pal, but when he and Tom turned up a week or so later, I felt easy with him. Free love was still alive and well in 1975. They were going to the Knebworth Festival. Pink Floyd, a favourite of the dope smokers, were top of the bill. Being skint, as usual, they were planning to bunk in over the fence without paying for a ticket.

It sounded like an adventure, and I'd never been to a music festival, so when they asked if I wanted to go with them, I grabbed my bag and a sweater without a moment's thought. They had the dope but suggested I carry it for them, as I looked such an innocent. I tucked it down my bra, safe and sound, and we set off.

We went in Tom's beat-up car, arriving at Knebworth in the early afternoon. The programme was well under way. There were still hundreds of people arriving in cars, on motorbikes and on foot.

Large men in plastic orange vests were clearly security, and were keeping an eye on anyone who tried to slip in without paying. We skirted the high fence for about a mile before we came to a bit that had partly fallen but was still six foot high. The boys lobbed me over the fence, where I fell on the other side, only bruising my hip. They yelled for me to go on and they'd find me later.

I tore off, not really knowing where I was going. I found myself in the thick of the crowd, who were sitting and lying on the grass listening to the bands. It was all very confusing and I wasn't sure what I should do.

I decided to sit on the edge of the grassy area and hope that Tom and Mark would find me. I still had the dope down my bra, but couldn't roll a joint without papers and, anyway, still hadn't mastered this particular art. A group sitting next to me was puffing away so I asked if I could have a toke of their joint.

Every now and then I'd wander off to another part of the field, still hoping to meet up with the boys. Each time I settled, I asked someone nearby if I could share whatever spliff was being passed around. Everyone was very generous.

I never did meet up with Tom and Mark, but ended up feeling very stoned. By the time Pink Floyd came on, late in the evening, I was well out of it and, although I appreciated the special effects of their set, didn't really hear the music. It had been a great day of peace, love and drugs, among gentle hippies.

I was not sure how I would get home. I didn't know the area, although it wasn't that far from St Albans – about fourteen miles. At the end of the festival, getting out onto the main road was a long, slow walk. The traffic, both motorised and on foot, was very heavy and people were milling about. I saw some hitching lifts, so I also stuck out my thumb and waited. A car soon stopped.

"Where you going, darlin'?" the driver asked through his open window.

"St Albans, but anywhere on the way will do," I said.

"Get in," he said. "I'll take you all the way home."

"Really? That's fantastic. Thanks so much."

As I got in I saw another man in the back seat. He introduced himself as 'Bob'.

"You been to the festival, then?" Bob asked.

"Yes. It's been a great day. Really good. What about you?"

The driver answered, "Yeah. We were there. Fucking great."

As we chatted, he was driving along roads that were unfamiliar to me. I wasn't concerned, as I did not know the route to St Albans. It was only when he drove down a track, which obviously went nowhere, that I realised I was in trouble.

First, I was dragged out of the front seat and pushed into the back. Then they both took turns in raping me, one sitting in the front while the other pushed me onto the seat and held me down. It wasn't difficult for them. I was a little woman and they were great hulking men. They only tore my jeans and pants off, without bothering with any other clothing.

When they had both finished, they left me sobbing in the back seat, scrabbling around to get my pants and jeans on again. They drove to a more populated area. It was only when they told me to get out that I realised they had driven me back to Knebworth. Although there were police officers around, I had the dope down my bra and was still very stoned. I was too frightened of being found out to report the rape.

There was nothing else I could do except try to get home by hitching again. Once more a car stopped fairly soon. This time I could see that there were two guys in the car. This time I knew that there would be a fare to pay. I got in the car anyway. Thankfully, it was only one of them this time who wanted sex with me. I was wordless, just waiting for it to be over.

I couldn't believe this was happening to me again. Was there something about me that shouted 'available to anyone'? Remembering the abuse in my teenage years, I felt that I was a target for marauding men who just saw me as a vagina on legs. Not a person, at all. Not someone who felt pain, humiliation and shame. Not someone real, like their sisters, mothers, daughters, wives.

It wasn't that I hadn't said 'No', but perhaps I was saying it in the wrong language. Instead of saying "No, please stop", perhaps I should have been saying "STOP RIGHT NOW, YOU FUCKING BASTARD SHIT!"

These men did drive me to St Albans, where they dropped me off in the centre of town. By the time I got home, dirty, bruised and sore, it was about three o'clock in the morning. Dany and Phil had only just gone to bed but heard me come in. Dany took one look at me and said, "You need a cup of tea." She drew me into their bedroom, sitting me on an easy chair, and threw a blanket over me while I shivered with shock and relief.

I told them what had happened, and they were both immensely kind and nurturing. There was no question of going to the police. We were all much too suspicious of the Old Bill.

In the days that followed, I found that I was bruised black and blue all over my body.

My spirit, too, was battered. I just wanted to retreat into my home, surround myself with familiar things and people. I was frightened to go out alone at night for a long time. I would take the long route walking home and avoid all those handy, but lonely, shortcuts.

All the terror of being raped when I was fourteen came back to me. Once again, I told no one, apart from Dany, how much this experience had horrified me, or how defiled and soiled I felt. I put on a brave face and, when Louise asked me about it, I told her, "It was just a fuck I didn't want." But in private I cried a lot.

Life went on and the summer of 1975 progressed. A referendum had the UK voting to stay in the Common Market,

Lord Lucan was named as the murderer of his children's nanny, and Margaret Thatcher was chosen as the Conservatives' new leader.

Just another year, and my life returned to some sort of normality.

Looking for Answers

By now I had developed an interest in self-development. This was certainly spurred on by Rose and her insistence that I should become more aware by exploring my psyche.

I really did not want to mirror her experience of going for psychotherapy. I wanted to do my own thing to find out more about myself: what made me tick, what were my influences and so on. I hoped to find a way to resolve the feelings I was left with after being sexually abused, both at fourteen and after Knebworth. I think that I also hoped it would make me a better person, and that it would have a positive effect on my relationship with Rose, who would approve of the experience.

I had read some of the work by R. D. Laing and was interested in his off-kilter approach to mental health, although Debbie had met him at a swinging party and told me he was rather unpleasant to her. In *Time Out*, an alternative magazine, I saw adverts for Encounter Groups. Now and then *Time Out* would run an article about these groups. Carl Rodgers, an American, had coined the term. He believed that people have the innate ability to heal themselves, and that by disclosing their thoughts and feelings in a group, they could learn to use similar techniques in other settings. The groups could have one or two leaders, and could take place over one evening, a whole weekend or several months.

Being impatient to get to grips with my inner self, I signed up for a whole weekend group; they called it 'intensive' and participants would be expected to stay for forty-eight hours. I was hoping for quick results.

Wrong.

The group consisted of ten participants, all young men and women, together with two female leaders. I'm not sure that these facilitators had any qualifications, although they were both confident.

We started with the usual icebreakers. Basically, these are games designed to get people talking to each other and are often a bit silly and rather fun. That was the easy bit. However, the exercises moved on to become ever more emotionally demanding. After each exercise, the group would reconvene to talk about their responses to whatever we had been doing.

I remember one exercise, which I think was about confronting our fears, where a man was lying on top of me, and I was trying to push him off. I just couldn't get him to move away from me, although I used all my strength. At the discussion afterwards, this man declared that "she could have easily pushed me off", implying that I simply had not tried hard enough. Instead of feeling empowered, I felt rather ashamed. Support from the leaders was lukewarm, which did nothing for my self-esteem.

Another exercise involved getting naked (no problem for me) and having a kind of 'show and tell' with the other participants, as if we were children and were particularly proud of our bits and pieces. It was completely asexual, and I don't think anyone became turned on, but if the intention was to empower, then it fell short of its mark. It just didn't work for me, and I felt silly going round the other group members, looking into their eyes and telling them that I had a pussy. Rather like Mrs Slocombe in *Are You Being Served?*

There was a lot of shouting and crying over the weekend and, as we became more and more physically exhausted, having very little sleep for forty-eight hours, my defences came down to the point where my throat was hoarse, my legs felt like jelly, my eyes were red from crying, and I longed to go home. And I'd paid good money for this!

At the end of the weekend, the facilitators said that they felt

I had not given my all to the process, and had held back. This would, they said, affect the benefits of the experience.

I was disappointed. Perhaps, I thought, I was doing it wrong. I was really very keen to discover myself. I signed up for a six-week group, meeting for a whole day each week. Talk about a glutton for punishment.

I did grow and develop. I am not convinced that this was entirely due to the experiences I had in Encounter Groups, but I did learn some techniques for dealing with problems and was able to put these to use in my everyday life. Perhaps I would have learnt these anyway.

I suspect that the one-to-one counselling and therapy I undertook later in my life was far more useful, although I did startle my therapist early on in our relationship by stating: "I killed my mother."

I meant, of course, that I had dealt with her hypothetically in one of the Encounter Groups.

Oh yes, it was fun, fun, fun all the way.

Kit Off Again

Dany's stripping success had an unexpected bonus for me. She suggested to the agents that she had a friend who could work as a topless waitress, and I started to get a few jobs. With my background of taking my clothes off in various situations, I had no trouble going topless. We even found work for Debbie occasionally. Dany and Phil had met her by now, and liked her almost as much as they liked me.

It was quite hard work, as the waitress had to go to various tables, take the orders, go to the bar, collect the drinks and take them back to the table. Most of the men drank pints so the tray of drinks could be heavy. I'd been told that the same rules applied to the waitress as to the stripper – in other words, the men could look but not touch. If any of the guys did touch, then we were at liberty to give them a slap or, my favourite, knock them on the head with my (empty) tray. The audience was, usually, good-humoured and did not give me a hard time. The money was good, being cash in hand, and was helped by the tips, which were frequently generous.

What to wear was a problem. I didn't want to be completely bare above the waist. I would feel too vulnerable. Dany and I found a compromise where I would wear a black mini-skirt, black tights and heels (agony after a few hours on my feet, but they looked better than flats). On my top I wore a white shirt, just like a real waitress, but I tied it under my breasts, which were naked, of course.

There was a protocol to observe, which was that the waitresses should never be moving around taking orders and giving out drinks while a stripper was on. It took the punters' attention away from the main attraction if they had breasts to look at nearer to their table.

The shows always included a comedian, sometimes just the one, who acted as MC, but sometimes there would be comedians who had their own spot. Many of the comics who went on to greater things on TV in the seventies and eighties, including Frank Carson, Jim Davidson and Mike Reid (who went on to star in *EastEnders*), started their careers at stag nights in working men's clubs, Rotary dinners and British Legion venues all over the country.

In the run-up to Christmas, the waitressing work really took off, but I was feeling very low and lonely. I loved Dany, but wanted to be in the company of some lesbians or gay men. Dany was utterly straight and, although she was empathetic, could never really understand what it meant to be a lesbian and on the fringes of a heterosexual society. Attitudes were beginning to change but prejudice was still rife out there at the end of 1975.

Living in St Albans was particularly isolating for a lesbian. It was probably much better in London, although meeting places were still thin on the ground. I was subscribing to a lesbian organisation called KENRIC. The name came from a group formed in 1965 by lesbians in Kensington and Richmond, but had now expanded to encompass the whole of the UK.

The way it worked was that members would organise outings, meals or events, some of which took place in their own homes. The details would be circulated via a monthly newsletter. Some of the dates on offer could be a group dinner or a West End show, but others would be far more pedestrian, such as an evening of board games. They also had a rule that any married members had to have the written permission of their husbands before joining!

I'd found one local event to attend. This was an afternoon in a Hertfordshire park playing rounders. Not a good choice for me, the least athletic woman in the West, but I went and found a nice group of hearty lesbians who were friendly and welcoming. I felt like a fish out of water and did not keep in touch with any of them, but still took the newsletter just in case anything else came up.

I'd managed to find a local Campaign for Homosexual Equality (CHE) group and went along to one of their social meetings. When I got there, I found that I was the only woman. The group was entirely made up of gay men. It wasn't a problem, though, because they were all absolutely sweet to me, taking the time to chat. I went to one or two more meetings over the next few months and, while it wasn't what I was looking for, I was very grateful to this bunch of lovely guys for being so kind, at a time when I needed someone to be kind to me.

Some years later I was able to repay their goodwill when I worked with people with AIDS. It felt like a chance to put something back into my community. And that, in turn, led me to a number of close friendships with gay men. I could enjoy the company of men... without the messy bit.

But back in 1975, as it got near to the festive season, my feelings of isolation grew. I phoned London Gay Switchboard late one night. I found myself talking for a long time to a gay man who was funny and made me laugh, lightening my mood.

"I'm not meant to do this," he said, "but my housemate and I are having a party at the weekend. Why don't you come?"

I was a bit surprised, but thought, *Why* not?

We arranged that I would meet up with his friend Babs, who would take me to the party, and that I should bring a sleeping bag, as it was bound to go on until the early hours. I wasn't sure whether he was making a blind date for me and Babs, but thought I could deal with that if the need arose.

I was quite anxious about it, but knew that having some dope would give me confidence, and would be an entrée into the in-crowd. The only hiccup in this plan was that I had not mastered the art of rolling a joint. I hit on a solution by taking a pipe. Not a cool dope smoker's pipe, made by impoverished children in India, but a real man's brown-stemmed pipe, with a large bowl for piling in the tobacco.

Meeting Babs was straightforward. She turned out to be a pleasant, shy butch of a woman. Not my type at all, and she was much too timid to make a pass, so that was alright.

We arrived at the address to find the party in full swing. The house was enormous, filled with antiques. It even had its own cranky lift. I'd never seen such an opulent house, not even in my swinging party days. In the largest ground floor room the music was belting out and men were dancing like crazy to 'Play That Funky Music' by Wild Cherry. A few women were in there, too.

As the music got louder, so the dancing got ever more frenetic. The men started taking their shirts off and the women followed suit. In spite of my history of taking my own clothes off, I was quite shocked. How odd. I wasn't ready for this. Time for a smoke.

I found the room where I would be sleeping and proceeded to fill the bowl of the pipe with shredded Silk Cut and crumbled dope. As I lit up, a couple of other people came into the room and sat down to chat. They gave me an odd look, but it was a while until I realised what a picture I must present: this little, fairly femme lesbian, smoking from a pipe like their dad. I offered them a toke, which was accepted, but felt bound to explain that I couldn't roll joints.

After they left, I just couldn't be bothered to join the party so unrolled my sleeping bag, had a fitful night's sleep and took off as early as possible in the morning. Back to real life.

Still, it was nice of the Gay Switchboard volunteer to invite me. It just wasn't what I was looking for. I knew what that was. I just didn't know how to make it happen.

End of the Dream

While she was in France, Rose and I were writing to each other and occasionally spoke on the phone. I tried to get a date from her as to when it would be good to make a visit, and we settled on sometime in early June.

However, a couple of days before I was due to go, she phoned to say she was not well and, anyway, would be coming home for a visit soon. I was disappointed but felt that we would soon be having a lovely reunion, which was bound to be romantic and passionate.

Which it was.

She spent a lot of time with her children, as was to be expected, but we had some good times together, going for hacks on ponies in the countryside or out for meals. We even had an evening in London at The Gateways. It was fun and felt like the time when our relationship was new and happy.

However, it became clear that she did not want me to visit her in France. She explained that she was using her time there to get her head clear, to grow and develop. She feared that my presence would be a distraction to that. I didn't argue with her. I had my new friendship with Dany to sustain me over the otherwise lonely days and evenings. And I was enjoying this relatively peaceful time in my relationship with Rose, so didn't want to rock the boat.

My unspoken hope was that she would finally get this need to gather a multitude of lovers out of her system, and we would settle down into a calm, loving, faithful relationship. I just wanted to be with her, with neither of us having other sexual encounters.

My fantasy was that we could have warm companionship, passionate lovemaking and an ordinary, everyday relationship – maybe with occasional rows about whose turn it was to take out the rubbish bins, but an otherwise serene life. Romantic, of course, but surely it's the way that thousands of people live?

She returned to France after the holiday to start the new term and we continued to write to each other – long letters full of angst usually, with me declaring my love for her on every other page, and her going off into a stream of consciousness, citing her psychotherapist and Jung, in particular, but other theorists too. She was finding herself. Again.

Rose came home for Christmas and we had the mother and father of all arguments, which came to a head in the kitchen, when she just would not stop going on and on about something or other. I was doing the washing up at the time and, just as I got to the end of it, with the bowl of tepid, greasy water in front of me, she paused for breath. I thought that she had finished, but no, she started up again. I picked up the bowl of dirty water and threw it over her. That shut her up. Then, of course, I had to apologise and mop it all up.

She went back to France to finish the last term of the exchange. She spoke French fluently by now but did not seem clear on how she might use this new skill.

She had sublet her room to another art student, Mary. I was never involved in these decisions on who I would be sharing the flat with. I had been lucky that she chose tenants who were nice to live with. Mary was not as outgoing as the previous subtenant, Lucy, had been, but she was pleasant as we bumped into each other in the kitchen or hall.

Finally, the time had come for Rose to return home. She phoned me to let me know the date and said that she had made friends with the daughter of her French landlady. She would be bringing Giselle for a holiday in England, as she had never been to Britain before. I agreed that I would get the little spare room ready for Giselle, and have a meal ready for them.

I was so happy that this extended break had come to an end and hoped that we could resume our relationship on a calmer footing now that we'd had so much time to reflect and grow. I cleaned and cooked like a banshee, determined that her homecoming would be a happy, positive occasion for both of us, and that her friend would feel welcome and comfortable.

Rose looked different. For a start she had a shorter haircut, a stylish bob instead of her usual long hair. She wore a skirt and knee-length boots, not her usual jeans and shirt. I guessed it was the French influence but it was a little unsettling. Giselle was tall and quite chunky but was also very chic. She did not speak much English so that it was difficult to converse, but we managed with Rose acting as interpreter.

At bedtime, Rose went into the spare room with Giselle to show her where things were while I went to bed next door in my room. I could hear them talking quietly, and then a long silence. And then a little moan. The kind of moan Rose made when she was kissing. No, no. I must have imagined it because Rose then came to bed with me, and we snuggled under the covers.

It had been a long time since we had made love and I wanted her. I was making all the usual moves but was not getting any kind of response from Rose.

"What's the matter?" I asked.

"I don't want to do that," she said. "I don't like it."

"Well, you always used to like it."

"I'm sorry. I suppose I'm just tired."

Well, they had been travelling all day, so I stopped and said, "Let's just have a cuddle then."

The next day, Rose was taking Giselle to see the Roman ruins in town, together with St Albans Cathedral. They would be gone all afternoon, doing the tourist thing. I thought that I would leave them to it, as I had already been to these places several times.

But I started thinking about what I thought I'd heard last night. Surely Rose wouldn't bring a new lover into our home when I was there? I couldn't help myself… I had to look at her journal to try to work it out. It was a revelation.

Rose had actually been in England for almost two weeks. She had gone to stay with John for a few nights before he went off on a business trip and Giselle arrived. Rose and Giselle had been sleeping at his chalet for a week, making love, going out for meals and going to The Gateways.

I felt sick. I was cold, yet sweating. I sat in the kitchen trying to make sense of it all when I heard their voices coming up the stairs. They were laughing. Well, they would be, wouldn't they? How pleased they must have felt to have completely fooled me, to have me falling over myself to make Giselle so welcome, so glad to see Rose. I wondered if they had a plan on when I would be told the truth.

As they arrived on the landing of the first floor, I came out of the kitchen and walked towards them, shouting at Rose.

"You bitch. You fucking, cunting bitch. How could you? How could you bring your new lover here, install her next to me, kiss her in the very next room. Why did you let me think you'd only just come home? When were you going to tell me?"

As I shouted, I got nearer and nearer to her until I grabbed her by the throat, pushing her backwards over the banister. I had strength in my hands and arms that I'd never previously been aware of.

Everything seemed to stand still, a frozen tableau where I was vaguely aware of Giselle at the top of the stairs. Julie was standing in the stairwell, Mary had come out of her room and was in her open doorway and Rose was staring at me with wide eyes, like a frightened rabbit, still bent over the banister.

For about thirty seconds I held her like that, feeling powerful at last, knowing her life hung in the balance then, just as quickly as it had happened, the overwhelming urge to hurt her left me.

I let go of her and dropped onto the floor. A moment later, a wail came up from my belly as I opened my mouth and howled. The pain encompassed my whole being. My humiliation was complete. I was aware of someone picking me up and holding me close, while I sobbed into their chest. It was Giselle. The irony did not escape me.

I pulled away and went into my room where I fell onto my bed, overwhelmed by a surge of grief. Grief in the knowledge that this woman, the very same one who had helped me find my true self, who had given me so much pleasure as well as pain, who had been tender and loving and fun, and had taught me about art, nature, music, dance, the beauty of nature and animals, had finally betrayed me, and this was surely the end of all those romantic dreams and hopes I'd had.

Well and truly finished. There could be no tearful reconciliation this time.

A tentative knock at the door. Mary. "Are you alright? Is there anything I can do?"

"No. Just leave me alone. There's nothing anyone can do."

I felt exhausted, so very tired. I wanted to climb into bed and stay there forever. A short while later, though, there came another knock at the door. This time I didn't answer, but the door opened anyway and Dany came in.

"Jan, you've got to get yourself together. Julie has called an ambulance."

"I don't care. Why has she done that? No one needs an ambulance, do they?"

"Well, you'd better start caring, because Julie has said that you need to be sectioned. They'll be carting you off to the loony bin."

The tears were still pouring down my face, and I was all snotty. Dany gave me a tissue and said, "Dry your eyes and blow your nose. I'll be back in a tick."

She was gone for a moment, and then returned with a damp flannel and a towel. She wiped my face and hands, drying them gently with the towel. "Where's your hairbrush?" she asked, and tidied my hair.

She pulled a clean T-shirt out of my drawer and helped me to take off the one I was wearing, which was unaccountably creased and stained, and put on the clean one. Then she sat me in the chair by the window and put a book in my hands. Just in time, as the doorbell rang at that moment.

The ambulance men found me sitting calmly in the easy chair reading an upside down book. They talked to me for a while, as I told them that there had been an argument with my flatmate, but it was now resolved and all over. Dany, who had shown them in, confirmed that it was just an argument between friends. I was so composed that they were clearly baffled as to why they had been called out and, after checking it out with me one last time, went on their way.

When the dust had settled, Rose told me that I would have to find somewhere else to live. She wanted me to move out so that she and Giselle could live together at Lemsford Road. But I was stronger now than the previous time she had turfed me out. I refused and told her it was her turn to move. I think she was a bit surprised that I was standing up to her and challenging her demands.

I went to the local Citizens Advice Bureau who confirmed that she had no right to ask me to move, as it was still my name on the rent book. When our landlord made his next monthly visit, I went to see him as quickly as possible, certainly before Rose could get to him, and explained the situation.

He was a nice man and embarrassed by this unexpected explanation of the nature of our relationship, but agreed that as I'd found the flat, and my name was on the rent book, he had no objection to me continuing to live at Lemsford Road.

So I stood my ground with Rose. I agreed that she could leave some of her belongings at the flat until she found alternative accommodation. It felt so good to have done that, to have asserted myself and been strong in a relationship where I'd so often been controlled and influenced.

Rose was not a bad person. She could be tender, funny, loving, but she could not understand or agree to my need for a monogamous relationship. Not only could she not adhere to such a notion, but she could not believe that my ideal was to commit only to her. Perhaps the way we met was too much of an underlying theme for us. It wasn't exactly a conservative way to form a lesbian relationship.

I think that she also saw me, who was just coming out and ten years younger, as someone she could mould and shape to the kind of person she thought I should be. And it worked for a while, until I started to mature and grow stronger.

In spite of all the pain, we did stay in touch on and off for a long time. She lived with Giselle both in England and France, where she worked as a teacher of English to French adults. Rose also completed an art therapy qualification, and went on to work with disturbed children.

Giselle, being a good Catholic girl, decided to end her relationship with Rose and got married. What goes around…

A long time after this, I met Rose's current lesbian lover. Although she looked nothing like me, I was shocked when I got to know the similarities between us and how Rose was encouraging her to develop.

She was also from a working class background. Rose had introduced her to Tibetan Buddhism and meditation, exactly as she had with me. She had encouraged her to go into therapy – ditto. They had blazing rows because Rose believed she was having affairs outside of their relationship… It was very strange and gave me a feeling of *déjà vu*. I wanted to tell this latest girlfriend to run for the hills.

I didn't, of course. I did, however, eventually cut off all contact with Rose. This was after years of therapy, exploring the nature of our relationship, which affected me for a very long time.

When writing this book, though, I found that I was curious about how her life had panned out and how her children were doing. I had been very fond of them. I found that she had an email address, and wrote to her. I think it was a chatty, friendly note.

She replied that it was a pity I had been so 'disturbed' at the time we were seeing each other. She took no responsibility for being the cause of any 'disturbance' I might have experienced. She even suggested that I had false memory syndrome. Her emails (there were several) were full of the old stuff she had subjected me to in the past: a diatribe, a stream of consciousness, full of psychobabble.

I felt the old anger surfacing again. This woman knew all the buttons to push to make me feel manipulated and bullied. There was clearly no point in continuing with this correspondence, and I wrote back to say as much, although I was sorry that we could not put the past aside and have a friendship.

Back then though, ending our tie to each other and unravelling the knots was so, so difficult and painful. In spite of everything, I still loved her and found the prospect of a life without her very bleak. She'd been the focus of my life for seven years and I was frightened to be without that.

Thank God for Dany, always there with a hug and a cup of tea. She was just a flight of stairs away and, as I gradually recovered and moved on, she was my rock, and gave her support and love generously and without conditions.

There was no way of knowing then that our friendship would continue for over thirty-five years, that our lives would change so radically, going down very different paths and that we would still love each other like sisters until the very end of her life.

5

Naked Ambition

One evening early in 1976, I was at a stag do somewhere in the Home Counties, doing a topless waitress stint. It was a posh function room, and quite a big event, with an MC, two comedians and three strippers.

One of the girls was Dany; another was Jacqui (real name Rosemary). Jacqui was a statuesque young woman who, at twenty-three, was a few years younger than Dany and me. She had trained as a ballet dancer but grew too tall. She had the grace and flexibility you would expect from a dancer, and this lent an unexpected twist to her routines. Dany had become friendly with Jacqui, who declared herself bisexual, although this was generally expressed by her laying her head on my breasts and singing "Heaven, I'm in heaven…"

The third stripper that night was Zizi. I never did find out her real name. Zizi was in her late thirties, so was probably one of the oldest girls on the circuit. Her first spot would be to perform a belly dance, gradually divesting herself of the scarves attached to her sequined underwear.

It was her second spot though that was a showstopper. She came on with a wicker basket, which contained her two pet pythons. These huge snakes would twist and curl themselves around her, while the audience of supposedly rough, tough men would visibly draw back in their seats as far as they could.

It was in between her two spots, and while Jacqui was on, that I nipped to the dressing room for a quick fag and natter to Dany. I leaned against the wall, kicking off my shoes for a moment, wearing my usual outfit of short black skirt and white shirt tied under my breasts. Zizi gazed at me, long and hard.

"You know wot?" she said. "You should be a stripper. Wiv those tits all you'd have to do is just stand there."

I laughed and looked at Dany, who looked back at me, raising her well-plucked eyebrows.

"Well, why not, Jan?"

"For one thing, I can't dance."

"Of course you can. I've seen you dance. It's just that you're a bit self-conscious."

"And for another thing, I'm too fat."

"No you're not," said Jacqui, who was just coming back into the dressing room, grabbing her robe. "Anyway, if you really feel you want to lose a few pounds, I can give you the name of my doctor in Harley Street. He'll sort you out with some pills to help you lose weight."

I had to get back to the waitressing, but a seed had been planted. The strippers earned far more than the waitresses, had a higher status in the hierarchy of the stag circuit and didn't have to mingle with the groping audience.

Jacqui was right; I wasn't really fat, but the words of the Bunny Mother at the Playboy Club saying that I needed to lose 5lb to be a Bunny Girl still rankled. If I wanted to do this stripping lark, I needed to lose a little weight if only to give me a bit more self-assurance. What's more, I wanted to lose it quickly, so a sensible diet and exercise just wasn't going to be the ticket. I got the name of Jacqui's doctor and made an appointment.

His consulting rooms on Harley Street were opulent, with floor-to-ceiling windows hung with heavy drapes. The parquet flooring was set off by huge, thick oriental rugs. The magazines on the coffee table were *The Lady* and *Horse & Hound*, and without a dog-eared page in sight.

Being shown in by the receptionist (the one with several plums in her gob), I found Dr C to be suave, Savile Row suited and sympathetic. I explained that I wanted to lose some weight quickly and had been given his name by Jacqui/Rosemary. He weighed me, took my blood pressure and wrote out a private prescription. It was that easy. He told me that the 'diet pills' might keep me awake at night, so he included a prescription for sleeping tablets. I paid the plummy receptionist and hot-footed it to the nearest chemist.

The diet pills were, of course, amphetamines. I'd not experienced taking speed before, but found that I loved its effects. If smoking dope made me the wittiest, most laid back person in the room, I found that whizz gave me confidence. Not only that, but it minimised appetite, so I was eating next to nothing, my mood was lifted and I had enormous amounts of energy.

So, before long, I was smoking both spliffs and Silk Cut like they were going out of fashion, and there were nights when I would be awake and buzzing until four in the morning. The sleeping pills would then kick in and I would sleep half the next day away. I think I probably became quite addicted to speed as I went back to Dr C for more supplies time and again over the next two years. Still, at least it would have been pure and not cut with anything unpleasant, as it might have been if I'd bought it from a street dealer.

Dany, Phil and I started to think about what I could do in my act, what the music should be and, most importantly, what my gimmick would be. (*You gotta get a gimmick.*)

General opinion was that I looked younger than my twenty-seven years and, being little, appeared to be something of an *ingénue*. Thus, we hit upon the focus of my first spot, when I would appear as 'An Old-Fashioned Girl'. I would wear the maxi dress I still had (and could fit into) from my swinging party days. It was cotton, pale blue with a black flower-sprigged pattern; it was fitted at the waist and had shoestring straps. This would be covered with a velvet tippet (a short cape) I had acquired. I would wear elbow-length gloves and heeled black T-strap shoes, and I would carry a parasol. My bra, basque, pants and G-string under the costume would be white, continuing the sexy virgin theme.

So that was the outfit. Then we only had the music to sort out. The clear choice to start with was 'Just an Old Fashioned Girl' sung by Eartha Kitt, finishing with 'Diamonds Are a Girl's Best Friend' sung by Marilyn Monroe.

The other spot was obvious. I still had my nurse's uniform, including apron, cloak and cap. There's a gimmick and a half: a genuine nurse's outfit, under which I would wear black underwear. Every man's dream, right?

I can't remember how, but I had acquired a huge, silver-coloured syringe. The barrel was about eight inches long, with a circumference of six inches. Heaven knows what it was really meant for, but I decided that I would fill it with body lotion, which I would 'ejaculate' onto my breasts and rub in when I was down to my pants. It looked really filthy. I was quite proud of this little piece of theatre.

I would come on to the Beatles' 'Dr Robert' and end up with their song 'Come Together', which was suitably slow and full of innuendo. The protocol was to have a spot that lasted for around nine minutes, so the music had to reflect this.

There was etiquette to the way in which our clothes were removed. The idea was to keep as many clothes on as possible, for as long as possible. Obviously, the top layer would come off first, but it would be done very slowly. Then the undies would be removed at a leisurely pace, until we were down to the G-string. This would only be taken off at the very last moment, so that the punters had the briefest flash of pubes – and we all had pubes. Brazilians were unknown in those days, unless they came from South America. And none of us wore pasties – those nipple-covering thingies with tassels.

There was also an expectation that the act would be a 'clean' one. Any sexual activity would be frowned upon by most of the strippers and comedians, although a certain amount of humorous interaction was alright, and faked sexuality was fine. For instance, one of the girls did some rapid humping movements, but did it as part of her dancing, not with a punter. Having said that, there were a small number of strippers who would go beyond the limits of what was acceptable, but these were in the minority. Really, we were good girls, we were. We just happened to take our clothes off for a living.

Getting the music and costumes sorted out took several weeks, during which time the weight was falling off me due to the amphetamines I now took every day. I found that I could do my ironing in a third of the time it usually took me, and walking back from the town centre with my shopping was now a brisk canter, rather than my usual leisurely stroll.

The next stage in my transformation to the shortest stripper in the business was to get some publicity photos done for circulating to agents and potential bookers. My old friend Bill had recently added a photographic studio to his portfolio of business ventures, so that was an obvious first stop. With his usual generosity, he arranged a studio and professional photographer for me, all at his expense.

I think that the photographer was more used to taking pictures for catalogues because he clearly wasn't sure what to do with me.

"Er... How about giving us a twirl, then?"

"Like this?" I said, whirling about, so that my nurse's cloak flew out, almost knocking the camera out of his hand.

"Maybe a bit less energy. Can you twirl slowly?"

Between us we came up with the idea of re-enacting my proposed performances as he took the photos. This seemed to work quite well, until I got to the point of having removed the dress, so was wearing bra, basque, pants, stockings and high-heeled shoes. Oh, and elbow-length black gloves.

"Let's have some of you sitting down on that couch," he suggested.

Well, it was a low, squashy sofa, which I sank into. It didn't feel right, so I edged towards the front of it so that I was sitting almost on the edge. The photographer clicked away, only suggesting that I leant forward or smiled. I didn't like smiling in photos. I thought it made my nose look big, but did it anyway.

When I saw the completed contact sheet a week or so later, I knew immediately that these pictures would not do. In the nurse's outfit I looked positively demented, a grinning full frontal nude, swirling my cloak like an extra from *Dracula*. In the sofa pictures, I appeared to be asking "More tea, vicar?" All that was missing was the teapot.

Back to the drawing board, then.

I had become friendly with one of the circuit comedians. We chatted easily and laughed a lot. Tony Gerrard was quite severely disabled, having had polio as a child. He was perfectly independent, though, and had a customised wheelchair that he could manoeuvre himself and drove an adapted car.

Tony and I did not really have a sexual relationship, although he liked to have a fumble now and then. We had a friendship that included going out for meals (always a pull for me), going to the cinema or staying in and playing Scrabble.

He told me he had a two-week contract to perform at a hotel on a Greek island, and would I like to join him as his 'carer'? It would be an all-expenses-paid gig for both of us. Naturally, I jumped at the opportunity of a holiday in the sun. I'd not been able to afford to go away on holiday for several years. Tony would be expected to give just one performance each week. The rest of the time he would be free to relax. And so would I.

It turned out that Tony was a keen amateur photographer. When I brought him up to speed on the publicity shot problems, he suggested that he take some pictures of me while we were away. I was a bit concerned that the angle might be wrong, given that he was in a wheelchair, but said we'd give it a go and see how they turned out.

During the first week I worked on my tan, which wasn't difficult. Having been blessed with olive skin, I turn brown very easily and we were ignorant then of the dangers of sunbathing. By the second week I was bronzed, rested and positively glowing. We took ourselves off to a secluded part of the hotel complex, complete with a number of outfits for me to pose in.

Dany and Me

Boxer short material kaftans
(and curtains)

Dany ready for work

The Glamour Model

Not regulations shoes!

To take account of Tony being in the wheelchair, I knelt in some shots and stood in others. I posed against flora and under a shower. I wore my hair up and down. I looked sultry in an open denim jacket; perky in a teeny bikini; saucy in a wet cheesecloth blouse; serene in a lace shawl, bikini bottoms and not much else.

We actually had a lot of fun taking those pictures and when, two weeks later, I saw the contact sheet, I was very pleased with the results. In spite of the unusual angle of some, they seemed to work. I decided to use two of these and one of the calmer shots of me in my nurse's uniform taken at the studio.

These were made up to form a sort of collage, together with my 'vital statistics' of '38-26-36'. I was ready to go, and appointments were made – using contacts gleaned from Dany and other friends – to see agents who might be able to offer me gigs. Simon (he of the boxer shorts material glut) had a partner who was a photographic glamour/soft porn model. She suggested that I also contact some of the agents she used for work, so I duly made appointments to see them, too.

The agents varied from professional to sleazy. One asked me to take off my top and bra so that he could see my breasts, and inspected me as clinically as a doctor. Another (a well-known publisher of soft porn) interviewed me at his huge, darkened studio apartment, then sat on his satin-sheeted round bed and said, "If you give me a blow job, I'll give you some work." Revolting man.

The offers of work as a stripper and glamour model started to trickle in. It would seem that there was gold in them thar hills, and that I'd been sitting on a fortune.

Let's Go On With the Show

So… I was on my way as a stripper. After that first gig at the Hackney pub, the work really took off, and I found myself travelling all over the country to stag nights and private parties.

I had bought a car from Phil, a yellow DAF, which constantly broke down and had to be repaired at great expense, usually involving a long wait for spare parts to arrive from Holland.

I'd had a few driving lessons and had driven with Phil or Debbie in the passenger seat, but hadn't passed my test. This did not stop me from trundling around in a car that would not go above fifty miles per hour. Consequently, it sometimes took me hours to reach my destination, not helped by the fact that I was hopeless at reading maps. I often found myself lost or having to stop to check my whereabouts. Eventually I realised that it would help to write out the route in very big letters before I started out. This did make it easier but I still frequently found myself arriving very late for gigs.

Indeed, by the time I arrived at one working men's club in the Midlands, they had thought that I wasn't going to turn up at all. When I did arrive and the MC announced, "The stripper's here!", a huge cheer went up and I performed to a standing ovation! They were very nice and good humoured about it, I must say.

After going to one job in Portsmouth, I started the long, slow drive home when the full headlights on the car stopped working. Only the side lights were coming on. If that wasn't bad enough, I managed to lose a contact lens at some point in the evening. I am very, very short sighted, so this was a major catastrophe, as I did not carry a spare lens or even a pair of spectacles in the car.

I found that if I covered the eye without a lens, I could see reasonably well, but couldn't drive with one hand up to my face. I'd worn a scarf that evening, so managed to tie it around my head, covering the problem eye. It looked a bit piratical but solved the problem.

So there I was, driving home at 1.00am, with a learner's licence, in a car with only its sidelights on and with a scarf covering one side of my face. What else could go wrong? I got lost, that's what. I found myself on a narrow country lane without any street lamps and without a clue where I was. I stopped the car and tried to make sense of the wretched map, using my one good eye to decipher the road numbers and names.

Then, out of the blue, there was a tap on the window. My heart shot into my mouth, out again with relief when I saw it was a policeman, then back again when I realised I must be breaking dozens of laws.

I had the wherewithal to push the scarf back on my head, so that it looked like it had just slipped over my face.

"Oh, hello, Officer," I simpered with what I hoped was a beguiling smile.

"Is there a problem, Madam?"

"I'm terribly lost, I'm afraid. I'm trying to get to the A3 but I seem to have taken a wrong turning."

"You certainly have, Madam. You need to go straight on until you reach the crossroads, take a right, then keep going until you come to a roundabout by a pub called The Dog and Duck and take the third exit. Keep going for about two miles and you will see a signpost for the A3."

I'd lost the plot after he got to the crossroads, but nodded and smiled and said, "Thank you so much, Officer." He didn't seem to notice that I wore a scarf at an odd angle or that I only had sidelights and did not ask to see my licence. I drove off very carefully until I was out of sight, which was when I had to re-adjust my headgear, so that I could see again. I finally managed to find my way home, arriving at around 4.00am.

Dany and I sometimes got bookings for the same gig. During that winter there was one occasion when we had a job at a private stag party. Unusually, it was at the home of one of the punters. I would have been nervous about going into a private house with a room full of men, but Phil drove us and sat in the kitchen, apart from when he oversaw the music for our acts. No one would dare take liberties with Phil in the next room. As it turned out, these were a group of about fifteen very respectful young men. They weren't even terribly drunk.

We used one of the bedrooms to get changed and the

evening went without incident, although we did get quite stoned in between our spots. At the end of the night, the organiser came to pay us and said, "Um… we were wondering… er… if we… um… had a whip round, would you… er… do a d-d-double act for us?"

"I think that would be OK," Dany said. "Are you up for it, Jan?"

"Why not?" I said.

"Just give us fifteen minutes to get organised," Dany said to the chap.

"Ooh. That's great. Ooh. Thank you, very much. Ooh."

When he left the room, we had a quick brainstorming session about how we would work this extra, unexpected performance. We'd never done a double act before so we had to think on our feet. We decided to cobble another costume together from our ordinary daytime clothes and bits from our costumes. Then we came up with a very loose plan for the act itself. Obviously, there would be a lesbian theme but it would all be simulated. There would be no real sexual activity, and the usual rules applied. In other words: no complete nudity until the very last moment.

So we had a plan, then we had another joint.

And so it came to pass that I tied Dany up to a chair with my woolly scarf, and then proceeded to beat her with a knitted hat with a bobble on it. It was hardly the stuff of erotica and we both got a terrible fit of the giggles in the middle of the action, but managed to conceal it with suitable noises of "Oh, yes. Aaah. Oh. Aaah. Yes!"

Our small audience was very quiet, with all eyes on us. I don't think any of those men even took a sip of their drink while we were doing our stuff. When we finished we returned to the 'dressing room' and the organiser came in with a pint glass stuffed with £5 and £10 notes, which he gave to us.

"Wow. That was amazing. Thanks so much. I'll never look at those photos in *Playboy* in the same way."

We graciously accepted his appreciation and the pint glass.

As well as the stripping jobs, I was also starting to get work as a glamour model. Some of these just involved baring the boobs, while others wanted full nudity. Most of these modelling jobs were straightforward cheesecake pictures, largely involving pulling my stomach in and thrusting the breasts out in a variety of coy poses.

Once or twice, though, the photographers expected more, taking revealing photos of me on my own, or with a man. The agent never told me what to expect from these jobs so I went along with it.

It was only after one of these shoots, when talking to Simon's girlfriend, that she said, "You don't have to do anything you don't feel comfortable with." I wish I'd known that sooner... or had been confident enough to refuse. Not that anything really awful was requested. It was soft porn. I never had sex on camera, no children were involved, and all of the Alsatians had given their written consent.

Heatwave

In spite of all this activity and my now firm friendship with Dany, I yearned for another relationship with a woman. Dany and I loved each other and would be tactile with hugs, but there was no sexual chemistry between us. She was most definitely heterosexual, and I was not attracted to her in that way.

I eventually placed an ad in the Lonely Hearts column of *Time Out*, a radical listings magazine. It read:

Lesbian, 28, small and voluptuous. My friends say I'm attractive, GSOH, likes reading, music, smoking and laughing would like to meet similar. Photo appreciated. Herts.

Not especially witty or eye-catching, but I received quite a few replies, including some from men who seemed convinced that if only I met up with them, I would realise that I was not a lesbian at all. I rejected all of those, along with the photos showing butch-looking women. That wasn't my cup of tea. I was left with three possibilities – women who looked attractive and had written nice letters.

The first one lived in Hertford, so was reasonably near. I phoned her, found out that her name was Rose and she had children. I was so spooked by the coincidence that I couldn't consider taking it any further.

Another one sounded interesting. She had also been married, but it turned out that her husband was gay and now she had come out as a lesbian. They still shared a house in Hampstead.

She had said in her letter that she was a hedonist. I didn't know what it meant until I looked it up in the dictionary, and decided that I could describe myself similarly. We met and went for tea on Hampstead Heath. I asked her what made her laugh and she replied, "There isn't much to laugh about, is there?" So that was that.

The last date I had was with a young American woman, Kerry-Anne. She had come to the UK with her dad, who was stationed at a US Army base in Suffolk. She lived outside the base with a boyfriend, but she was exploring her sexuality and wanted to experiment.

Now, I've always had a bit of a crush on Americans, generally. I think it's the result of watching all those Hollywood films in my formative years. They always seemed so glamorous, with their sun tans, hamburgers and big cars. We wrote to each other a few times, spoke on the phone and then decided to meet. She would come to St Albans and would then drive us to her place in Suffolk.

She was lovely. Not overly tall, with a womanly figure and blonde bobbed hair. Clearly anxious about our proposed weekend together, she was shy, which made me feel like a woman of the world – very confident and taking the lead. We shared a spliff before setting out on the journey to Suffolk.

It was a long drive and, by the time we got there, had talked non-stop about our lives, hopes and dreams. She stopped off at a friend's place briefly and, when she came back to the car, announced that she'd scored some coke.

I'd never had cocaine before, but as usual was up for trying something new. When we got to her place she tipped the white powder onto a mirror, cut it up into several lines with a credit card and inhaled some through a rolled-up £1 note. I did the same and caught a horrible taste at the back of my throat.

It took a short while for the drug to affect me, but then my mood soared, along with my confidence. I was witty, sexy and alert. I felt on top of the world and never wanted this feeling to end. It seemed only a short while later that we started to feel tired, so we had another line and it all started again.

Meanwhile, we made love and, although my senses were heightened, I think that it was not very satisfactory for either of us. Still, that is what we had met for and we both seemed to just want to get it over with.

I stayed overnight with her, hardly sleeping at all. She said that she was working the following day, so I got myself back to St Albans via public transport.

I never saw her again, and it was many years before I had the opportunity to try coke once more, but I loved the effects and can understand how people get addicted to it.

June and July in 1976 saw a heatwave in the United Kingdom. Temperatures reached 35.9°C (96.6°F), which led to the worst drought in the country since the eighteenth century. Not only was there a hosepipe ban, but we were also encouraged to save water in all sorts of other ways: use the contents of the washing-up bowl to flush the toilet; share the bath water with several members of the family and so on.

We watched the grass in our garden get increasingly brown, the earth baked to a hard, cracked surface. We all adopted the European ways of having the windows open and the curtains closed to try to keep the rooms cool. In spite of only wearing our boxer-shorts-material kaftans, we were still melting in that heat, and could manage little more than to sit around, listening to music, chatting, drinking endless cups of tea, snacking and smoking dope.

On one of these blistering afternoons, Tom came to visit. He had just scored some hash, so he got busy rolling and passing joints. Phil was, unusually, out somewhere and not at home. The schools were on holiday, so the children were at home, playing in their bedroom. When the doorbell rang, we assumed it was another of our usual crowd come to hang out and have a smoke.

I think Dany answered the door, but suddenly their sitting room was filled with burly-looking blokes. At first I thought they were villains, catching up with Phil for something or other, but then they were shouting, "This is a raid. Nobody leaves this room!"

Tom, sitting on the window seat, promptly dropped his stash out of the window into the long grass and weeds beneath. I just sat and gawped. One of the coppers announced that they would be searching the place and promptly started with Phil's armchair.

The children, surprised but not alarmed by all the noise, wandered in and Dain said to the policeman poking around the chair, "That's where my daddy keeps his special tobacco." With this, the officer said, "Perhaps someone could look after the kids for a bit."

I immediately rounded them up and took them, now hugely excited, to my flat where we made lemonade floats from fizzy pop and ice cream. I settled them down with some coloured pens and paper and worried that my flat would also be searched. I had a couple of acid tabs hidden away in a box made for me by Rose. This box could only be opened by undoing the little screws in each corner. I hoped that it would just look like an ornament and they wouldn't open it.

After what seemed an age, a policeman came to my flat and asked me about my relationship with Dany and Phil. He then proceeded to search the room, feeling around the door mantle, behind and under the gas fire, all over the bed, pillows and mattress. He was pretty thorough and, just when I thought he'd finished, he picked up the little box on the mantelpiece and said, "What's this?"

"It's a box. My friend made it for me."

"Hmm," he said, shaking it. "What's inside?"

"Oh, just some earrings she gave me. It was for my birthday last year. Pretty isn't it?"

Later, in the post mortem, we thought that maybe I just looked too innocent to be someone who used drugs, or perhaps he just couldn't be bothered, because at that point he left and went back downstairs.

They hadn't found any large quantity of marijuana downstairs, but in the old stables at the end of the garden they found a drum of white powder. They assumed it was cocaine and Phil was charged with possession and intent to supply.

However, upon examination it turned out to be lignocaine – the anaesthetic used by dentists – which was not an illegal drug, so all charges were dropped. I never did find out what Phil was doing with a drum of lignocaine, or how he had come by it. Phil did get charged for possession of marijuana but it was a tiny amount so he got off very lightly.

So the sun continued to shine on all of us and we thought that summer would never end.

Clothed Ambition

In spite of the stripping and modelling work, which was now being offered fairly frequently, I was still always broke. Somehow the money just slipped through my fingers and I always seemed to be surviving on an overdraft.

When Louise, my nursing friend, said that she had been working the night shift at a private nursing home for the elderly, but was now leaving, it was a chance to step in and earn a bit more. The home was just minutes away from Lemsford Road so was very convenient.

The owner, Mrs P, was so happy to find a replacement for the night shift that the interview was a mere nod in the direction of suitability. No references were asked for or given. She asked if I could provide my own uniform, which I could, of course. I didn't mention that it would also be doing duty as one of my stripping costumes.

The home was in a Victorian house, not unlike the one where I lived, albeit rather better maintained. The ground floor housed the kitchen and a residents' lounge, together with private accommodation for the owner, her husband and two teenage sons.

The three upper floors had been converted into single and double or triple rooms for the residents. None were en suite, and there were shared bathrooms. There was no lift or chairlift, so anyone who was not ambulant would not be able to use the lounge area. It was a small concern, with only twelve elderly people living there. A few of these were able to live relatively independently but most needed care of some sort.

The nighttime drugs were given out by Mrs P or one of the qualified daytime staff. My duties would be uncomplicated. First thing was to go round to the residents offering them a nighttime drink of Horlicks or whatever. Then go back and collect the cups, make sure everyone was comfortable for the night, help them to the lavatory or commode if necessary, plump up pillows, tuck in blankets, put incontinence pads in place, put cot sides up and turn off the bedside light if the resident was unable to do this for themselves.

After washing up the used crockery, the next task was to set up the breakfast trays ready for the morning, and get the porridge ready in the double boiler, ready to be heated in the morning.

Then all I had to do all night was to make an occasional round of the residents to (a) check that they were dry, (b) change the incontinence pad if they were not, (c) ensure they had not fallen out of bed and (d) check they were still alive. It wasn't rocket science, and I could spend the rest of the night watching TV until the programmes ended (they did not go on all night in those days), reading or even have a snooze, as long as I set an alarm clock to wake up every hour or so to do my rounds.

What really shocked me about this home was that the residents who were alert were accommodated in the most comfortable rooms on the lower floors, with carpeted floors, heavy drapes at the window and rather nice furniture.

There were two residents, however, who had advanced Alzheimer's and who were incontinent. These were housed in the attic rooms. They walked on bare boards, which stank of urine, the wood having absorbed it for years and suggesting that toileting was not a regular feature of their lives, and nor were incontinence pads.

There were no curtains and only the minimum of furniture. I've no idea what the relatives of these people were paying, but I'm sure they could not have visited or they would have made sure changes were made to the care of these elderly people. It was truly awful and so very sad to see how neglected they were, yet I felt powerless to change anything. There were no checks and inspections of homes in the seventies.

I didn't last long in this job. Not only did I find some of its practices distressing, but I really didn't like Mrs P, the owner, who was imperious and arrogant.

Finishing work one morning, I went to the shops before going home. When I arrived at Lemsford Road, I found a note from Dany waiting for me on the stairs. It was headed 'BEWARE!!!'

Craig is in your room. The time is 11.15am. He found Louise with Mick last night in Mick's room. You can imagine the hustle that went on. Craig chasing Mick up the road, frying pan in hand. He clouted Louise. Mick stayed clear – going up the street like a flash of thunder.

Anyway, Jan, Louise stayed in your room last night, and Craig crashed out at Tom's. BUT he returned, up the drainpipe to your room. No Louise. She was up with Mick again. Craig took 10 moggies and passed out for a few hours in your room, by which time the cowards retreated very, very quietly.

Craig came down to us at 8.30 this morning, then went upstairs to Mick's, but the door was locked. Craig tried to kick the door in. I stopped him, brought him downstairs and convinced him they'd gone. Then he went back to your room and crashed. Oh yeah!

See you later.

It summed up the craziness of life in Lemsford Road, but made me laugh then… and still makes me laugh now. We took it all in our stride and just carried on living our bohemian existence, with the kaftans, dope, music and (mostly) love and peace, man.

I loved the hippie lifestyle and the relatively easy money from stripping and modelling, but woke up one morning thinking that I really couldn't form a lifetime's career on taking my clothes off in one place or another, whether it was an artist's studio or a working men's club. And I wasn't getting any younger. Those huge boobs would start drooping soon.

I thought about Rose and how she had managed a higher education when much older than your average student, and I was envious of that. I knew that if I followed suit, I wanted an education that would lead to a job. Something as vague as Philosophy, Humanities or Linguistics wouldn't do – even if I knew what they were.

I remembered when Rose had been so ill in hospital with asthma, and how impressed I had been with the ministrations of the physiotherapists in particular. However, when I looked into getting a qualification, I found that there was a minimum height requirement and, being under five foot, I didn't meet it.

What else could I study? There must be other degrees that would lead to a proper occupation.

I acquired a book on further education and careers in the caring professions and found that the local polytechnic at Hatfield did a four-year degree course in Applied Social Sciences, which was combined with a Certificate and Qualification in Social Work.

Now, what I knew about the role of the social worker could be written on the back of a very small stamp, but the course clearly met my wishes: higher education leading to a degree, which also provided a practical professional qualification… and it allowed one to work with people. Social work wasn't the reviled profession it is these days. People didn't sneer when the words 'social worker' were mentioned, although they might look vaguely bored.

I assumed that the entry requirements would be the same as those Rose had to meet for her degree course. Three GCE 'A' Levels would be needed – which I didn't have. Hell, I didn't even have 'O' Levels. Only some Pitman certificates in shorthand, typing and book-keeping. I would need to take this one step at a time and get some 'O' Levels. It might take a while, but if I could be patient, I felt positive that I could make it. This was to be a long-term plan.

I made an appointment to see the principal of the local further education college. When I met him I believed that I would have to take 'O' Levels before going on to 'A' Levels. However, he surprised me by suggesting that I just went for the 'A' Levels.

I knew that three of these were the usual requirement for entry into a degree course, so we agreed that I would go for all three in one year. He pointed out that this would be demanding, but I was in a hurry. A long-term plan was all very well, but I wanted to get going, and any way that I could cut corners to achieve a new career was to be considered. I decided on English, Sociology and History.

I found out that I would not be able to sign on for the dole when I was studying for 'A' Levels, as I would not be 'available for work'. I applied for a grant but was only provided with a discretionary grant of £75 per term. Now, even in 1976 this amount of money was not enough to live on, so it was clear that I would have to continue with my stripping and modelling gigs for the moment.

Starting classes that autumn, I found that all the other students were much younger than me. In spite of that, I found a group of rather sweet young people who asked me to go for coffee with them on a regular basis. I never disclosed my 'other life' to them or the lecturers, so it was all a bit odd really, being a student by day and a stripper by night.

I really did try to get to all the classes but was often too tired to make it, having been out working until the small hours. I had to drop the History, but persevered with the English, which I loved. Having always been an avid reader, I found that the required books were stimulating, and I liked analysing the literature.

Sociology was more of a challenge. It was difficult to get my head around this way of looking at the world, but once I got it, then I really got it and was fascinated by the study of society and understanding human social activity.

Meanwhile, I was offered a three-day gig in Southampton with a couple: Dave, a comedian and MC, and Khadine, his wife and a stripper. We would be performing at three different venues in the area, and the booker had included payment for staying in a hotel for the duration. However, Dave suggested to me that we pocket this extra money and sleep in their camper van, instead. It sounded good to me. I didn't mind roughing it for a few days.

The camper van was well equipped with a little cooker and sink, but it only had one double bed so I found myself sleeping in a hammock slung between the two sides of the van. It was actually surprisingly comfortable.

The only real downside was keeping clean. I found the local swimming pool for a shower and at one point I had a complete wash down and hair wash in the ladies' toilet of one of the venues. Fortunately, I was able to do this during the day before any staff or punters were around, although a couple of waitresses did turn up when I was drying my hair under the hand dryer. They gave me an odd look but I brazened it out. It was worth the inconvenience for the extra dosh.

Another three-day gig came in for me for the New Year celebrations. This time I would be on my own, and the job was in Glasgow. Now, I had heard awful stories about the gigs in Glasgow – a tough crowd, they said. So I was a little nervous. I was staying in the same hotel that I would be performing in, and was anxious about bumping into punters at breakfast. Consequently, I barely left my room for three days except to go to work.

I used room service for all meals. Not a happy time. I felt so lonely in a strange place over the holiday period. In fact, the audience were fine, if a little rowdy, but I was glad to go home, albeit with the sizable fee tucked into my bra for safety on the train journey.

It had been terribly cold in Glasgow but back in London the weather was quite mild. I resumed my 'A' Level studies and submitted an application for the Hatfield Polytechnic degree course I'd noted earlier.

The interview at Hatfield Poly was quite intensive and involved writing a short autobiography, which was submitted with the application. I talked about my working class origins, my avid reading habit and my beliefs in compassion, justice and equality, but left out any reference to sexuality or taking my clothes off for a living.

The interviews were held in March 1977 at the Poly's Hatfield site, where I was seen individually by four tutors. They represented various aspects of the course and their questions related to each area of expertise. I was very nervous, but reasonably articulate and mostly gave well-thought-out answers, although I may have been a little naïve on some social issues that came up.

Although this four-year programme would mostly attract school leavers, albeit with a minimum entrance age of nineteen, it was made clear that the course was also interested in taking on mature students who had life experience to offer and who might be better placed to empathise with clients.

I received a letter in the post less than a week later telling me that I had been accepted onto the course. The offer was not dependent on 'A' Level results, so the pressure to get good results was off. I decided to take the GCE exams anyway.

Terrified and excited in equal measure, I began to plan for my future. I wasn't sure that I would be able to keep up with degree-level study, or how I would manage financially. After experiencing the demands of trying to combine studying and stripping, I knew that this mix did not work. Local authorities still gave student grants then, so I applied for one, but carried on working my socks (and knickers) off until I started at the Poly.

The Sisterhood

The mid to late seventies were a time of exploration for me, together with a growing awareness of political issues. I got involved with issues which were important. There was Rock Against Racism – marches and concerts set up to challenge racism through music. Gay Pride marches, where there were very few women until much later, saw me stomping along in rain and sunshine. Later on, I was drawn to Reclaim the Night, a feminist movement challenging male violence. This last one had obvious importance for me.

I had become interested in the Women's Liberation Movement, although didn't think that I could join, as bra burning was not an option for me, being a 36D cup. I needed my support. I hadn't realised that the well-publicised cremation of underwear was meant to be symbolic rather than actual. It was intended to suggest a protest against the oppressors of women.

I was reading about the issues of equal pay, sex discrimination and domestic violence, having acquired a copy of Erin Pizzey's book

Scream Quietly or the Neighbours Will Hear. The themes being discussed gave me food for thought, and around 1974 I found a magazine entitled *Spare Rib*. I began buying it regularly – or whenever I saw a copy in the newsagent, as not every shop would agree to stock it.

Many of the articles resonated with me. One recurring topic suggested that rape was not about sex but more to do with violence, power and control against women. Thinking about how I had felt as a victim of rape, it made a lot of sense.

I was not in accord, though, with all the articles. I remember one that suggested sex workers (and strippers, who were included rather erroneously under this heading) were undermining the women's movement.

There was no acknowledgement that many sex workers and, indeed, strippers may not have any other means of earning a living so were promoting their independence of men by having their own income. Of course, the articles were invariably written by middle class young women who would have no concept of what it was like to be poor, either financially or in terms of education and employment opportunities.

Scattered throughout the magazine were advertisements, mostly for women's discos, benefits, socialist journals and so on. However, there was also an advert for Sappho, a lesbian organisation named, of course, after the ancient Greek poetess.

Sappho had its own newsletter, edited by Jackie Forster, who I later discovered was a flamboyant lesbian actress, chock full of charisma and brio. Taking out a subscription I found that the newsletter was a rough mimeograph (this was before photocopiers were widely available) printed on cheap paper and stapled together. Unlike KENRIC, there were no rules about married women having to inform their husbands and it had a tendency towards the saucy. I loved it.

Sappho also held monthly meetings at The Chepstow pub in Notting Hill. They had speakers such as Anna Raeburn, Mikki Doyle from the *Morning Star* and author Maureen Duffy, who read her poetry.

Going along to my first meeting at The Chepstow, I felt shy and nervous as I made my way through the pub and upstairs to the meeting room. As I went in, I was pounced upon by Jackie Forster who exclaimed, "You're new, aren't you? I don't remember seeing you before. Do you know anyone here, darling?"

I had to say that I did not know anyone, and Jackie took me over to three women sitting at one of the tables, saying, "This lovely is new. Take care of her, will you?" And they did. I was immediately made to feel welcome, bought a drink and chatted to these new friends, who were as warm and hospitable as Jackie herself. I found out that everyone adored her, and that she was central to the whole organisation.

I started going to Sappho regularly, although it was a bit of a trek from St Albans, and met a nice young woman, Terri, who was just coming out. I offered to take her to The Gateways, off the King's Road, where I had continued going now and then over the years. It was an institution by then, made famous by featuring in the film *The Killing of Sister George*, and a pilgrimage for any aspiring lesbian.

I didn't really have any sexual ambitions towards Terri but one thing led to another and we found ourselves in bed eventually. She was sweet but it was never going to be a grand passion for me. We saw each other for a while and then it faded away into the occasional phone call. Still, it was nice to have soft, warm, smooth flesh to snuggle with for a while, although she was a bit too slim for my tastes.

Anyway, there was a lot going on for me, what with 'A' Levels, stripping, modelling and a degree course coming up. I didn't have the time or inclination for a full-blown affair. Although it was something that I still yearned for, this fantasy would have to wait a while.

In April, my latest flatmate left. She had finished her foundation course at the art college and was moving on to a degree course. Rose returned to collect a few last items she had left in the house. We managed to have a civil conversation and it emerged that she was now living and working in France with her Giselle. I felt oddly removed from her. Our time together already seemed like a soap opera; the passion and drama that we'd shared had become the stuff of dreams (or nightmares).

I had been occasionally seeing Peter, one of the regular visitors to the house. He was funny and easy-going, although hopeless in bed. Still, it was a body to cuddle with and there's no such thing as a free lunch, or free cuddle.

As well as enjoying the dope smoking, Peter was also a heavy drinker. We would go out to the pub, where he would insist that I kept up with his rate of drinking. Since he was a big lad, his capacity was far greater than mine, and I often found myself so drunk that I could barely walk home.

Peter asked if he could move into the now vacated room and I agreed. The sexual relationship died a death quite soon afterwards, which was actually quite a relief. Nice guy, but we had nothing in common apart from smoking dope. Actually, I think that he only initiated a sexual relationship with me because he wanted to move into Lemsford Road. Ho hum. The benefits of hindsight, eh?

In June I received the result of my 'A' Levels. I passed, but only just. I had dropped History, but it was still really over ambitious to try to take two in one year, especially while working such odd hours.

Taking all those drugs probably didn't help, either.

6

Educating Janet

In September 1978 I had a gig booked at a hotel on the outskirts of East London. I was reliably informed by the MC that it was for the local police... and the local villains. I wasn't really surprised. Corruption in police forces was a hot topic at that time. In fact, soon after this, it was acknowledged by the Home Office that there was widespread dishonesty within the London police services. Operation Countryman, an investigating unit, was set up in the late seventies. It resulted in police officers, at every level, being checked out and some were prosecuted.

Most punters were aware of the 'no touch' etiquette and, while they might make bawdy jokes about the girls, would adhere to the protocol. The audience of this gig, though, was not playing by the usual rules. This particular stag party was rowdy and heavy-drinking from the start.

There was no stage for the girls to perform on. Instead the tables had been set out around a dancefloor. When I was half way through my first spot, and dancing quite close to the tables, I found myself grabbed and pulled into a crowd of baying men who proceeded to grope me in any place they could reach.

I was really frightened and it raised all sorts of unpleasant memories for me. I tried slapping them, not too hard, but giving a message that this was not acceptable. What I really wanted to do was to scream "Get me out of here!", but that would have been unprofessional, and might have resulted in the agent hearing about it and not giving me more work.

I think that one of the men must have sensed my terror

under the fixed smile, because he called time on the groping, saying, "That's enough now, boys."

They let me go and I carried on with my act, but was very careful not to stray onto the edge of the dancefloor again.

It was shortly after this gig that I decided enough was enough, and informed my various agents that I was no longer available for stripping or modelling. It would make a huge difference to my income but I had been so freaked out by that last experience that I just couldn't face another roomful of drunken, feral men.

In any case, I was due to enrol at the Poly in October and would be starting my studies, so working into the early hours would not fit into my anticipated regime.

I felt sick with nerves on enrolment day. I tried to look cool as I entered the portals of the Poly, taking stock of the organised chaos around me. Not only were there umpteen forms to fill in, but there was also a sort of market place where students were being encouraged to join all sorts of societies. There was the Christian Society, the Film-making, Philosophy, Gay (hmm… might be interested in that), Drama, Rugby (I don't think so, thank you), Photography Societies…

It was all a bit overwhelming.

I started attending lectures shortly afterwards, finding myself in a group of about forty people. Most of these were young women, around nineteen or twenty years old, although there were a couple of men in that age group. There were about six mature students, from a variety of backgrounds – teaching, nursing, a housewife – but no other strippers (as far as I know).

The syllabus consisted of a number of subjects, including Economics, Social History, Social Policy, Politics, Law, Psychology, Society and Culture, and Sociology. Some of these I found interesting and engaging but others (particularly Economics) were a mystery and I really struggled.

I was commuting to and from the college by bus. It wasn't a long journey but the buses were unpredictable. I had met a young woman, Corinne, on the course, who had to pass my road every morning. She was only nineteen but was funny and friendly. She said she could give me a lift on her motorbike so we fell into a routine. It was good for me, as it meant that I had to be ready to leave by quarter past eight every morning. Left to my own devices, I would have probably just turned over and gone back to sleep when the alarm woke me.

I was glad of her friendship, as cliques had started to form among the freshers. As a mature student I found that the others in my age group were rather too staid and sensible. I preferred the company of the younger participants, but found that they did not always want to engage with an oldie like me, being as I was now thirty years old.

There was a particular group of young women that I felt attracted to. These were clearly bright, articulate, vocal girls who always seemed to have interesting conversations about the course content and life generally. I was very much on the periphery, but when I saw one of them in the students' union bar reading *The Female Eunuch* by Germaine Greer, I sat down next to her, asking what she thought of it. She blanked me, more or less. That was that, then. I couldn't think of another way to sidle my way into this clique.

Meanwhile, back at home, I was trying to study, writing essays and seminars. I was still using amphetamines and downers, and smoking spliffs, but was managing to get the work done on time. The biggest problem was Phil's music, which he played very loudly in their sitting room, immediately below my room. I had to ask him to keep it down from time to time. My friendship with Dany was unchanged, although I had less time to spend with her. I think we both missed the constant contact we'd had for the past few years.

We spent that Christmas together as usual. The children came upstairs to wake me and Debbie, who was staying with me for the holiday, at around eight o'clock on Christmas morning. They presented us with stone cold cups of tea and explained that they were not allowed to open their presents until we came downstairs.

Dany and I cooked lunch, having a couple of capons. Unfortunately, we had forgotten to take the plastic bag of innards out, until the birds had been in the oven for twenty minutes or so. Well, we were stoned. We managed to retrieve the situation before the bags melted.

We had the dishing up down to a fine art. We would set all the plates out on the table, Dany would then carve and put portions of capon on each plate, while I took over the veg, dolloping a spoonful on each plate: peas, peas, peas. Then carrots, carrots, carrots. And so on. When we sat down for lunch, there was quite a crowd of us. As well as Dany, Phil and the children, there was me and Debbie, Simon, Tom and Bob, plus one or two others who just dropped in.

Many years later, Dany wrote:

It seems the most memorable times of all centred on Christmas…
I don't know why, but our place was like a magnet. It attracted
people.

When others head off home to be with family, the majority
of people we knew came to our place.

It was great! Hard work, but great fun. I would like to say
that we all shared the work. There would be roughly twelve to
fifteen people for dinner, but generally only two of us doing the
cooking: me and Jan. We would be in the kitchen preparing, and
smoking the evil weed, but we would be laughing!

These Christmases were the best I'd ever had. I loved them from start to finish. I loved the kids opening their presents; I loved the first joint of the day with a cup of tea and a mince pie; I loved helping Dany to cook the lunch; I loved the rest of the day spent smoking, watching TV and listening to music. And Dany would tell me, "You *are* part of my family, Jan." I loved that, too.

In January 1979, all the tenants in the house received a letter from our landlord. He wanted to sell the property, and was giving us a year's notice to find alternative accommodation. It wasn't a surprise. We'd known for some time that this would be on the cards eventually, but still the thought of leaving this beautiful house where so much of my adult life had been played out was heart wrenching. Dany and I had become used to the luxury of having our best friend just a staircase away. I had wanted it to go on forever.

On the plus side, at least there was no rush to leave, although we were aware of how quickly a year would pass. Dany and Phil put their names down for a council house, and I approached the college to see if they could help me with accommodation.

I found the end-of-year exams a challenge. I had such limited experience of sitting real exams that I didn't know there was a method to getting through them, for example: answer your best question first; attempt all questions if time is running out; and make notes or bullet points. I only found this out later when the mature students were offered a seminar on 'Returning to Study'. A bit late, seeing as it was in my second year.

Probably as a result of this, I failed three subjects but was offered an opportunity to re-sit them. Determined to get through to the second year, I applied myself to studying and managed to pass two and, although I never did pass Economics, was allowed to continue the course.

At the end of that first year, we had to complete a residential placement of six weeks. I fancied being in Brighton, partly because of its reputation as a lesbian and gay Mecca, and partly just because I thought it would be fun to be by the seaside in the summer.

So I packed my bucket and spade and set off…

A Mature-ish Student

I had found a placement at a home for single mothers. Although social attitudes to unwed mothers had relaxed over the past decade, there was still a stigma attached to having a baby outside of marriage.

This particular home was owned by the Church of England, and was managed by a warden and her assistant who both lived on the premises. It housed about ten young women in various stages of pregnancy until they had their baby.

They had all been rejected by their families, and all had elected to keep their babies, rather than terminate their pregnancy or give up the children for adoption. After the birth, they would return to the home, pending an offer of a council flat. This was usually within six months.

The atmosphere in the home was fairly relaxed. No men were allowed in the girls' rooms (although this was bolting the stable door…), and the warden had some odd ideas about how to treat staff.

I would be living in for the duration of six weeks, and found that my ground floor room had nails banged into the window frame which prevented me from opening the window more than three inches, presumably to stop me having male company.

She was also unhappy about me appearing outside of my room in a dressing gown, even on my day off. She felt that it would give the girls the impression that it was alright to slob about. And what's wrong with that, eh? I'm all for a bit of slobbing, but there you go.

Her assistant, Margaret, was a young woman who was a right goody two-shoes. A regular churchgoer who was never seen outside her room in her night clothes, it became clear that she was held up as a role model for both the residents and myself. She was alright, I suppose, just awfully decent, emanating a glow that could only come from leading a life free from sin or naughtiness.

Part of my role was to clean the communal areas every week. It didn't much resemble social work, but the warden justified it by suggesting it showed the girls that cleaning should be done regularly and thoroughly. (My work was inspected by the warden.)

I suggested to the warden that it might be useful for the residents to learn how to do some basic cooking, ready for when they took up their new life in their own flat. She agreed, but vetoed my suggestion of showing them how to cook a shepherd's pie, one of my signature dishes.

"I would rather you demonstrated how to bake bread," she said.

"Well," I hesitated, "I've never done that. Can't I show them something I know how to cook?"

"No. Baking bread is a very useful thing to know how to do. You can follow a recipe with them. That will also be a useful thing for them to learn."

So a date was set and the girls and I assembled around the table in the kitchen. I explained that I would be following a recipe and that they could help me with this. Although I'd encouraged them to call me 'Janet', they had problems with this and always addressed me as 'Miss'.

"Miss… can I sit down, cos me back's killing me?" asked Delia, eight months gone.

"No problem, Delia. You get yourself comfy. Right, let's get going. So when we're cooking, what's the first thing we do?"

"Get out all the bits."

"Find the recipe."

"Wash our hands."

"Yes, yes and definitely yes. And can you put your cigarettes out, please."

"Can I smoke if I sit over the other side of the table?" asked Delia.

"No. Sorry. You can't smoke in the kitchen while we're cooking. And, anyway, it's bad for the baby."

"I've told her that," said Susan, her best friend, holding her newborn to her ample chest. "She reckons that the baby will be alright because she only smokes roll-ups."

"Yeah. Cos roll-ups keep going out, so you smoke less. It's obvious, innit?" said Delia. "Anyway, you smoke, don't you, Miss?"

"But she's not pregnant, you twit," Shona interrupted.

"Have you had a baby, Miss?"

"No. I've managed to avoid that. And do you know how I've avoided it? I've used contraception." (OK – I was a bit economical with the truth, but it was in a good cause.) "Do you know what that is?"

"Yeah. It's rubber johnnies, innit."

"Well, yes. But there are other things you can use to stop you getting pregnant."

The cooking session quickly turned into a health education session, but I wasn't too bothered as it seemed to me that this was at least as important as knowing how to cook, and their knowledge of contraception was clearly sparse.

Eventually, I returned to the bread baking and we got the flour, yeast, oil, salt and water measured. Following the recipe seemed straightforward and we proceeded to the point where the dough was left to prove. Time for a fag and coffee break, so we went into the garden for an hour or so, still talking about coils, Dutch caps, the pill and what a bloke might do when he said, "I'll be careful."

I liked the girls. On the whole they were bright and chatty, although one or two were quieter and needed to be drawn out. And there were a couple who were not the sharpest knives in the box.

They would ask lots of questions about my private life and while I answered honestly whenever possible, there were some areas that remained private. I was new to all this and so often had to think on my feet as to which questions could be responded to and which ones had to be side-stepped.

It was time to put the bread into the hot oven. We had time for another fag break before taking it out and tapping the base to see if it sounded hollow, and therefore cooked.

However, the loaf that came out of the oven felt as heavy and solid as a brick, and definitely not edible. The girls were much amused by this.

"Look," I said chucking it into the bin, "if you want bread, I suggest you go to Sainsbury's and buy some."

Later, the warden asked the residents how the cookery session had gone. They were great; all agreed that it had been delicious and that they were now confident of being able to put what they had learnt into practice. I quietly rescued the discarded loaf, just in case it was discovered, and took it into town to dispose of in a public waste bin. Shame, really. If I'd had a few hundred of them, I could have built a shed.

When the placement ended, I stayed on for a while in Brighton. I'd bumped into Craig (the proverbial bad penny) who was living there, and had met his new girlfriend, Amy. We came to an arrangement that I could stay with Amy for a nominal rent. It worked out very well, and I had a lovely summer getting to know The Lanes, the flea market, the pier and the stony beach.

I went back home to St Albans a few weeks before the new academic year started. I'd become quite friendly with Sandra and Patrick, the young couple who were part of the St Albans dope-smoking crowd. They had brought a friend of theirs, Rob, over a couple of times. He had a well-trimmed beard, was short, wiry, blonde and about my age. Sandra and Patrick relayed to me messages of the 'My friend fancies you' variety.

Well, he was attractive, working and single, so why not? We started seeing each other and I found him to be a considerate lover. He was articulate and sensitive. Unfortunately, he was also a man. Not his fault, of course, but what I yearned for was a connection with a woman. Still, any port in a storm, eh? This was the first real relationship I'd had since Rose, and it was nice to be a proper girlfriend again, doing things that couples did. We had meals out or I cooked for him. We went to the cinema or to hear bands. We held hands and cuddled on the sofa. Ordinary things, but kind of stabilising.

His family was having a party for some notable event. Rob asked me to join him, as it would be a good opportunity for me to meet them. We arrived in good time, although most of the other guests had already arrived. He ushered me through to the sitting room where most of the family sat.

Before I could shake hands with anyone, his sister's Jack Russell dog attached itself to my leg and started to enthusiastically hump it. The wretched thing even clung on when I shook my leg about. In the end, someone forcibly removed my new best friend, and I was able to recover my composure.

Rob usually came over to me on Friday evening and left on Sunday evening. Occasionally we would spend the same amount of time at his place; he lived with his parents, but they were relaxed about us sleeping together there.

I think that they were hopeful that he would settle down with me. I liked them, and it was clear they liked me. It emerged that Rob's grandfather was Jewish so there were no anti-Semitic issues with them as there had been with Tony's family.

When he told me that he loved me, I reciprocated, but truthfully my heart wasn't in it. I suppose I thought, rather unfairly, *It'll do*. If I couldn't have what I really wanted, this would be the next best thing. He knew that I had slept with women and, like so many heterosexual men, found it an exciting fantasy. So that was not a problem, either.

The college had found me accommodation in student halls, but had evidently taken my mature student status into consideration because they offered me a small flat in what used to be a resident tutor's space. It was contained within a huge Victorian house and consisted of a bed-sitting room with a separate kitchen and bathroom, and overlooked some rather lovely gardens. It was small, but perfect for me. The flat was particularly handy for the college, being only ten minutes' walk away.

That year the Social Sciences course had moved to the Balls Park site in Hertford. The main building was a beautiful mansion house built in 1640. The campus was situated in over a hundred acres of parkland. It had been an educational establishment since 1947, and was certainly more attractive than the redbrick functionality of Hatfield Poly's main site.

It was hard to leave Lemsford Road in St Albans. Dany and

I shed a few tears and promises were made to keep in touch. I had only a few possessions to move, as my flat had been let as furnished, so Rob helped me to shift the black bin bags and cardboard boxes containing my life so far. The college had provided the basic furniture of bed, dining table, fridge and so on.

Once he left, I set about making the place mine: putting up pictures and lacy shawls on the walls; arranging my pots, pans and crockery in the kitchen; a mattress on the floor was covered with an oriental throw and cushions piled upon it, so that it formed a kind of sofa. My tiny TV went in one corner, and my record/cassette player in the other corner. And when I'd finished, yes, it looked like home.

Lectures started shortly after this. The syllabus had some new areas for study, such as Psychodynamics and Statistics, but the dreaded Economics had been removed.

The students who had been in halls for their first year were now all living outside of the college in rented accommodation, with many house sharing.

Corinne was living with her boyfriend and the girls in the clique were all sharing houses. They seemed to be as unreachable as ever.

My birthday is in October, and I happened to mention this to Corinne a week or so before the event. When she asked me what my plans were, I explained that my boyfriend would be coming over at the weekend after my actual birthday, so we would go out then.

I was surprised when, a few days later, one of the clique said to me, "Corinne says it's your birthday on Tuesday. Why don't you come over to ours for a birthday celebration?"

I was a bit wary, but turned up at their house as arranged. I was amazed when they pulled out all the stops, not only cooking a lovely meal, served with wine, but also did a cake complete with candles. This group of girls actually seemed to like me. I must have completely misread the signs.

After that evening, I was definitely in with the in-crowd. And

I was right; they were bright, funny, challenging and articulate. It proved to be something of a watershed for me. I still struggled with some subjects but discovered that I wasn't the only one.

What I also found out, though, was that by discussing a particular issue around the refectory table with my new friends, it would gradually make sense. I began to steam ahead in my understanding and arguments in essays and seminars. Suddenly, I loved being in a learning environment, soaking up unfamiliar information like a sponge. It was stimulating and stopped being a chore, something to get through for the piece of paper at the end.

They were a group of eight who were living in two shared houses near to Hertford. Inevitably, I bonded more with some than with others. My particular friends were Corinne, Sue W and Sue C, Naomi and Katherine. These last two were the dope smokers in the group, and the three of us started to spend more and more time together.

They were both very young, only twenty years old, and I was impressed by how mature they seemed compared to my own twenty-year-old self.

Katherine was from Northern Ireland and had been brought up on a farm. She was relaxed about the Troubles, saying, "Well, you hear of something happening down the road but it never seems to affect our lives particularly." She was fun, although could be a bit over-sensitive and rather prickly if roused.

Naomi was the product of a very middle class home, and had attended a Girls' Public Day School Trust fee-paying school until she was sixteen, when she moved to a college of further education. She had that easy confidence I had noted in other middle class girls. She was clever, laid back and in no doubt of her abilities or self-worth.

She had blonde highlights in her hair and dressed like Annie Hall, wearing jeans with a dark waistcoat over a man's shirt. Naomi seemed cool and sophisticated way beyond her tender years.

One evening I invited Katherine and Naomi over for a

meal. After dinner, we rolled a joint or two and talked about our lives. The dope loosened our tongues and I told them that I was bisexual, and Naomi said that she'd had a one-night stand with a woman. She said she wondered what might have happened if she had let the tentative experience continue.

She was lying on the makeshift sofa with her head in my lap when she told us about how she had to look after her mother following her parents' messy divorce. I was touched by her youth and vulnerability, which was just visible beneath the veneer of poise, and found myself wanting to stroke her hair. I wanted to kiss her.

I resisted, of course, but found myself thinking about her more and more over the next few weeks. I knew that I was going to have to talk to her about my attraction, but just couldn't find the right opportunity or the bravery to do it.

Then there was a student party we both went to. I was with Rob at the party; I got drunk and knew it was now or never. I found us a quiet corner in the kitchen and just said it to her: "I'm very attracted to you."

She didn't scream or back off. She just said, "I don't think it's a very good idea for us to get involved, what with being on the same course for the next three years."

She was so grown up, so reasonable. I felt like a lovesick adolescent. I wanted the floor to open up and swallow me, but took a deep breath and said, "Right. Of course, you're right. But I had to say it, you know, because I've been thinking about you so much. Can we still be friends?"

I was trying to be adult and retrieve my dignity. Not easy when you've drunk around a litre of cider. I may have slurred a bit.

"Of course we can be friends," she said. "I would hope that we're both able to go on getting to know each other better because I do like you and want you as a friend."

I went off to find Rob and told him that I wanted to go home because I wasn't feeling too good.

And that was that. Once I'd sobered up, I was glad that I had come clean with her. I told myself that, having confessed all to her, it took the energy out of my longings, and that I could now get on with life.

Rob went back home, as usual, on Sunday evening. I had not told him of my crush on Naomi, or that I had propositioned her. I just wanted it to go away. So I was surprised to find her knocking on my door on Monday, after lectures for the day had finished.

"Oh, hello. Come in. Do you want a cup of coffee?" I said, startled and flustered, but trying to appear blasé.

She came in and sat on the bed. "I've been thinking about what you said on Saturday. I was a bit taken aback and had to think on my feet."

"Yes. Well. I'm sorry about that. I was very drunk, you know, and it just came out. I didn't mean to upset you…"

"No, no. I'm not, wasn't, upset. It's not that. It's, well, I've had a chance to think about it, and I've changed my mind."

We had one of those conversations that should have thought bubbles over our heads. What came out of our mouths was reason, objectivity and logic, with a plan that included being non-exclusive and remaining friends, whatever.

What was in the invisible thought bubbles was: Let's make love!

And an hour or so later, that's what we did.

Falling in Love again

Naomi was passionate and adventurous in the bedroom, a quick and enthusiastic learner who soon became an accomplished lover. We would spend hours and hours making love, then sleeping, missing lectures, before making love again, pausing only for refreshments to keep our strength up.

We talked a lot, too, and I found that she was sensitive, with an insight into herself far beyond her years. We told each other many, many secrets in those first few weeks. We wanted to be together as much as we could manage to discover each other's bodies and minds.

I felt as if the ground had been whipped away from beneath my feet, and I was floating on a cloud of physical desire and mental stimulation. Everything was heightened. All sensation was intense. I was in love. And, joy of joys, it happened for her, too. We quickly became almost inseparable.

I saw Naomi most days during the week, while at weekends I was still seeing Rob. I don't know how I found the energy, but that's love/lust for you. I had to tell him, eventually, of course. Oddly, it did not end my relationship with him. It probably helped that we had a few threesomes.

The thing with threesomes is that they never really live up to expectations. There is always someone who is left out, or has to go to the toilet, giving the other two an opportunity to talk about them, or just finish having sex, without the third person in the room.

Sometimes at weekends we would all go out together to see a band or to the cinema. Or, as Rob had a car, we'd go over to see Dany and Phil at Lemsford Road. It was always good to spend some time with Dany, and we had an ability to pick up where we'd left off. It was always as if I'd last seen her yesterday, instead of several weeks ago.

I'd stopped using speed and downers by now. There was no withdrawal period, no detox or rehab. I just stopped. Not for any moral or health reason, it has to be said, but just because I couldn't afford it anymore. I still smoked dope, but much less than I used to. Again, this was more due to finances than anything else, although I'd woken up to the fact that I couldn't study and be constantly stoned.

My second-year placement was at Blackfriars Settlement, a community centre in Southwark. I was, as usual, very nervous about getting in there and having an interview. It was a very popular placement for students and competition for placements was high.

The organisation was originally established as the Women's University Settlement in 1887 and aimed to assist the poor women of the area. In 1961 it changed its name to Blackfriars Settlement, as both an acknowledgement of men's involvement and as an attempt to include the local community in its work.

I was accepted and placed in the Welfare Rights Unit, which gave advice to local people on a range of issues, such as housing, employment, problems with debt, benefits and so on.

I took to the work like a duck to water. I found that I had an ability to talk to people of all ages, classes and backgrounds, taking a mass of information from them and breaking it down into manageable and comprehensible bite-size pieces.

Not only that, but I was rather successful at sorting out the problems they had. I had a brilliant supervisor there who would let me get on with the work, knowing that I would refer to him if I was unsure of what to do or who to contact. He even let me loose, with another student, with a 'Mobile Advice Unit' (a clapped-out van), which we took onto the Rockingham Estate, a notorious housing estate at Elephant and Castle where the police patrolled in pairs.

My sister, Debbie, lived in Southwark at that time. Her married MP lover had installed her in a basement flat in one of his many properties. She, being a whizz at all things DIY, had built a spare room at the end of her garden, practically single-handed, from the foundations to the roof.

It had built-in furniture of bed, drawers, shelves and wardrobe, as well as a tiny sink with running water and a Baby Belling cooker, and was more or less self-contained, apart from a bathroom, which was housed in Debbie's flat. While I was at the full-time placement in Blackfriars, I stayed here. It was cosy and private, and I felt that I was living in a doll's house. And it was good to be able to spend some quality time with my sister.

The Hippy

The Student

Falling in love again - with Naomi

The Graduate

Her flat was just around the corner from Morley College, an adult education centre. I had worked there in the past as a life model, so checked out whether they could use me again. It turned out that they did want a model for two evening classes, and so I went back to my old occupation of taking my clothes off for a living. Surviving on a grant, it was a useful (and almost respectable) means of extra income.

The placement came to an end without any problems and I sat the end-of-year exams, doing much better this time around, with good marks and no fails.

I spent the summer of 1979 working as a temp for Blue Arrow. My typing speeds were still good, and I had no problems with getting jobs.

The accommodation provided by the college came to an end, as students were only allowed one year in halls. I looked around for a flat share and found one in a modern flat in Ware.

I would be sharing with Elaine, who had removed all of her eyebrows then drawn them back on again with pencil. The result was that she looked permanently surprised. My other flatmate was a young Dutch woman, who was friendly, but had her own social circle so didn't mix much. Elaine, on the other hand, turned out to be a bit of a nightmare – bossy, mouthy and brash. I spent a lot of time in my room, at Rob's place or with Naomi.

The flat in Ware was very convenient, though, for my next placement. This was to be at the Ware Social Services office of Hertford Council. I wasn't too keen on completing a social services placement, as I felt that I had found my niche in the voluntary sector. Still, it had to be done, as it was a requirement of the Certificate and Qualification in Social Work (CQSW).

The work there was certainly very different from my previous placements. The clients tended to be middle class people dealing with issues of ageing and disability, and the settings were mostly rural. The work was interesting enough, particularly in view of the contrasts, but not very demanding.

Naomi had not been getting on with the girls she was sharing a house with, so had also found new accommodation. She would be sharing a house out in the countryside, in Waterford. It was a lovely village, with a shop, a pub and a church with beautiful windows by the William Morris factory, including one by Edward Burne-Jones. Her housemates were two young men: Phil, who had recently graduated as a surveyor and taken up work for Hertford Council – the council house had been part of the deal, as he had moved south from Nottingham; and Martin, a vicar's son, who had also recently graduated. I met them very soon after Naomi moved in and found that they were both nice guys.

My affairs with both Naomi and Rob continued with the usual rota of seeing Naomi during the week and Rob at the weekends.

I'd stopped taking the pill years ago, when I was seeing Rose. It seemed unnecessary if I wasn't having heterosexual sex. When I found myself having the occasional one-night stand or three-month affair with men, I had to think again about contraception. I'd had a Dutch cap in the past, but found it messy and inconvenient. I also knew that I was likely to get caught up in the moment and not bother to put it in. Consequently, I had opted to have a coil. The insertion of this was one of the most agonising things I have ever experienced. Apparently, it was far less painful for women who had had children. Still I managed to get through the procedure, although found that my periods were then so heavy that the bath water would turn red.

Rob had complained that, when we made love, he could feel the wire that was attached to the coil, and which protrudes just a little from the cervix. I'd gone back to the FPA clinic, and they had clipped the wire, making it shorter.

In October my periods stopped then started again. This happened several times. I wasn't worried to begin with. I thought that perhaps the stress of moving yet again, and starting a new academic year and a new placement, were taking their toll. However, by the third time of these stop/start periods, I went to see my doctor. He confirmed that, in spite of the coil, I was about ten weeks pregnant.

My first reaction was delight. I was in a steady relationship with Rob (although it was somewhat unconventional, what with my weekdays with Naomi) and I thought that he would be prepared to be a hands-on father. When I told him, he was shocked, but willing to continue our union to the extent of talking about marriage. We started making plans. His parents were pleased and supportive. I bought baby books and started to look around Mothercare. Even Naomi was pleased for me and said that she would help in any way she could.

Then, at thirteen weeks, I started to bleed again. Not just spotting but almost as heavy as a period. When I saw the doctor I was told that the bleeding was probably due to the coil still being in situ, and that continuing with the pregnancy could result in my own health being at risk, or that of the baby. It wasn't inevitable but the odds were fairly high.

It was decision time. And that decision would have to be made soon as the clock was ticking in relation to a safe termination. I talked about it with Rob, Naomi, Debbie and Dany. I just didn't know what to do for the best. It was one thing to have a healthy child, but giving birth to one with disabilities was a different matter. In the end, I asked for a termination and was quickly admitted to the local hospital. I was fourteen weeks pregnant by then.

I'd had to do a lot of thinking and decision-making in a very short time. I knew that I did not want to continue a relationship with Rob. He'd done nothing wrong, but was always going to be second best as I faced up to what I'd known all along. I wasn't bisexual really. My affairs with men were the result of loneliness and desperation.

I'd had to acknowledge that I was a genuine lesbian, a dyke, a sapphist of the first degree. And, with that, I was clear that this was the last relationship I'd ever have with a man. I felt as if a huge weight had been lifted from my shoulders and, in spite of the anxiety and sadness about the impending abortion, was happy to have an unambiguous vision of my future sexuality.

One morning while we were still in bed, a few days before I was due to go into hospital, I told Rob that it was over and that I had opted to have a termination. I sensed his relief that he would not be a daddy just yet, nor would he be required to walk up the aisle. It was all very amicable, and we parted as friends.

The operation was completed without any fuss, although the ward sister was brusque with me. When I complained of post-operative pain, she retorted, "Well, you should have thought of that." I was shocked and upset by her comment and told Naomi when she came to visit me later that day. She was so cross about it that she challenged the ward sister, telling her that I had wanted to continue with this pregnancy and had been very distressed at having to choose a termination. I was so proud of her, this young woman who had so much chutzpah that she could confront an older woman… who actually listened to her and apologised.

Mind you, Naomi also told me that she and Katherine had slept together while I was in hospital. I was not pleased. It reminded me of stories about men who played away from home while their partner was in labour.

On the other hand, Naomi was still so young, and it was inevitable that she would want to experiment and sow a few wild oats. I couldn't expect her to be one hundred per cent faithful, particularly as our relationship had been so irregular up to that point. So I did not make a fuss, but tried to be terribly avant-garde about it, willing myself not to feel betrayed by either of them.

Once I was discharged from hospital, I had a few days off to recover, then went back to my social services placement.

I'd been back at work for ten days and life went on as normal. I'd bought some fish for my supper, storing it in the office fridge until I went home. Then Naomi rang me and asked me to come over that evening, so I left my proposed supper there, as Naomi did not eat fish. I thought it would be alright until the following night.

I'd gone to Naomi's straight from work and, after having a meal together, we'd gone to bed and made love for the first time since my operation. Later, drifting into sleep, I became aware of a warm, sticky sensation around my bottom. Upon investigation, I discovered the bed soaked with blood.

I woke Naomi and told her to call an ambulance, while I tried to remember what to do in the event of a haemorrhage. I felt quite calm and lay on the floor with my legs raised against the bed, although the blood didn't stop seeping out of me.

The ambulance arrived and I was taken on a stretcher into the emergency vehicle. Then it was blue lights and sirens, which I was only vaguely aware of, starting to slip in and out of consciousness. I can't really remember what happened next, or the sequence of events, but I know that I had blood transfusions and was taken to the operating theatre and had a general anaesthetic. Later, I was told that the termination had been incomplete, and this was my body trying to tidy everything up.

I was in hospital for about a week then, on the day of my proposed discharge, I started to bleed heavily again, so that meant more blood transfusions and another operation.

A further week on, I was finally discharged home. My personal tutor had been in touch to tell me that I had missed so much of my placement that it would have to be cancelled and I would have to repeat the social services experience elsewhere, probably over the summer break. So I never returned to Ware Social Services.

I've often wondered what happened to the fish that I left in their refrigerator, and how long it was before someone threw it out.

Village People

Christmas 1979 was our last at Lemsford Road, as Dany and Phil had been allocated a council house nearby. The children were excited about the move, but Dany and Phil knew that it would be the end of an era. Debbie and I spent the festivities with them, as was tradition. And, as usual, we had a wonderful time, but we were all moving on and everything was changing. The photos I have of that Christmas, though, show me looking pale and wan, still recovering from being so ill.

I went home with Naomi to her mum's for New Year. Naomi had come out to her mother by now, and I'd met Eileen when she came to visit Naomi in the Waterford house. I loved Eileen from the moment I met her. She was gentle, gracious and warm. So different from my own mother. I envied Naomi that, although I had a far better relationship with my sister, Debbie, than Naomi had with her sister, Linda, who was about my age.

We'd stayed with Linda when we went to a feminist conference in Leeds, as she lived there. I found her to be a direct and no-nonsense person. She had also come out as a lesbian, although Naomi maintained that she was a 'political lesbian', in other words one who had made a conscious decision to sleep with women as a statement of her feminist beliefs. Whatever. I liked her.

Back home in my shared flat with Elaine, things became untenable, as my landlady decided that the only way to clean a kitchen floor was on one's hands and knees, and that she didn't want me to cook fish in the shared kitchen as it smelt too much and, what's more, she didn't like my friends, Naomi in particular. I think that she'd cottoned on to the fact that we were lesbians, and that was the real problem.

I started looking for another flat share. I'd been spending more and more time at her digs, so Naomi suggested that I move into the house in Waterford, although it meant that I would be in the box room. I didn't mind this at all. I got on well with Phil P and Martin, her housemates.

Being in the little room meant that I would be paying less rent than I had at Elaine's, so that was good, too, as I was in my usual financial mess. I was glad to be going into a situation where I would be living with Naomi. I enjoyed the domesticity of living with a lover and sharing those everyday moments of intimacy, jokes and affection.

I moved in February 1980. The house was at the end of a row of terraced houses. The front of the house had a view of fields, horses and a stream with swans, while the back of the house overlooked the manor house of Goldings Estate. This made for a beautiful setting, but it meant that the house was exposed to the elements on both front and back. It was freezing.

There was no central heating, and we kept warm with great difficulty. The back boiler, which supplied heat and hot water, was only put on if a bath was planned, as it was expensive to run. Otherwise, we had electric bar heaters. In the sitting room we would sometimes have two of these glowing at opposite ends of the room, and we could still have frost on the *inside* of the windows. Naomi and I would take a bath together, in six inches of water, keeping our thermal vests on until the very last minute, when they would be whipped off for a quick splash.

The village was about two miles from Hertford Station, and there was a bus to Waterford that ran once each hour. This service stopped at around six in the evening, so getting home from college or a night out could be a bit of a problem. It meant walking home (which was decidedly scary in the dark, going past woods and things that go bump in the night), riding my bike or persuading Phil P to come and collect me and/or Naomi in his car. I must say he was very accommodating on the whole, and only occasionally grumbled.

I was still grieving for the baby I had lost at the end of the last year, frequently feeling tearful, thinking about how things might have been, how old the baby would have been by now and how they would be developing. I found a weekend workshop at The Women's Therapy Centre in Holloway Road, which focused on termination of pregnancy. Attending the event that April was painful. I cried for six out of the eight hours I attended on both

Saturday and Sunday, only stopping for lunch and buying a new pack of tissues. It was cathartic, though, and cleansing. I came back from the weekend feeling drained but ready to go forward.

I needed to make up the time I had lost on my social services placement, so over the summer holiday I went to the Essex Road office of Islington Social Services. This was known to be a radical practice that was progressive and open to new ideas, mixing social work theory with that of community work, and committed to a client-centred approach and self-determination.

Islington was, at that time, a very mixed bag in terms of its demography. Run down houses, homes to poverty-stricken families, could be found side-by-side with the homes of wealthy, middle class citizens. It was very different from my Ware placement, and one where I could employ the skills I'd developed in my voluntary sector placements. My placement tutor was kept busy with her own caseload but still found time to give me useful supervision. There were no problems with this placement and the six weeks of full-time work just flew by.

Sometime that June, Phil P and Sue W from college got together as a couple. They had been casting glances at each other for some time, but both had been with other people until that summer. They were sweet together and it was lovely to see their romance develop.

Of course, we had no idea then that they would still be together over thirty years later, and that I would be with them when both their daughters were born. In 1980, though, they were young, in love and in lust, without much thought of the future.

Naomi and I were increasingly committed to the ideals of feminism. We had read that some women were attending Consciousness Raising (CR) groups. The idea behind these was that women were isolated from each other, so the issues raised as problems in their lives were often seen as personal, rather than the result of oppression. CR groups gave women the opportunity to meet and discuss their lives, without the interference or involvement of men.

If that all sounds rather serious and worthy, it's because it was. It was important stuff, and there was rarely anything to have fun with in those early days of feminism.

Now, with hindsight, I can see that the feminist movement had to go through this period, with its rather heavy-handed approach, before we could find a middle way. It could be exhausting at times, too, constantly having to challenge men and meetings; going on marches and protest meetings; campaigning and generally being that 'strident feminist' so abhorred by the media.

Exploring feminist politics and issues, I found that once I'd seen what the problem was, I couldn't 'un-see' it. So, I was increasingly aware of the ways that women and girls were oppressed by men, by society, by organisations.

Naomi and I decided to take the bull by the horns and start a CR group locally.

We placed an advert in *Spare Rib*, and had eight women contact us. Hey – we had a CR group! We started to meet weekly at each other's houses, and occasionally had a social evening at a local restaurant. They were all nice, middle class women – some in relationships, some not – and all were heterosexual. And we did have gossip and fun, too, over shared bottles of wine and the occasional joint.

Within the group we discussed all the current issues being raised by *Spare Rib*: abortion, rape, domestic violence, equal pay, pornography, stereotypes and so on. These were serious issues, but it was stimulating, and it was exciting to think that we might be in the vanguard of a revolution for how women were treated and perceived.

Though the wheels of change do move exceedingly slowly, the next few years did see considerable social and political transformations for women and girls. Equal pay, ending employment discrimination, changing police attitudes to rape and domestic violence, and challenging stereotypes are just a few of the areas that have changed as a result of the feminist movement at that time. I am proud to have been a small part of that.

I get very cross when I hear women saying, "I'm not a feminist", because if it wasn't for women like Naomi and me, they would not be earning enough to buy their own property; they would be trapped in abusive relationships; they would have unwanted babies; they would be treated as sluts following rape. I could go on. Being a strident feminist still has its place.

Back in the day, it was a time of exploration, revelations and honest discussions. One evening, I was with my sister Debbie and we were talking about the issues raised by feminism, including how previously taboo issues were being brought into the open.

Then she dropped a bombshell.

"I was sexually abused by Dad."

What? Did I hear that right? My lovely daddy, abusing my sister? I kind of went into shock; I felt my hands and feet get very cold, my voice seemed to be coming from someone else and it seemed as if we were characters in a film, acting a role. None of it felt real.

I gradually came back into the room and a kind of consciousness. She told me that he had started sexually abusing her when she was eleven years old. He didn't have intercourse with her, but used to rub his penis against her back until he had an orgasm. I suppose that was marginally better than actually having sex with her, but not much.

Apparently it had continued until she was seventeen. He would wait until everyone was asleep, then get up, seemingly to go to the toilet in the yard, but really he would sneak into her bedroom. Or it would happen when everyone else was out of the house. On one occasion, he took her on a 'holiday' to Scotland, where they stayed in the same room.

I knew from my reading that it was fairly common for just one child in the family to be the focus of sexual abuse. Anyway, my eldest sister, Sheila, had been evacuated from when she was nine years old until she was a teenager, so had not been exposed to the risk of his abuse.

And what about me? He died when I was nine years old. It made me wonder, though, if he had been alive, whether I would have experienced something similar.

I'd always had my dad up there on a pedestal. He was my hero, my saviour if Mum was being particularly aggressive. I loved my dad, but now it seemed as if I'd been hoodwinked and betrayed by him.

Meanwhile, Debbie and I agreed that she needed to talk to someone about her experiences. I was too close to both her and Dad, but I remembered seeing something in *Spare Rib* about incest survivors. We found details of a group for her to attend, which led to her being in a documentary on television.

This was her 'coming out' as an incest survivor to the rest of the family. Our sister, Sheila, refused to believe Debbie's story (another common reaction in the families of abused children) and they did not speak for a very long time. I never disbelieved her for a moment. I think that it made Debbie and me even closer than before, although we were already friends.

It wasn't until many years later, when I was having therapy, that I resolved the anomaly of the two sides of my father: one being the kind, loving, affectionate man I had known, and the other being the sly, selfish abuser of young girls. I was able to see that my own relationship with him was unchanged. He was still my lovely daddy, who had been the perfect father to me. I was able to get a distance between this man and the other very different one. I could still love the father I had, while despising the one that Debbie had.

Almost There

The new academic year meant a new placement. This would be the final year of the degree, and our professional placements would need to be reflected in a dissertation, so it was an important one. The dissertation would be a major piece of work, and would include my own research, as well as references to a substantial body of published work. It would bring together theory, practice and methodology.

Sometimes I had to pinch myself to feel that all this was real. I had come a long way in such a short time. Underneath the academia, I was still that girl without even an 'O' Level, whose most lucrative career had been getting naked. It still, at times, felt like this story was happening to someone else.

I found a placement with a voluntary organisation, The Piccadilly Advice Centre, which would involve welfare rights advice once more, but this time the focus would be the young, homeless population. It was based, as the name suggests, right in the centre of London, very near to Piccadilly Circus, which was, at that time, a well-known 'meat rack' for young rent boys. Many of our clients were living on the streets, selling themselves for a warm bed and a free meal under some punter's roof.

The placement suited me. I found, once more, that I was able to talk to people at all levels and that I was effective in dealing with housing and benefit issues for our service users. My supervisor was the uber-posh Hattie, who lived with two lovers and swore like a trouper.

Naomi, meanwhile, had found a placement with the British Pregnancy Advisory Service (BPAS), an organisation that offered counselling and termination of pregnancy to women. It was a non-profit-making organisation and, although it did charge for termination, these fees could often be met by the NHS. Naomi's supervisor there was a manager called Anne, who was only about six years older than Naomi herself.

Naomi was full of admiration for Anne. She told me that her new supervisor was sensitive, professional, experienced, had insight, was wise and had a great body. Well, no, she didn't exactly say that, but it didn't take a clairvoyant to sense that Naomi was sexually attracted to Anne.

But it was OK, because Anne was heterosexual and in a long-term relationship with a man, so no threat there, then.

In fact, Naomi invited Anne to come and meet me over lunch at our house. I cooked, of course, and the meal was a great success. I'd made crème caramel for pudding and Anne was fulsome in her praise of it. I didn't like to say that it had come out of a packet, and was rather caught on the hop when she asked for the recipe. I blustered a bit, and said I'd write it out and send it to her via Naomi. When she'd left, I had to find a suitable recipe in one of my cookery books to give her. Oh, what a tangled web...

I didn't much like Anne. She was a working class woman from up North. She'd done well educationally, getting a degree straight after school, but I thought she was pretentious and full of herself. Very serious, without much humour, she was full of feminist and socialist theories. And had a great body.

So Naomi and I would commute every day from Waterford, riding our bikes to Hertford Station, and then getting a train into King's Cross before travelling on the tube to our respective placements. These were full-time placements for several months, and we were revising for final exams in January, as well as writing extended essays that would be assessed as part of our degree. It was an exhausting time, but we still managed to find the energy to make love and sometimes go out to one of the lesbian discos that were now fairly common in London.

All too soon January 1981 dawned and, with it, the start of our finals. We were still on placement, too, but this was now on a part-time basis. We were so tired, but ploughed on. We both looked gaunt, ill and very thin.

As part of my dissertation research I had visited Centrepoint, the hostel for young, homeless people in London's Soho. They had suggested that I spend a night there to really experience what it was like. In all honesty, I didn't want to, but felt that it would give my research street cred to do it.

I'm glad I did, because it was an eye-opener, albeit an uncomfortable one. I arrived in time for supper. Shepherd's pie and baked beans, if I remember rightly. Then there was time for chatting with that night's intake, as well accompanying the workers to the entrance to answer the doorbell and do a quick assessment of anyone wanting to stay the night.

There was a limit on how many nights a person could stay, and they had to be aged between sixteen and twenty-five. Anyone younger than this could come in but the relevant services would have to be informed, and they were told of this proviso.

No one who was clearly drunk or under the influence of drugs would be allowed in, and again it was made clear that anyone found with booze or drugs would be asked to leave.

There were showers, a launderette and a television, and books and magazines were provided, along with a rail of second-hand clothing that could be used by anyone needing it. The whole place was scruffy, but clean and warm.

There were two dormitories, one for boys and one for girls, both with as many bunk beds squeezed in as possible. It was lights out at eleven, so I found myself a bed and snuggled into the sleeping bag I'd brought with me.

However, if I was hoping for a good night's sleep, I was soon disabused of that notion. For a start, the doorbell rang incessantly as late arrivals tried to get a bed for the night; there was a limit on how late they could be admitted. Then there was the coughing, sneezing, swearing and farting (due to those supper-time beans, perhaps?) of the other people in the dorm. I tossed and turned, and probably slept now and then.

By the time we were roused at around seven in the morning, I was very, very tired and just wanted to get home for a real sleep. I guess I was lucky that I had a place to go and do this. A cup of tea and a bowl of cornflakes were on offer, before everyone was turfed out onto the streets for the day.

It had been a valuable experience for me as a researcher and a would-be social worker, but also as a member of the tabloid-reading public. It really was no fun being homeless, and I could not imagine that anyone would choose that life.

That experience, my placement and my research had made it clear to me that homelessness and unemployment were inextricably linked: you can't get a job without an address, and you can't get an address without a job. References are required for both, and it's a non-starter until one of these requirements is met.

Our final placements ended in March 1981, and then it was back to college for lectures, although we also had our dissertations to finish, plus one or two exams still outstanding, so the stress of study didn't end until April, when we could finally breathe again.

We had an end-of-course barbeque at Sue W's place, where everyone on the course came together for one last time until graduation. Of course, we still had to get our results, but for the moment we could relax and have fun until real life kicked in and we'd have to look for jobs.

Having left her placement, Naomi was now developing a friendship with Anne and was seeing her at least once each week. When she came home from these outings it was 'Anne this' and 'Anne that' and 'Anne the other'. I could see, of course, the way this was going, but tried to keep my jealousy in check.

Naomi was still so young, and had had limited experience of lesbian relationships, although she had slept with a couple of other women since we'd been together. I thought that if I could go with the flow, then this new crush would burn itself out, as her other infatuations had.

I started temping as a secretary for one of the local agencies in July. It was something I knew I could do to earn some reasonable money until the time came to look for a social work post. I was fairly confident that I had passed both the degree and the qualification, but thought that I might merely scrape by. Our year had been a dry run for an honours degree, so we were working to that level, although would not be able to claim honours status. That would be the privilege of subsequent students.

In mid-July our results were available. I had passed and gained a degree 'with commendation'. This meant that it was the equivalent of a 2:1 degree, a very respectable result and one that I had never imagined that I could aspire to. In fact, all of my closest friends gained degrees with commendations; our group had turned out to be the brightest of the bunch – and that included me. I couldn't have been more surprised at my inclusion in this faction. And Naomi got an award as 'Student of the Year'.

That wasn't her only prize. She also went to stay with Anne for a weekend, where they consummated their relationship.

She was very open and honest with me about it. We'd never had any secrets but, even so, it hurt a lot, especially when she told me that her desire for Anne had been so powerful that she'd practically raped her. I didn't believe, for a moment, that Anne had been unwilling, but it was telling that Naomi's desire for her had felt so out of control.

I think that was the evening when I broke down. I hit out at Naomi, who became frightened and called out for Phil P. When he appeared in the doorway, he held me very tightly while I sobbed against him, my heart breaking.

But life went on. We resolved that conflict in the way that we always had, by falling into bed and making love.

Naomi and I were still living together, although this would soon end, as Phil P had a new job in London. His tenancy was linked to his post and ended when he left the organisation, so we would all have to leave this lovely, though freezing, house in its idyllic, rural setting.

Naomi was looking for a job and accommodation in the capital. She wanted to change her living arrangements, saying that she felt constricted living with me, although she told me that she still loved me. It was all very painful, with so many changes to deal with all at once.

Meanwhile, a distraction in the form of a royal wedding was offered. Prince Charles married Lady Diana Spencer on 29 July 1981. We all sat and watched this fairytale couple make their vows, although I'm sure I wasn't the only one to be saying, "She seems too young. I hope she knows what she's letting herself in for."

In August, Naomi and I went on holiday to Spain for three weeks. We were meeting up with her dad and his second wife. They had an apartment in Alicante. The Spanish sun shone, and we swam and sunbathed and ate well, sleeping in a double bed where Naomi announced she was too hot to cuddle, and certainly too hot to make love. It was a strange time. We were together, yet drifting steadily apart, still bound together by a tenacious love, yet unable to shake off those intrusions that threatened our connection.

Upon coming home, Naomi went to her mother's place in Cambridge, and I set about clearing up and packing. I was moving to Debbie's flat to stay in the little Hansel and Gretel cottage at the end of her garden. I knew that I wanted to work in London, as that was where the most interesting jobs were, so it made sense to make my base there, planning a more permanent home when I knew what location I would end up in.

Meanwhile, Naomi got the first job she was interviewed for, while I filled in application form after application form, went for umpteen interviews, and kept getting turned down. My confidence, always a fragile thing, had been knocked by the wreck of my relationship with Naomi, and I was very, very nervous in interviews. I would go completely blank and be unable to answer questions that were really quite straightforward.

To try to overcome this, I took to carrying a miniature bottle of brandy, which I would swig just before going into the interview. I now suspect that alcohol could be smelt on my breath, which is not the best presentation for a newly qualified social worker.

In the meantime I ordered the cap and gown I would need for my graduation ceremony, and bought a new dress for the occasion. I invited my sisters, Debbie and Sheila, to the ceremony, and Naomi invited her mother, Eileen.

I was ready for the next step, the moment I'd worked so hard for over the past five years, getting those 'A' Levels, and now a degree and a social work qualification.

Fancy that.

7

What Janet Did Next

I could not have been more proud of what I had achieved. I was the first member of my extended family to complete higher education and gain a degree. It would be my passport to a different place.

I had discovered an intelligence, a desire to learn, grow and develop. I had found a profession that would draw on my natural abilities of communication and empathy. I never knew that I had those qualities until I explored this new world.

I could have ended up unhappily married with 2.5 children, without any real career, bored and miserable. Or I could have become a substance abuser, swapping soft drugs for a dangerous addiction.

Instead, I now had a piece of paper that would lead to stimulating, interesting, demanding jobs, which in turn would lead to abiding, much valued friendships.

It wouldn't always be plain sailing, but I would go on to work with the young homeless. Then I would be the first person in the UK to be employed solely to work with people with HIV and AIDS. I would move between the voluntary and statutory sectors, becoming a well-respected manager in social services.

Gaining my degree also meant the start of a new life where, after a while, my old one would seem unreal, like remembering a film about a rebel wild child, who abused drugs and who was abused by men. It was a fresh start, which I embraced completely. I am a walking, talking testament to the value of education, and feel so privileged to have been able to have that opportunity.

And what of relationships? I never had another relationship with a man. I had a few more with women, but ultimately made a decision that I'd had more sexual encounters than most women have had hot dinners and, frankly, could do without it.

Dany had split up with Phil, finally, a few years after we left Lemsford Road. Although it was completely out of character, Phil had begun to be violent towards her. She left the children with him, although it broke her heart, coming to stay first with me and then with Debbie. Phil and the children moved in with his mother, who lived in a large house by the sea. Dany and Phil managed to remain on friendly terms, and they both loved those kids to bits. We were always best friends, although there were long periods when we did not see each other, usually when she took up with some unsuitable boyfriend or another.

Many years later, I returned to our lovely house in St Albans. By then it had been turned into a rather posh hotel, where Debbie and I stayed for a night. It was a very odd experience, knowing the building so well, but trying to assimilate it with its new persona. I sent a text to Dany saying 'I'm at Lemsford Road, now a hotel. It's not the same.' She replied 'Of course it's not the same, Jan. You're not stoned.' Which made me laugh.

When she was fifty-eight, Dany was diagnosed with lung cancer. I last saw her a week before she died. At that visit, she was very ill, yet when we said our last goodbye she held me with such strength, telling me she loved me. I knew I would never have another friend like her, and told her so. She was only fifty-nine, and I still miss her every day. She has, however, left me the most wonderful legacy. I now have a much valued friendship with Lisa, her daughter, she of the yellow knitted jacket, who I used to babysit.

I stayed friends with Naomi for a long time, and had sporadic contact with Rose.

In spite of all the trials and tribulations with Rose, she had shown me that loving women could be passionate, tender and warm. She had introduced me to the delights of classical music and dance, and a love of the countryside and animals; she encouraged me to read authors I might not have otherwise encountered and showed me the peace that meditation can bring.

And Naomi? With her I had discovered feminism, politics and a delight in discovering that sexuality could be fun and sensual. And she taught me how to play backgammon.

And they both showed me that I was capable of being loved for who I was. They believed I was beautiful inside and out. They respected my intellect and gave me the space to develop it. They gave me priceless gifts, and I will always love them for that.

My sister Debbie and I became ever closer and she is now my best friend. We live together in happy domestic chaos, sharing two and a half cats (the half being a stray who regularly visits) and a rescue dog named Twiggy.

I regret nothing. There were some incidents that I would rather not have had, but all of my experiences have made me the person I am today, and I think that I'm OK – loved and loving. I have a circle of friends who are there for me, and who know that I would be on their doorstep should they ever need a cup of tea and a hug. My glass is usually half full, and I know that I am lucky.

But I'm not perfect; I haven't exactly developed into a well-rounded, healthy in mind and body type of do-gooder person. Slightly rounded, you could say, as I struggle with my weight every day, but flawed. I get angry with people who are racist, homophobic and who drop litter. I am impatient when my friends are indecisive about where we should meet up. I'm bossy and like to control the TV remote. I like non-PC jokes, particularly ones about farting. I flirt inappropriately, especially when I'm drunk. I swear far too much, and constantly resolve to stop using such bad language, but then think, *Oh, sod it.*

But in spite of all that, in spite of having a mum and dad who may have fucked me up, in spite of a complicated route to achieve my ambitions, here I am. Still a tiny bit of a rebel, who believes most rules were made to be broken. All grown up now.

So there.

Acknowledgements

Where do I start? There are so many people who have influenced my life and my writing.

First of all, there is Debbie, my wonderful big sister, who has believed in me, right from our earliest encounter (she was nine and I was two weeks old). She was always proud of me, encouraging and supportive. She has read umpteen versions of these memoirs and pronounced each one 'Brilliant', although I think she may be biased.

I have to thank Dany, precious friend, without whom a large section of this memoir would not have been written. I remember her every day.

Appreciation to Cath Jackson, a close friend, a talented journalist and editor, who read the drafts and offered constructive criticism (which was not always well received – sorry, Cath!) and who encouraged me in my writing abilities. Thanks, too, for being very funny and listening to me chunter on endlessly.

Mark, another friend who read an early draft, who was supportive and is so proud of me that he introduces me to new acquaintances as 'Janet – she writes!' Not forgetting Tony, his partner and my old boss. They are wonderful to spend an evening with, as we drink Espresso Martinis, and I get squiffy.

Penny, Alison, Kay, Lisa, Sue and my niece Jemma who have all been so patient over the very long time it has taken to complete my memoirs, always interested, but never nagging. Patrick and his husband, Colin (another aspiring author), have provided a sounding board and valuable ideas.

Not forgetting Sir Nick Partridge, who I worked with at Terrence Higgins Trust. We have remained friends for over thirty years. He and his spouse, Simon, are a consistent cornerstone for me.

Tanya Solomon was a brilliant structural editor, correcting my dodgy grammar and punctuation and making suggestions on the draft manuscript. Troubador, my publishers, have been helpful and patient with this fledgling writer, so thanks to them, too.

I must mention the tutors on the many creative writing courses I have attended over the years. All have been helpful, but special mention must go to the Arvon Foundation tutors, Sathnam Sanghera, Melanie McGrath and Marina Benjamin who, as published authors, offered particularly invaluable advice and were so encouraging.

Finally, thanks to the anonymous woman in the smoking room at work who commented, "What an inspirational story", when I told her about my journey from unqualified school leaver to social work manager – and that was without the more exotic details! She sowed the seed for me to write these memoirs.

And finally, finally… love and thanks to my hairy family: The various cats and rescue dog who have provided cuddles, comfort and laughter whenever they were needed. Not to mention fur which sheds all year round.